# Google Cloud Certified Professional Cloud Developer Exam Guide

QvR. 2/22

Modernize your applications using cloud-native services and best practices

**Sebastian Moreno**

BIRMINGHAM—MUMBAI

# Google Cloud Certified Professional Cloud Developer Exam Guide

**Group Product Manager**: Vijin Boricha
**Publishing Product Manager**: Shrilekha Inani
**Senior Editor**: Alexander Powell
**Content Development Editor**: Mrudgandha Kulkarni
**Technical Editor**: Nithik Cheruvakodan
**Copy Editor**: Safis Editing
**Project Coordinator**: Shagun Saini
**Proofreader**: Safis Editing
**Indexer**: Pratik Shirodkar
**Production Designer**: Ponraj Dhandapani

First published: July 2021

Production reference: 1070721

Published by Packt Publishing Ltd.
Livery Place
35 Livery Street
Birmingham
B3 2PB, UK.

ISBN 978-1-80056-099-4

www.packt.com

*To my girlfriend, Belén Sarrás, for her love, support, and inspiration.*

*To my family, Luisa Espinosa, Francisca Moreno, Josefa Saavedra, and Puppy, for showing me how talent and creativity evolve.*

*To my friends, James Martinson, Nicolás Nilo, and Rudighert Schalchli, for their unconditional support.*

*– Sebastian Moreno*

# Contributors

## About the author

**Sebastian Moreno** is a former Google Developer Expert for Google Cloud Platform. He is working on multiple projects using cloud technologies, such as cloud innovation, virtual agents, application modernization, and data analytics. He has more than eight cloud certifications with multiple cloud providers. He is a Google Cloud Certified Professional Cloud Developer.

# About the reviewer

**David Saleh** is an IT professional and holds a BSc. in electrical engineering and other professional certifications in cloud architecture, data engineering, and cybersecurity.

With over 20 years of experience in IT, including software architecture and development, David is currently the director of cloud architecture at one of the largest banks in Canada. He has extensive competencies in cloud-native application design and development, enterprise architecture, and cybersecurity.

> *To my parents, who raised me to be who I am today. You are always there for me, you are amazing, and your efforts have not gone unnoticed. I greatly appreciate and love you.*

# Table of Contents

# 2
## Security Fundamentals and Best Practices

# Section 2: Developing and Modernizing Applications on Google Cloud Platform

# 3
## Application Modernization Using Google Cloud

# 4
# Using Cloud Functions and Google App Engine

# 5

# Virtual Machines and Container Applications on Google Cloud Platform

# 6

# Managing APIs on Google Cloud Platform

# Section 3: Storage Foundations

# 7

# Handling Unstructured Data

# 9
## Data Management and Database Strategies

# 10
## Optimizing Applications with Caching Strategies on Google Cloud Platform

# Section 4: SRE for Developers

## 11

## Logging on Google Cloud Platform

## 12

## Cloud Monitoring, Tracing, and Debugging

# Section 5: Analyzing a Sample Case Study

## 13
## HipLocal Sample Case Study Preparation

## 14
## Questions and Answers

## Other Books You May Enjoy

## Index

# Preface

*Google Cloud Certified Professional Cloud Developer Exam Guide* is a book for learning more about Google Cloud services used by those working in a cloud developer role on a daily basis. Covering the most important services and best practices, this book will help you to design and develop cloud-native applications, reduce operational tasks, and improve the deployment speed of new features.

This content will allow you to prepare for the Google Cloud Certified Professional Cloud Developer exam by reviewing the entire exam guide through the course of the book, providing sample questions, and by covering a sample case study included in the exam.

## Who this book is for

This book is intended for developers, cloud engineers, and anyone preparing for the Google Cloud Certified Professional Cloud Developer exam. Basic to intermediate development skills are required to make the best of this book.

## What this book covers

*Chapter 1, Google Cloud Platform Developer Fundamentals*, covers the fundamentals for developers and good programming cloud practices on Google Cloud.

*Chapter 2, Security Fundamentals and Best Practices*, covers the essentials tips and acceptable security practices for your cloud applications.

*Chapter 3, Application Modernization Using Google Cloud*, covers how to take advantage of all the cloud benefits, such as autoscaling, fully managed services, and cost saving.

*Chapter 4, Using Cloud Functions and Google App Engine*, covers resource optimization and cost saving using two of the most popular serverless solutions on Google Cloud.

*Chapter 5, Virtual Machines and Container Applications on Google Cloud Platform*, covers three different compute options for deploying containerized applications on Google Cloud.

*Chapter 6, Managing APIs on Google Cloud Platform*, covers how to implement, expose, manage, and secure APIs on Google Cloud using three different services.

*Chapter 7, Handling Unstructured Data*, covers how to store and consume unstructured data in an efficient way using Google Cloud services.

*Chapter 8, Databases and Event Messages in Google Cloud*, covers topics, SQL, and NoSQL database services on Google Cloud for storing your data and decoupling your applications.

*Chapter 9, Data Management and Database Strategies*, covers different use cases and best practices regarding data management in the cloud.

*Chapter 10, Optimizing Applications with Caching Strategies on Google Cloud Platform*, covers how to create, implement, and manage caching strategies using Google Cloud services.

*Chapter 11, Logging on Google Cloud Platform*, covers how to detect errors and diagnose issues in your application faster using Google Cloud services.

*Chapter 12, Cloud Monitoring, Tracing, and Debugging*, covers how to create dashboards, automated alerts, and trace, profile, and debug applications to understand your application's issues and optimization opportunities.

*Chapter 13, Hip Local Sample Case Study Preparation*, covers a detailed review of the sample case study with a draft of a solution that meets the needs of the case.

*Chapter 14, Questions and Answers*, covers questions and answers related to the public exam guide for the Google Cloud Certified Professional Cloud Developer.

# To get the most out of this book

To get the most out of reading this book, install the following software in order to be able to run the multiple code examples from each chapter:

| Software/hardware covered in the book | OS requirements |
| --- | --- |
| Node v 10.16.0 or later | Windows, macOS X, and Linux (any) |
| Google Cloud SDK v 317.0.0 or later | Windows, macOS X, and Linux (any) |

You can find the instructions to install Node by following this link: `https://nodejs.org/en/`.

You can find the instructions to install the Google Cloud SDK by following this link: `https://cloud.google.com/sdk`.

**If you are using the digital version of this book, we advise you to type the code yourself or access the code via the GitHub repository (link available in the next section). Doing so will help you avoid any potential errors related to the copying and pasting of code.**

# Download the example code files

You can download the example code files for this book from GitHub at `https://github.com/PacktPublishing/Google-Cloud-Certified-Professional-Cloud-Developer-Exam-Guide`. In case there's an update to the code, it will be updated on the existing GitHub repository.

We also have other code bundles from our rich catalog of books and videos available at `https://github.com/PacktPublishing/`. Check them out!

# Download the color images

We also provide a PDF file that has color images of the screenshots/diagrams used in this book. You can download it here: `http://www.packtpub.com/sites/default/files/downloads/9781800560994_ColorImages.pdf`.

# Conventions used

There are a number of text conventions used throughout this book.

`Code in text`: Indicates code words in text, database table names, folder names, filenames, file extensions, pathnames, dummy URLs, user input, and Twitter handles. Here is an example: "Where `YOUR_IMAGE` is the path to the image of your application in Google Container Registry."

A block of code is set as follows:

```
{
  "steps": [
    {
      "name": "gcr.io/cloud-builders/gke-deploy",
      "args": [
        "run",
        "--filename=kubernetes-resource-file",
        "--location=location",
        "--cluster=cluster"
      ]
```

```
        }
    ]
}
```

Any command-line input or output is written as follows:

```
gcloud iam service-accounts set-iam-policy sa-id policy-file
```

**Bold**: Indicates a new term, an important word, or words that you see on screen. For example, words in menus or dialog boxes appear in the text like this. Here is an example: "In the **Host and path rules** and **Frontend** configuration sections, we do not make any changes."

> **Tips or important notes**
> Appear like this.

# Get in touch

Feedback from our readers is always welcome.

**General feedback**: If you have questions about any aspect of this book, mention the book title in the subject of your message and email us at customercare@packtpub.com.

**Errata**: Although we have taken every care to ensure the accuracy of our content, mistakes do happen. If you have found a mistake in this book, we would be grateful if you would report this to us. Please visit www.packtpub.com/support/errata, selecting your book, clicking on the Errata Submission Form link, and entering the details.

**Piracy**: If you come across any illegal copies of our works in any form on the internet, we would be grateful if you would provide us with the location address or website name. Please contact us at copyright@packt.com with a link to the material.

**If you are interested in becoming an author**: If there is a topic that you have expertise in and you are interested in either writing or contributing to a book, please visit authors.packtpub.com.

# Share Your Thoughts

Once you've read *Google Cloud Certified Professional Cloud Developer Exam Guide*, we'd love to hear your thoughts! Scan the QR code below to go straight to the Amazon review page for this book and share your feedback.

https://packt.link/r/1-800-56099-0

Your review is important to us and the tech community and will help us make sure we're delivering excellent quality content.

# Section 1: Welcome to the Google Cloud Developers' Guide

In this section, you will understand the basic programming concepts to consider when developing in Google Cloud and the most crucial security fundamentals and best practices.

This section comprises the following chapters:

- *Chapter 1, Google Cloud Platform Developer Fundamentals*
- *Chapter 2, Security Fundamentals and Best Practices*

# 1
# Google Cloud Platform Developer Fundamentals

In this first chapter, you will learn about the fundamentals and best practices of developing in **Google Cloud**, and how these differ from traditional on-premises application development. You will learn about concepts that allow you to take your developments to decoupled, resilient, highly available, and scalable architectures, in addition to delegating the most significant responsibilities to Google's self-managed services in a secure way.

In this chapter, we're going to cover the following main topics:

- The differences between IaaS, CaaS, PaaS, and serverless
- The fundamentals of a microservices ecosystem
- Delegating responsibilities to Google Cloud services

# Technical requirements

There are no specific technical requirements for this chapter.

# The basics that every developer should know about Google Cloud infrastructure

There are many people who think that programming in the cloud is simply a matter of programming in another environment, but I could not disagree more with that statement.

Depending on which cloud service you use, for example, a **virtual machine**, **Platform as a Service (PaaS)**, or **Function as a Service (FaaS)**, your code could need to handle life cycles and unexpected program terminations.

When you program in the cloud, you should pay attention not only to good coding but also to which platform or service you are using, since many things can change depending on this factor.

For example, programming in an IaaS service is different from programming in a CaaS or FaaS service. (We will explain what these acronyms mean very shortly.)

In this section, you will learn about the most important differences between the different services offered in the cloud, what the regions and zones are, and why concepts such as high availability and latency are so important in a cloud solution.

## Regions and zones

A *region* is a specific location where you can choose to host your services and computing resources with one or more zones.

A *compute cluster* (a layer between regions and zones) is a physical infrastructure in a data center with independent power, cooling, network, and security services.

A *zone* can be hosted in one or more clusters and allows the resource load to be handled and balanced within a region.

Choosing multiple zones and regions allows the application to reduce latency to final users and handle failures, transforming your application into a high-availability service.

If a specific zone presents an outage, your application can keep operating using another zone.

If a specific region presents an outage, your application can keep operating using another zone in another region.

Having instances of your application in multiple regions and zones increases your costs as well as your application's availability.

# What is X as a Service?

One of the most important things before starting development in the cloud is to understand what the different types of service are and how the shared responsibility model works. But when we start working in the cloud, we see acronyms everywhere, such as the following:

- **IaaS**: **Infrastructure as a Service**
- **CaaS**: **Container as a Service**
- **PaaS**: **Platform as a Service**
- **FaaS**: **Function as a Service**
- **SaaS**: **Software as a Service**

We will start with IaaS. In this case, the cloud provider gives you an infrastructure, generally represented as a virtual machine with an operating system based on a virtualized image. In this kind of service, there is a charge for use. An example of IaaS on **Google Cloud Platform** (**GCP**) is **GCE**, or **Google Compute Engine**.

In the case of CaaS, the cloud provider gives us an environment where we can deploy our application images. In this kind of service, there is a charge for use.

With PaaS, the cloud provider will provide us with a platform where we can load a previously compiled artifact and configure exposure rules for services and versions. In this kind of service, there is a charge for use. An example of PaaS on GCP is Google App Engine.

If we decide to use FaaS, the cloud provider will give us a platform where we will only have to code and configure the corresponding dependencies, without the need to compile or generate an image. In this kind of service, there is a charge for the number of executions and the time of these executions. An example of FaaS on GCP is Cloud Functions.

And finally, in the case of SaaS, the cloud provider will deliver the software in such a way that the user can directly consume the functionality. For this kind of service, there may be a charge for use or a subscription. An example of SaaS on GCP is **Data Studio**:

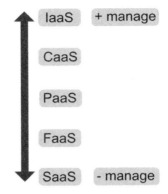

Figure 1.1 – From IaaS to SaaS

When you choose to code using IaaS, you should take care of operating system patches and updates, accepting more responsibilities but also having more options to customize your server. That means more management tasks.

When you choose to code using PaaS, you only need to take care of the business logic of your application, accepting fewer infrastructure responsibilities but also having fewer options to customize your server.

As explained in the introduction to this chapter, each service involves different considerations when we start programming.

Among the most important concepts from the preceding list of services is the control of the execution life cycle of our applications. This was not a concept we needed when we programmed on IaaS, because normally, the servers were always on and it was not necessary to worry about telling the server that our asynchronous executions had finished successfully to turn it off.

This is just one of many points that we will review in this chapter and that will help you to program applications in the different GCP services.

# How to reduce latency to your end users

Generally, when we have to solve a problem through coding, the first thing we worry about is that the code does what it has to do, no matter how we achieve it. After this, we focus on ensuring that the code does not have any security vulnerabilities, and finally, we might try to optimize or refactor various methods or functions in the interest of efficiency.

In some cases, this is not enough, and we must plan not only how our code will run in the cloud but also where it will run.

You will probably wonder why some streaming or video services are so fast and others so slow. Various factors may be responsible, such as the speed of the user's internet connection, which unfortunately is not something we can control. However, there is a factor that we can control, and that is how close we can bring the content to our end users.

When a user enters a web page to consume content, and in this particular case we are going to assume that the user decides to consume a video, the user has to go to the source, in this case, the server, to access the content.

Depending on how far the user is from the server where the video is stored, the speed with which they download the content to their computer may be higher or lower. This is known as **latency**.

The distance between the source and the consumer directly affects the latency, and that is why the closer we bring the source to the consumer, the lower the latency and the higher the speed of consumption of the information.

In GCP (and in most clouds), there is the concept of a **Content Delivery Network (CDN)**, which acts as a content cache. This means that the content is replicated on a different server than the originating one, in order to reduce the requests to the original server and also, in this case, to bring the content closer to the end consumer in order to increase performance.

When content is consumed for the first time, Cloud CDN, the Google Cloud solution CDN implementation, will consult the content on the server to find the source of origin and will replicate it in its nodes so that in future requests, the content is available to be delivered directly to users.

For this feature, Cloud CDN uses a **cache key**, based on the query URL, to determine whether or not the content the user is trying to access is already replicated on the CDN nodes. This is called a **cache hit**. When the content is not found, this action is called a **cache miss**. If you need to configure how long the cache content will exist on the CDN node before revalidating the content at the origin, you can use the **Time to Live (TTL)** configuration in seconds. The default TTL for content caching is 3,600 seconds (1 hour) and the maximum allowed value is 1 year:

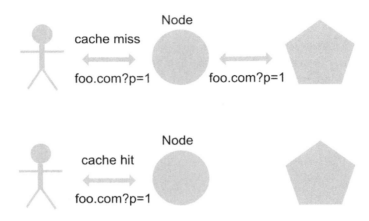

Figure 1.2 – CDN workflow

In summary, Cloud CDN is a solution that allows us to bring content efficiently from the source to consumers, such as images, videos, and files, by replicating the content in different nodes worldwide in order to reduce response times for the final consumer.

## Graceful shutdowns

In the world of microservices applications, containerized applications controlled by an orchestrator are generally used. The best-known one is **Kubernetes**. Kubernetes has the ability to shut down any of the existing microservices (called **pods** in a Kubernetes cluster) at any time in order to free up resources or maintain the health of the application.

If the design of the application does not support graceful shutdowns, we could run into problems, such as the execution of a call to our application not being completed. That is why it is important to control shutdowns gracefully via the SIGTERM execution termination code.

When our application receives the termination code from SIGTERM execution, our application must close all the connections it has open at that moment and save any information that is useful for maintaining the current state prior to the end of execution.

In Kubernetes, this can be done with the **preStop hook**, which we will explore in *Chapter 5, Virtual Machines and Container Applications on Google Cloud Platform*.

But Kubernetes workloads are not the only case where we need to handle graceful shutdowns. For example, GCP has a GCE virtual machine type called a **preemptible VM instance**. A preemptible VM instance can be purchased with a discount of up to 80% as long as you accept that the instance will terminate after 24 hours.

In that case, you can handle a graceful shutdown using a shutdown script. This script will be executed right before a virtual machine instance is stopped or restarted, allowing instances to perform tasks such as syncing with other applications or exporting logs.

You can also use a shutdown script when you are using other GCP solutions, such as **Managed Instance Groups** (**MIGs**), in order to gracefully shut down your instances when the MIG performs a scale-out operation (deleting instances inside the group).

# Top tips for developing and implementing resilient and scalable applications

Having presented some of the fundamentals of programming in the cloud, it is important to now address one of the topics that is probably the most mentioned but least understood: **microservices**. In this section, we briefly introduce the microservices ecosystem and explain how to correctly manage user sessions, create traceability logs in order to detect and solve errors, implement retries in order to make our solution reliable, support consumption peaks through autoscaling, and reduce server consumption through information caching.

## Microservice ecosystems

Microservices are an architectural design pattern that allows the separation of responsibilities into smaller applications, which can be programmed in different programming languages, can be independent of each other, and have the possibility of scaling both vertically (increasing CPU and memory) and horizontally (creating more instances) independently in order to optimize the cluster resources.

Although microservices have been widely accepted by both start-ups and established organizations, on account of their great advantages, such as decoupling business logic and better code intelligibility, they also have their disadvantages, which are mostly focused on problems of communication management, networking, and observability.

It is therefore important to decide whether the use of a microservices pattern is really necessary. The size of the solution and clarity in the separation of responsibilities are fundamental factors when making this decision. For simpler or smaller solutions, it is perfectly acceptable to use a monolithic-type architecture pattern, where instead of having many small, orchestrated applications, you have just one large application with full responsibility for the solution.

In *Chapter 3, Application Modernization using Google Cloud,* we will go into greater detail on the technologies used in GCP in order to support an ecosystem of microservices, mitigating the disadvantages mentioned previously:

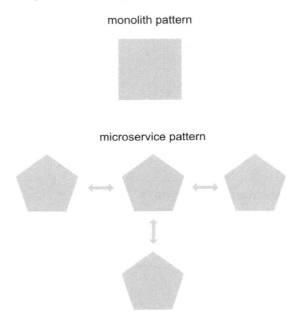

Figure 1.3 – Monolith versus microservice pattern

# Handling user sessions and the importance of stateless applications in the autoscaling world

Probably, if you are a developer who comes from an old-school background, you will be familiar with managing user sessions on the server side. For a long time, this was how you knew whether or not a user was already authenticated in an application, consulting the server for this information. These types of applications are called *stateful.*

With the advent of the cloud and the ease of being able to create and destroy instances, horizontal autoscaling became very popular, but it also brought with it a big problem for applications that already existed and were based on querying the server status.

Horizontal scaling consists of the ability to create and destroy instances of our application to deal with high demand at peak times. One example of a trigger for horizontal scaling could be the number of calls received in a specific period of time.

Stateful applications don't work well using horizontal scaling because in this kind of application, the state information is stored in the instance itself, leaving all the other instances inside the horizontal scaling group without the state information. One example of this is when a user with a user session created and stored in one instance of the application accesses another instance of the group without the information from this user session.

To solve this problem, we can use access tokens, which enable session information to be maintained by the user, not by the server. Applications that store state information outside the instance itself are called *stateless*.

When a user logs in for the first time, an access token is generated, which is signed by an authorizing entity with a private key (which is only stored in that server or instance) and is verified in each of the other instances or servers with a public key, to verify that the access token has been effectively generated by our application and not by a third party:

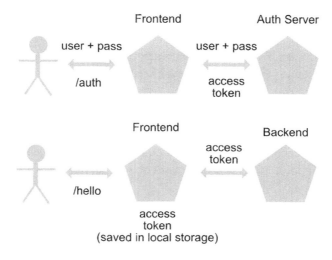

Figure 1.4 – Authentication flow

There are also access tokens of the **JSON Web Token (JWT)** type, which, in addition to having information about the signature of the token, can contain non-sensitive information such as the user's name, email, and roles, among other things.

In conclusion, although there are still applications that maintain their states based on the server, if an application requires horizontal scaling capabilities, it is necessary to adopt an authentication strategy using access tokens that are stored on the client side, using a stateless application solution.

# Application logging, your best friend in error troubleshooting

Before the advent of microservices, there were only monolithic applications, in which the complete solution was kept in a single instance. This allowed application debugging and troubleshooting to be much simpler, since all the logs were stored in one place.

With the advent of microservices, solutions stopped relying on just one instance and this began to make debugging and troubleshooting activities more complex.

Now we need to be able to stream the logs generated by the various microservices to a centralized logging service in order to analyze all the information in one place, transforming our application to stateless.

We need also to revise the way in which logs are generated in our applications to facilitate debugging.

Now the logs have to not only indicate whether or not an error existed, but also somehow allow the generation of a trace from whichever service the call was initiated because an error now depends not only on a single instance but also on multiple actions executed on different servers.

Among the most common solutions to address these problems is the addition of custom headers to each of the calls that are generated between microservices, resulting in the traceability of the origin of the system and unique event codes:

Figure 1.5 – Trace example

These options are an excellent element in microservices ecosystems to facilitate both the debugging and troubleshooting of applications.

## Why should your microservices handle retries?

In any computer system, anything can fail and that is why our application has to be prepared to control these errors. In the world of microservices, this problem is even greater since, unlike an application built with the monolithic pattern, where all communications are generated in the same instance, each of the calls between microservices can fail. This makes it necessary to implement retry policies and error handling in each of the calls that are made.

When retrying a call to a microservice, there are some important factors to consider, such as the number of times we are going to retry the call and how long to wait between each retry.

In addition, it is necessary to allow the microservice to recover in the event that it is not available due to call saturation. In this case, the *truncated exponential backoff strategy* is used, which consists of increasing the time between each of the retry calls to the microservice in order to allow its recovery, with a maximum upper limit of growth of the time between calls.

Some service mesh solutions (a dedicated layer to handle service-to-service communications) such as Istio come with automatic retry functionality, so there is no need to code the retry logic. However, if your microservices ecosystem does not have a service mesh solution, you can use one of the available open source libraries, depending on which programming language you are using.

Understanding that service-to-service communication can sometimes fail, you should always consider implementing retries in applications that work with microservices ecosystems, along with the truncated exponential backoff algorithm, to make your solutions more reliable.

## How to handle high traffic with autoscaling

Before the arrival of the cloud, it was necessary, when starting a computer project, to first evaluate the resources that would be required before buying the server on which the application would live. The problem with this was, and still is, that estimating the resources needed to run an application is very complex. Real load tests are generally necessary to effectively understand how many resources an application will use.

Furthermore, once the server was purchased, the resources could not be changed, meaning that in the event of an error in the initial estimate, or some increase in traffic due to a special event such as Cyber Day, the application could not obtain more resources. The result could be a bad experience for users and lost sales.

This is why most of the applications that are still deployed on on-premises servers have problems when high-traffic events arise. However, thanks to the arrival of the cloud, and the ease of creating and destroying instances, we have the arrival of **autoscaling**.

Autoscaling is the ability of an application under a load balancer to scale its instances horizontally depending on a particular metric. Among the most common metrics to manage autoscaling in an application are the number of calls made to the application and the percentage of CPU and RAM usage:

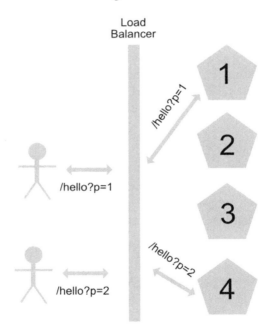

Figure 1.6 – Scaling out or horizontal scaling

For applications implemented in services of the IaaS or CaaS type, it is necessary to consider, for the correct management of the applications' autoscaling, the warm-up and cool-down time, in addition to application health checks.

**Warm-up** is the time it takes for the application to be available to receive post-deployment calls. This time must be configured to avoid an application receiving calls when it is not yet available.

**Cool-down** is the period of time where the rules defined in the autoscaling metrics are ignored. This configuration helps avoid the unwanted creation and destruction of instances due to short variations in defined metrics such as CPU, memory, and user concurrency calls.

For example, if you have a 60-second cool-down configuration, all the metrics received in that period of time, after the creation of new instances, will not be considered to trigger the autoscaling policy. If you don't have a cool-down configuration, the autoscaling policy could trigger the creation of new instances before the warm-up of the application in those first created instances, generating the unwanted triggering of the autoscaling policy.

The health check is a status verification used for determining whether a service is available to receive calls (it is related to warming up) so that the load balancer has the possibility of sending traffic only to instances that are able to receive traffic at that time.

For applications implemented as serverless-type services, no special configuration is required, since they support the ability to auto-scale automatically.

Depending on the services supported by the cloud provider you use to implement your application, it may be necessary to perform additional configuration steps to correctly control autoscaling policies.

# Avoiding overload caching your data

Although it is possible to control an increase in traffic by autoscaling the application, this action is not free, since it means both the temporary creation of new instances to be able to support this load and, in the case of serverless services, an increase in costs for each call made.

To reduce costs and also increase the performance of the calls made, it is therefore necessary to use a data caching strategy:

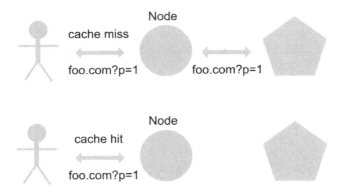

Figure 1.7 – Caching example

Implementing a caching strategy consists of saving in a database, in memory, queries that are made recurrently (using a key that corresponds to the query). To see whether a user returns to make a query that was made previously, it is saved in the database and thus there is no need to re-process the request, thereby reducing both response times and costs.

The first thing to do before implementing a caching strategy is to evaluate whether the scenario allows this strategy to be implemented. For this, it is necessary to identify the frequency with which changes are made to the data source that the application service consults. If the data change frequency of the source is 0 or very low, this is the ideal scenario to implement a caching strategy. Otherwise, if the data change frequency of the source is very high, it is recommended not to implement this caching strategy since the user could get outdated data.

Depending on the frequency with which the data changes in the source, it will be necessary to configure the lifetime of the cache. This is to avoid the data in the cache becoming outdated relative to the data in the source due to modification of the source, in which case users would get outdated information.

This strategy allows us to optimize our application to achieve better use of resources, increase responsiveness for users, and reduce the costs associated with both the use of resources and money for serverless solutions.

# Loosely coupled microservices with topics

When designing a microservices architecture, it is important to ensure that calls made between each of the applications are reliable. This means that the information sent between microservices has retry policies and is not lost in cases of failure. It is also important to design the application solution so that if a microservice needs to be replaced, this does not affect the other microservices. This concept is known as **loose coupling**.

To implement a loosely coupled strategy, and also to ensure that messages sent between microservices are not lost due to communication failures or micro-cuts, there are **messaging services**.

In GCP, we have a messaging service based on the publisher/subscriber pattern called **Pub/Sub**, where the publisher makes a publication of the message to be sent to a topic, and the subscriber subscribes to a topic in order to obtain this message. There are also two types of subscriptions: pull-type subscriptions, in which the subscriber must constantly consult the topic if there is a new message, and push-type subscriptions, where the subscriber receives a notification with the message through an HTTP call:

Figure 1.8 – Loosely coupled microservices

In a loosely coupled ecosystem of microservices, each microservice should publish its calls using messages on a topic, and the microservices that are interested in receiving these calls as messages must subscribe. In Pub/Sub, upon receiving a message, the subscriber must inform the topic with an **ACK**, or **acknowledge**, code to inform the topic that the message was received correctly. If the subscriber cannot receive or process the message correctly, the topic will resend the message to the subscriber for up to 7 days in order to ensure delivery.

Each microservice that acts as a subscriber must have the ability to filter duplicate messages and execute tasks idempotently, which means having the ability to identify whether a message has already been delivered previously, so as not to process it in a duplicate way.

The use of messaging services in microservices ecosystems allows us to have robust solution designs, loosely coupled and tolerant of communication errors.

# Don't waste your time – use cloud management services and securely run your applications

In this section, we review some of the existing services to which we can delegate specific responsibilities so that we can focus development efforts on what really matters, which is business logic.

We will also review how we can communicate with these services in a secure way through service accounts, and how to ensure communication between services.

## Don't reinvent the wheel

GCP offers multiple services that allow us to perform tasks just by invoking the available APIs without having to code a solution completely from scratch.

In this section, we will review 10 of the most used services in GCP. In later chapters, we will review each of these services in detail. The services are as follows:

- Cloud storage
- Pub/Sub
- Cloud SQL
- Firestore
- Memorystore
- Compute Engine
- Google Kubernetes Engine
- Google Secret Manager
- Cloud logging
- Cloud monitoring

**Cloud Storage** is an object store that allows unlimited storage of information in different regions, storage classes (the possibility of reducing costs, changing the pricing model, and the availability of the objects required by the solution), and life cycle policy configuration for existing files. It also allows access to information in a granular way and the hosting of static data web applications.

**Pub/Sub** is a serverless messaging service under the publisher/subscriber pattern, used for communication between two services in a reliable and decoupled way. It has automatic autoscaling and allows messages to be stored for up to 7 days in case of subscriber failures.

**Cloud SQL** is a self-managed solution for **Online Transactional Processing (OLTP)** databases such as MySQL, PostgreSQL, and SQL Server. It allows you to configure the type of machine on which the databases will run, create read-only replicas, and generate backups on a scheduled basis.

**Firestore** is a serverless NoSQL database solution that allows you to store information in the form of documents based on keys and values, allowing you to access the information very quickly.

**Memorystore** is an in-memory database solution for technologies such as Redis and Memcached, used when you want to optimize the use of resources, reduce costs, and increase performance in calls to data sources that have zero or very low modification frequency.

**Compute Engine** is the IaaS solution for getting virtual machines on-demand using the GCP infrastructure.

**Google Kubernetes Engine** is the self-managed solution for Kubernetes clusters. It offers management of the master node in a totally self-administered way, and provides a host of configuration and monitoring options through the GCP console.

**Google Secret Manager** is a secret storage solution. It is used in order to comply with security standards, obtaining the secrets to use in on-demand applications instead of hardcoded values.

**Cloud Logging** is the logging and visualization solution. It allows you to store an unlimited number of logs and query the logs.

**Cloud Monitoring** is the solution for viewing metrics and scheduling alerts.

These are some of the most used services on GCP. In all, over 100 services are available for delegating different responsibilities within the solution design of your application, allowing you to focus on the development of business logic and the delivery of value to the end user.

# Accessing services in a secure way

When we delegate the responsibilities of our solution to one or more services, we must have a way of communicating securely from our application to each of those services.

For the consumption of services and APIs in GCP, two types of authentication are used.

If the application needs to consume GCP services such as Cloud Storage, authentication is carried out through **OIDC**, or **OpenID Connect**, an identity layer that utilizes the **OAuth 2.0** protocol for authorization, allowing the identity of the consumer to be verified.

If the application is to consume any of the Google APIs hosted on `googleapis.com`, OAuth 2.0 is used, the standard protocol to manage authentication and authorization.

However, in most cases, it will not be necessary to use either of these protocols and connecting to any of the services will be possible simply by using the libraries of the available programming languages and a service account with the necessary permissions.

A service account is an account that is used by services to consume other services, unlike users who use a username and password. Roles are assigned to the service account (this process is called binding), which has one or more permissions already defined in order to facilitate the consumption of services.

If it is necessary to consume a service from a resource in a GCP project, simply access the project's metadata and select the service account to use. This will allow the service to have access to the service account private key path through the `GOOGLE_APPLICATION_CREDENTIALS` environment variable and the client library will handle the authentication using the private key and sign the access token.

On the other hand, if the application needs to consume a GCP service and the application is not inside a GCP project, it is necessary to generate a private key of that particular service account, download it, and save it safely in the resource. You can then expose it in your application through the `GOOGLE_APPLICATION_CREDENTIALS` environment variable:

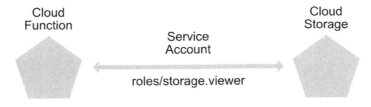

Figure 1.9 – Service account

In this way, it is possible to consume the different GCP services both for resources within the platform itself and as resources in other clouds or in environments within their own data centers.

## Summary

In this chapter, we learned about the differences between the different types of services offered by GCP, from IaaS-type services, which offer the greatest flexibility but, at the same time, impose greater responsibilities, to SaaS-type services, which provide direct access to functionalities without the need to code the solution. We also reviewed concepts such as region, zone, high availability, and latency, and discussed what types of solutions we can apply to our designs in order to meet the needs in these areas.

We had a general introduction to the world of microservices, understanding the importance of structuring and writing logs that allow the traceability of unique events so that debugging and troubleshooting can be carried out. We understood that it is necessary to create tasks within our applications in an idempotent way in order to allow retries and anticipate the failure of calls between microservices.

We reviewed concepts that are key to implementing an auto-scalable solution, such as stateful versus stateless, and were able to understand the importance of designing a loosely coupled solution. In the next chapter, we will learn about security concepts and best practices to protect your applications in the cloud.

# 2
# Security Fundamentals and Best Practices

In this chapter, we look at the best security practices for your applications on **Google Cloud Platform** (**GCP**) in order to reduce the attack surface of your services and protect them from any unauthorized access to information or actions. You will learn about the following topics:

- What the **principle of least privilege** (**POLP**) is, and why it is critical to the security of your applications

- What a service account is and how we can integrate it with our applications to access Google Cloud services

- How to avoid hardcoded passwords in your application using Google Secret Manager

- How to apply Google Cloud best practices to your application

# Technical requirements

For this chapter, you will require the following technology:

- Google Cloud SDK 317 or later (`https://cloud.google.com/sdk`)

# Reducing the attack surface with POLP

Often, we find ourselves in a situation where, to speed up the development of our application, we grant permissions without understanding what we are really doing, just to make the code work. The problem with this strategy is that by assigning more permissions than the application needs to perform its functions, we increase its attack surface. This increases the possibility of vulnerabilities arising in our application, with the risk that these will be exploited by malicious actors. This is why **POLP** exists, and we will look at this in detail next.

## POLP

The idea behind POLP is that *each application must have the minimum permissions it needs in order to operate, so as to prevent an application from performing actions for which it was not created.*

In order to comply with this principle, it is necessary to identify in the application design phase the dependencies of the services to be consumed and the actions that they will perform on these services, in order to create a privilege matrix and thus be able to determine what the permissions are that each application should have.

In an application designed with a monolithic pattern, the application will have a key with all the permissions needed to consume the services that the application requires for its operation.

In an application designed with a pattern of microservices, each microservice will have a unique key, where each of these keys will have the necessary permissions for its operation.

An overview of POLP can be seen in the following diagram:

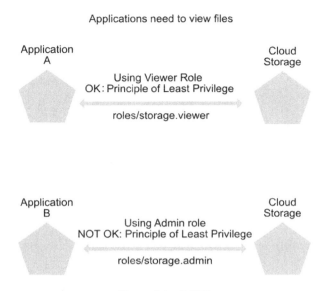

Figure 2.1 – POLP

In the next section, we will review in detail what a service account is and how to assign roles and permissions both to applications designed with a monolithic pattern and to those with a microservices pattern.

# How to authenticate client-to-service and service-to-service solutions

Whether our application is designed with a monolithic pattern or a microservices pattern, in most cases, it will be necessary to consume a service as a client (a user logging in to a web application) or as a service (a microservice called to another microservice or a self-managed service).

For both cases, it is necessary to understand concepts such as authentication, authorization, **identity and access management (IAM)**, and service account (among others), and we will review these concepts in this section.

# IAM

Using basic created roles, it is possible to quickly select the necessary permissions to execute certain activities in each of the services. The task of associating one or more members (such as user accounts) with a single role is called **binding**, and a collection of those bindings is called a **policy**.

The basic existing roles are **Owner (roles/owner)**, **Editor (roles/editor)**, and **Viewer (roles/viewer)**. These roles allow you to start working in GCP quickly but have very broad permissions, so it is always recommended to change roles and permissions after the creation of a project in order to be able to comply with POLP.

Each service also has predefined roles, which allow different activities focused directly on the capabilities offered by the service.

If you need to assign a role to a specific user, you can use the following Google Cloud SDK command:

```
gcloud projects add-iam-policy-binding PROJECT_ID
  --member=MEMBER --role=ROLE
```

The fields appearing in the preceding command are explained here:

- PROJECT_ID: The project ID
- MEMBER: The member to add the binding for (for example, user account)
- ROLE: The role to assign (for example, **roles/viewer**)

If the existing predefined roles do not meet the needs of both the user and the application that will consume these services, it is possible to create custom roles, adding the necessary permissions for our application's needs.

Because assigning roles can be a complex task, GCP offers a recommendation service that uses machine learning to make suggestions in order to reduce permissions and thus comply with POLP.

If you want to grant public access to a resource—as, for example, in the case of unstructured files within a Cloud Storage bucket—you can use the allUsers identity, which represents any internet user. This feature is useful when you want to have videos and images from a web application without an authentication requirement.

If you want to grant access only to authenticated users, you can use the allAuthenticatedUsers identity. This feature is useful when you do not want to restrict access to a particular resource but you want to know who is consuming that resource. In the following figure, you can see how the assignment of roles works in IAM.

Figure 2.2 – Identity, roles, and resources

# IAM hierarchy

Google Cloud offers the following ways to organize resources:

- Organizations
- Folders
- Projects
- Resources

This hierarchy is depicted in the following diagram:

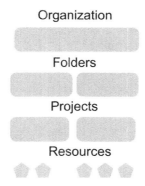

Figure 2.3 – IAM hierarchy

As we can see in *Figure 2.3*, the organization is the entity with the highest position in the hierarchy, then folders. The latter are optional and are generally used to order projects into business units; then come the projects, and finally, the resources.

It is also very important to understand how the granting of permissions based on the IAM hierarchy works, whereby the permissions granted higher in the hierarchy will join with the permissions assigned lower in the hierarchy.

For example, if user A has an **Owner** role at the organization level and in project B is assigned a **Viewer** role, user A will have an **Owner** role and a **Viewer** role in project B, because an *organization* is an entity at a higher hierarchical level than a project.

This is why it is important to understand how to organize your resources within GCP, as well as how permissions and roles are affected according to the IAM hierarchy, as this will allow you to have greater control and understanding over the access rights that each of the identities will have on each of the resources.

## Service accounts

Service accounts are used to establish authentication between two services to perform operations on an **application programming interface (API)**.

For this, it is necessary to first create a service account, which is an entity that does not represent a user but, rather, an application.

Unlike a user account, which has a username and password for authentication, a service account is associated with a private and public key that are used to authenticate in GCP. A service account will, depending on the management system selected, have a pair of public and private keys.

If the keys are managed through GCP, Google will store both the public and private keys and will periodically rotate the keys in order to prevent them from being used for unauthorized access in the event of a leak. Furthermore, Google will never access the private key directly, but will grant access through APIs in order to be able to create a signature on behalf of the service account.

This type of management is generally used when the service being used is part of Google, such as Cloud Functions. In the following figure, you can see how Cloud Function uses a service account in order to access Google services.

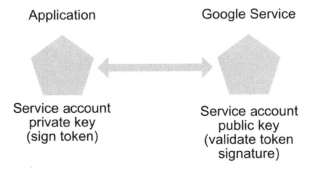

Figure 2.4 – Cloud Functions service account

If the keys are managed by the user, Google is only responsible for storing the public key, and the private key is used by an application that requires a signature on behalf of the service account in order to authenticate.

When key management is undertaken by the user, it is essential to store the private key in a secure way; otherwise, it could mean the leakage of the private key and access to unauthorized resources.

We can also use the concept of impersonating service accounts in order to give a member (such as a user account) access to all the resources that the service account can access or the ability to create **Open Authorization (OAuth)** 2.0 access tokens. This option is useful when we want to give access to a user without directly giving them the private key of the service account.

To allow a member to impersonate a service account, we can use the following Google Cloud SDK command:

```
gcloud iam service-accounts set-iam-policy sa-id policy-file
```

The fields appearing in the preceding command are explained here:

- `sa-id`: The ID of your service account
- `policy-file`: The path to the policy file with the bindings

If we want to allow a member to access all the resources that the service account can access, we need to use the **Service Account User** role (`roles/iam.serviceAccountUser`). If we want to allow a member to create OAuth 2.0 access tokens, we need to use the **Service Account Token Creator** role (`roles/iam.serviceAccountTokenCreator`).

To create the policy file with the roles mentioned previously, you can use the following template, replacing the member and the role to use:

```
{
  "bindings": [
    {
      "members": [
        "user:member@example.com"
      ],
      "role": "roles/iam.serviceAccountUser"
    }
  ],
  "version": 1
}
```

# Authenticating with Google services

If we want to save unstructured data such as images or videos, use machine learning services for the identification of images, undertake **natural language processing (NLP)**, or save information in a non-relational document database (among other activities), it is necessary to authenticate with Google Cloud services.

To authenticate with Google services, the first thing to do is create a service account and assign it a role with the necessary permissions to consume the selected GCP service(s). If the service account does not have the required permissions to consume the service, we will receive a status code of type HTTP 401 UNAUTHORIZED_ERROR. Otherwise, if the service account does have the corresponding permissions, we will receive a status code of type HTTP 200 OK.

If your application runs inside a Google Cloud environment such as **Google Compute Engine (GCE)**, **Google Kubernetes Engine (GKE)**, or Cloud Functions, and you are using Google Cloud Client Libraries to access Google services, **Application Default Credentials (ADC)** can be used automatically to find your service account credentials.

For example, if you want to make an authenticated call to a Google service such as Cloud Storage and get a list of the buckets inside, you can use the following code:

```
//Google Cloud client library for Cloud Storage
const {Storage} = require('@google-cloud/storage');

// The client library will use ADC to get service account
credentials.
const storage = new Storage();

async function listBuckets() {

    const results = await storage.getBuckets();
    const [buckets] = results;

    buckets.forEach(bucket => {
        console.log(bucket.name);
    });
}
listBuckets();
```

In most cases, it will only be necessary to use Google Cloud Client Libraries to consume the service, depending on the programming language we are using.

Should you need to authenticate to a Google service such as Cloud Functions or Cloud Run to call a custom endpoint, you will need to create a **Google-signed OAuth ID token** (a **JSON Web Token (JWT)** that expires approximately an hour after creation), with `aud` (**audience**) set to the **Uniform Resource Locator (URL)** of the receiving service, and then include the ID token (such as a bearer token) in the `Authorization` header.

In the code snippet that follows, you can see how to get a Google-signed OAuth ID token and then use the token to make an authenticated call to a Google service.

This code was taken from the official Google Cloud documentation (`https://cloud. google.com/run/docs/authenticating/service-to-service#nodejs`):

```
// Make sure to `npm install --save request-promise` or add the
dependency to your package.json
const request = require('request-promise');


const receivingServiceURL = ...


// Set up metadata server request
// See https://cloud.google.com/compute/docs/instances/
verifying-instance-identity#request_signature
const metadataServerTokenURL = 'http://metadata/
computeMetadata/v1/instance/service-accounts/default/
identity?audience=';
const tokenRequestOptions = {
    uri: metadataServerTokenURL + receivingServiceURL,
    headers: {
        'Metadata-Flavor': 'Google'
    }
};


// Fetch the token, then provide the token in the request to
the receiving service
request(tokenRequestOptions)
    .then((token) => {
        return request(receivingServiceURL).auth(null, null, true,
token)
```

```
  })
  .then((response) => {
    res.status(200).send(response);
  })
  .catch((error) => {
    res.status(400).send(error);
  });
```

In the event that user authentication is required against Google services, it will be necessary to implement an OAuth 2.0-type authentication model, which we will look at in the next section.

## OAuth 2.0

The OAuth 2.0 protocol is used to authenticate from one application to another application, without the need to share credentials such as usernames and passwords.

The protocol is depicted in the following diagram:

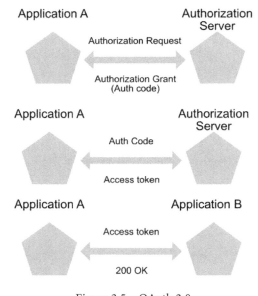

Figure 2.5 – OAuth 2.0

As can be seen in *Figure 2.5*, when a user wants to log in to application **A** from application **B**, the first step to be performed by application A is to generate an authorization request, which will show in pop-up mode a window of application B for the user to enter their username and password, in addition to accepting which permissions application A needs to perform its tasks.

After the authorization request, an authorization grant is received with an authorization code.

With the authorization code, an authorization grant is made to the authorization server in order to obtain an access token, which is used later in the calls from application A to application B to perform the actions that were accepted by the user.

Application A must be previously registered with application B for information such as the name, website, and callback URL.

With this information, application B will provide application A with a **Client ID** and **Client Secret** in order to carry out the authorization activities indicated previously.

In this way, by using the OAuth 2.0 protocol, it is possible to securely authenticate between two systems without compromising the user's credentials.

## Identity-Aware Proxy

**Identity-Aware Proxy (IAP)** allows you to manage user authorization at the application level in order not to depend on network-level tools such as firewalls and **virtual private networks (VPNs)**.

The use of IAP is recommended when you need to apply access control policies on applications.

An example of using IAP would be to allow access to an application for the sales business unit but to block access to the maintenance business unit.

The operation of IAP is based on the use of a proxy that allows users to access the application as long as they have assigned a policy previously defined in IAM. In the following figure, you can see the different layers of authentication and authorization of IAP.

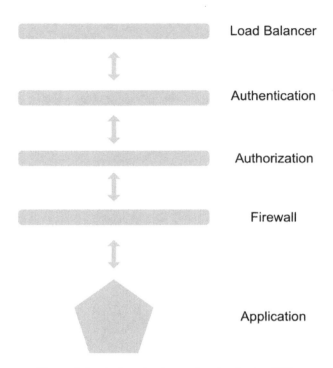

Figure 2.6 – Authentication and authorization IAP

As seen in *Figure 2.6*, the first step when a user makes a call to an application protected by IAP is verification of the load balancer, which verifies that IAP is enabled to consume the backend.

If IAP is enabled, IAP checks whether the user has previously logged in using the browser credentials. In the event that no credentials are found on the browser side, IAP asks the user to log in using the OAuth 2.0 protocol in order to obtain an access token and save it in the browser for subsequent access, thus validating the user's authentication.

If authentication is successful, it is necessary to proceed with the authorization of the user, verifying that the current user has the permissions to access the application.

If the user has the IAP-secured Web App User role configured in IAM, IAP will allow the user to access the application.

It is important to note that IAP works at the load balancer level. This means that if a resource within a project wants to directly access an application without going through the load balancer, it could perform this action. That is why it is important to perform a correct firewall configuration within the VPN or **virtual private cloud** (**VPC**) of the project. Otherwise, resources within the project could be able to access the application without the need to go through the load balancer, bypassing the IAP validation.

# Managing secrets with Google Secret Manager

Most applications require the use of credentials or keys to authenticate with either GCP or third-party services. The correct storage of these credentials and secrets is essential to avoid security problems and leakage of this information. It is recommended to use a vault of secrets to securely store all the credentials required by an application.

In this section, we will explore the benefits of using a vault of secrets in applications and look at the service GCP offers to fulfill this function.

## How to store your sensitive data in a secure way

Have you ever checked the source code of an application and found that the code stores sensitive information such as keys or credentials of databases or third-party services?

Storing these types of secrets in the code can mean a serious security vulnerability, allowing people who have access to the source code to access these resources and perform actions that were not contemplated during the creation of the application.

To avoid this problem, secret vaults were created. These are services that allow us to store sensitive information such as keys and credentials outside of the source code and request these values only when an application requires them, to prevent them from being exposed and thus being used maliciously.

In addition, a vault of secrets allows the management of all the secrets of an application in one place, which makes it easy to change a secret that could have been exposed or filtered, without the need to make changes to the source code of the application.

Another advantage of a vault of secrets is the possibility of constantly rotating keys and credentials, in order to prevent a secret that could have been leaked being used in a malicious way.

The use of a vault or secret manager in our application is a necessity if we want our application to be more secure, by preventing unauthorized access to resources that only our application should access. In the following figure, you can see how Google Secret Manager works.

Figure 2.7 – Google Secret Manager

## Google Secret Manager

**Google Secret Manager** allows you to store sensitive information in a centralized way, to prevent the information being obtained by a team member who has access to the source code of an application but who is not authorized to access those resources.

The sensitive information that can be stored includes API keys, credentials, and certificates, among other aspects.

Because it is possible to configure replication policies, secrets can be stored and replicated in regions, which allows the secrets to have greater availability and thus avoids service unavailability due to the inability to obtain secrets from Secret Manager in the event of an outage.

It is also possible to perform versioning on the secrets, in order to conduct an audit of changes that have been made in the rotations of keys or credentials.

Furthermore, thanks to IAM, it is possible to separate the responsibilities of the entities, authorizing access to the secrets only to applications and, on the other hand, authorizing the modification of these secrets to a member of the organization assigned exclusively to this type of task.

It is also possible to rotate the secrets, using the available Secret Manager APIs, to reduce the risk of unauthorized access to resources due to the leaking of secrets.

Finally, Secret Manager allows auditing of all the actions carried out on the stored secrets, such as reading, writing, and deletion, in order to meet the compliance standards required in organizations.

These combined characteristics allow our application to access secrets for calls to services from both GCP and third parties on demand, with the assurance that the information will be available through regional replication, encrypted by default, and with a rotation policy in place to prevent unauthorized access through undue exposure of sensitive information.

# Cloud Key Management Service

**Cloud Key Management Service** (**Cloud KMS**) is a service that allows you to manage encryption keys using Cloud IAM and also encrypt and decrypt data using those keys. The keys stored in Cloud KMS are part of an object called a key ring. One key ring can store multiple keys.

To create a key ring, you can use the following Google Cloud SDK command:

```
gcloud kms keyrings create KEY_RING_NAME --location LOCATION
```

The fields appearing in the preceding command are explained here:

- KEY_RING_NAME: The name of the key ring to create
- LOCATION: The location where the key ring will be created—this could be a **Regional**, **Dual-regional**, **Multi-regional**, or **Global** location

After creation of the key ring, we need to create a key that will be used to encrypt and decrypt our data. You can use the following command to do this:

```
gcloud kms keys create KEY_NAME --location LOCATION --keyring
KEY_RING_NAME \
--purpose "encryption"
```

The fields appearing in the preceding command are explained here:

- KEY_NAME: The name of the key to create
- KEY_RING_NAME: The name of the key ring to use
- LOCATION: The location where the key will be created—this could be a **Regional**, **Dual-regional**, **Multi-regional**, or **Global** location

After creating the key inside the key ring, we can use Cloud KMS encryption to encrypt data.

For example, if we want to encrypt data in plaintext, we can use the following command to create a new file with the encrypted data:

```
gcloud kms encrypt \
    --location LOCATION \
    --keyring KEY_RING_NAME \
    --key KEY_NAME \
    --plaintext-file FILE_TO_ENCRYPT \
    --ciphertext-file ENCRYPTED_FILE
```

The fields appearing in the preceding command are explained here:

- KEY_NAME: The name of the key to use
- KEY_RING_NAME: The name of the key ring to use
- LOCATION: The location where the key will be created—this could be regional, dual-regional, multi-regional, or global
- FILE_TO_ENCRYPT: The path of the file to encrypt
- ENCRYPTED_FILE: The path where the encrypted file will be saved

If you need to decrypt your file, you just need to change the command using the decrypt action, as follows:

```
gcloud kms decrypt \
    --location LOCATION \
    --keyring KEY_RING_NAME \
    --key KEY_NAME \
    --ciphertext-file ENCRYPTED_FILE \

    --plaintext-file FILE_TO_DECRYPT
```

# Google Cloud best practices

In this section, we review the best practices recommended by Google to make our developments safer, using the tools we've learned about in this chapter.

These practices are important because they help us to balance the focus given to the development of new functionalities in an application with the analysis and implementation of effective security measures. In this way, they substantially reduce the likelihood of having security incidents when the application gets to production.

## POLP and roles

If a role has many permissions that are not used by your application, it is recommended to create a custom role with only the necessary permissions, thereby following POLP and reducing the application's attack surface.

## Create one service account per microservice

If you are creating an application with a pattern of microservices, create a service account with POLP for each microservice and do not reuse the private keys of service accounts in any of the microservices. In this way, if a private key of a service account is exposed or accessed by an unauthorized user, it is necessary only to disable that service account key without having to disable all the service accounts of the application.

## Avoid using Owner, Editor, and Viewer roles

Although when creating a project the simplest thing is to use the basic IAM roles, this is not recommended because they have very high permissions that do not comply with POLP. It is always advisable to use predefined or custom roles, even though this requires more work.

## allUsers versus allAuthenticatedUsers

Use `allUsers` when you need to publicly expose unstructured data in a Cloud Storage bucket, and use `allAuthenticatedUsers` when you need to obtain information from the user or application that is consuming the information, without the need for authorization.

## Understand how the IAM hierarchy works

Remember that, depending on which level of the hierarchy you apply a role policy to, the policy can be overwritten by policies at higher hierarchical levels. Note that if a user has Owner permissions at the organization level, they will have these same permissions on all projects in the organization, regardless of whether they are assigned a Viewer role in a particular project.

The most permissive permission will always overwrite the least permissive permission.

## Use Google management keys whenever possible

Whenever possible, it is recommended to use the key management of a service account through GCP, because keys are then more protected and Google takes care of automatic key rotation. However, if this is not possible (for example, because the application that requires use of the key is outside of GCP or on account of some compliance issue), it is recommended to use a key vault tool such as Google Secret Manager. Failing that, take the greatest possible precautionary measures to avoid leakage and access by unauthorized personnel.

## Use OAuth 2.0 instead of sharing credentials between applications

If application A has to connect to application B to obtain information or perform an operation, never share the user's credentials directly with the other application. Instead, use the OAuth 2.0 protocol, which allows—through authorization flow—an access token to be obtained to enable authenticated operations to be performed on an API.

## Use IAP when possible to authenticate and authorize users inside your organization

If you have systems within your organization that only collaborators can enter, it is recommended to enable the IAP functionality in order to facilitate the management of the authentication and authorization of the systems.

It is important to remember that authentication is performed at the load balancer level, so appropriate security measures must be taken in the configuration of firewalls to prevent any malicious calls from going through the load balancer and then directly back to an application.

## Always use a key vault for the storage of secrets

If your application needs to store secrets such as private keys, or users and passwords to consume third-party services, never store these secrets in the source code of the application since anyone with access to the code could obtain the secrets and gain unauthorized access to resources.

Instead, always use a key vault such as Google Secret Manager to store, manage, or rotate secrets in a centralized way.

# Summary

In this chapter, we have learned what POLP is and seen how it helps to reduce the attack surface of our systems. We learned how to authenticate with GCP services, using service accounts with the roles and permissions required for an application to operate. We found out about IAM and related concepts such as identity, roles, and resources, and the association of these concepts through a policy. We looked at the hierarchy of resources within Google Cloud, and saw how this hierarchy affects the permissions that an entity may have on specific resources.

We examined the OAuth 2.0 protocol and how it relates to authentication between our application and GCP services, and learned how to manage secrets in a secure way using Google Secret Manager.

Finally, we reviewed the good practices recommended by Google for the development of our applications in order to create secure applications in the GCP cloud.

# Section 2: Developing and Modernizing Applications on Google Cloud Platform

In this section, you will learn the best practices of how to develop and deploy your applications in the cloud using the different components offered by Google Cloud Platform. You will also understand when to use each of these components and what acceptable practices you should consider in your developments.

This section comprises the following chapters:

- *Chapter 3, Application Modernization Using Google Cloud*
- *Chapter 4, Using Cloud Functions and Google App Engine*
- *Chapter 5, Virtual Machines and Container Applications on Google Cloud Platform*
- *Chapter 6, Managing APIs on Google Cloud Platform*

# 3
# Application Modernization Using Google Cloud

Many people think that just using a lift and shift strategy with their old applications will bring all the benefits of using the cloud.

Suppose you want to take advantage of all the benefits of the cloud such as autoscaling, fully managed services, and cost-saving. In that case, you need to create or refactor your existing application so that it works with those services and takes all the cloud's benefits. This is known as application modernization.

In this chapter, we're going to cover the following main topics:

- Preparing your environment for developing applications on Google Cloud
- Be sure that your application will work fine on the cloud with testing
- Improving your delivery speed with continuous integration and delivery pipelines
- Application modernization best practices

# Technical requirements

You will need the following technical requirements for this chapter:

- A computer with an internet connection and access to a web browser
- Node 10 or later: `https://nodejs.org/en/`

# Preparing your environment for developing applications on Google Cloud

Before you start any development process, it is necessary to prepare your local environment with the tools needed to manage **Google Cloud Platform** (**GCP**) resources.

In this section, we will review how to emulate GCP services in the local development environment, create a project to organize all our resources, install and configure the Cloud SDK, and use the developer tools to facilitate our development work.

## Emulating Google Cloud services for local application development

Some GCP resources allow you to execute and test locally to facilitate development, and thus avoid the need to constantly deploy your application to the cloud to perform tests.

With the **Functions Framework**, it is possible to develop serverless applications that run both in our local environment and in GCP, without the need for us to make changes.

The Functions Framework defines a `PORT` to specify functions triggered by HTTP calls, a `FUNCTION_TARGET`, which determines whether the function is called through HTTP or a specific event (such as the creation of an object in Cloud Storage or the arrival of a message in Pub/Sub), and a `SIGNATURE_TYPE`.

The Functions Framework can be executed via the command line in your Terminal or through a library as a dependency of an application.

In this case, we will explore an example of the Functions Framework by using Node.js in our Terminal.

The first step is to create a Node.js project using the `npm init` command.

If this is your first time creating a Node.js project from scratch, it is important to know some basic concepts about the preceding command.

The npm init command creates a package.json file that includes the dependencies of the project and metadata such as the project's name, description, and author.

When we execute this command, we will need to supply the following information:

- **Package name**: Name of the project
- **Version**: Version of the project
- **Description**: Description of the project
- **Entry point**: Main file of the project
- **Test command**: Command to test your project
- **Git tepository**: The URL of the GitHub repository
- **Keywords**: Words related to your project
- **Author**: Your name + <email> (optional) + (website) (optional)
- **License**: The license of the project

Then, create an index.js file with the following code:

```
exports.helloWorld = (req, res) => {
  res.send('Hello, World!');
};
```

Next, install the Functions Framework library with the npm install @google-cloud/functions-framework --save-dev command.

(--save-dev is used for modules that are used in the development phase; it is not required when you're running in a production environment.)

Edit the package.json file and add the following command to the scripts section:

```
scripts:
{
"start":"functions-framework -target=helloWorld"
}
```

Finally, execute the npm start command and, in a browser, go to localhost:8080.

# Creating Google Cloud projects

A GCP project is a space where all the resources that you will use in your application are organized. It is generally recommended that you create a project for each environment. For example, if we have an application that has separate development, integration, and production environments, three projects should be created in GCP:

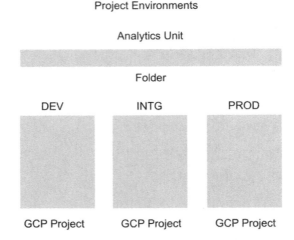

Figure 3.1 – Project environments

Each project has three basic elements that must be identified:

- **Project name**: A friendly project name for easy understanding
- **Project ID**: A manually generated unique identifier for the created project
- **Project number**: An auto-generated unique identifier for the project

To create a project, it is necessary to have a Google account and then go to `https://console.cloud.google.com`. If you are creating a project for personal use, you will have the necessary permissions to execute the operation. However, if you are working inside an organization, you will need to have the `resourcemanager-projects-create` permission assigned to your Google account.

You can create the project in several ways, such as from the GCP web console, by using the GCP SDK, or through a direct call to the GCP APIs. The most common way to create a project in GCP is through the GCP web console, but creating one by using the SDK or APIs is also possible (and highly recommended) when you must automate these processes at an organizational level.

To create a project through the GCP console, we must perform the following steps:

1.  Go to the **Manage resources** section of the GCP console.

    A. Under the hamburger menu, look for **IAM & Admin**, and then **Manage Resources**. Alternatively, go directly to `https://console.cloud.google.com/cloud-resource-manager`.

    B. (Optional) If you are working inside an organization, select the corresponding organization.

2.  Click on **Create Project**.

3.  Enter the name of the project. If you are working with your personal account, you will have to select a billing account, which is where billing for the use of project resources will take place.

4.  Click on **Create**.

By following these instructions, you will have your GCP project ready so that you can start creating the necessary resources for your application.

## Using the command-line interface withCloud SDK

To manage existing resources in your GCP projects, it is necessary to install Google Cloud SDK locally. Depending on which operating system you are using, you will have to follow the corresponding instructions at the following link: `https://cloud.google.com/sdk`.

Once the Cloud SDK has been installed and the project profile has been configured, you can use the following commands in your Terminal:

*   `gsutil`: Used to perform operations on Google Cloud Storage

*   `gcloud`: Used to perform operations on the GCP platform

*   `bq`: Used to perform operations on BigQuery

While it is possible to use the GCP console to create and configure most of the existing functionality, some tasks are only available if we use the GCP SDK. Also, if you want to perform automated resource creation and configuration tasks, you must use the GCP SDK.

The GCP SDK commands are ordered hierarchically according to the following syntax:

```
gcloud [release version] GROUP COMMAND [args]
```

An example of this is `gcloud beta compute instances`.

If the `gcloud` command is followed by the word `beta`, this means that the version of the command is not in the **General Availability (GA)** phase yet. The `gcloud` command can be followed by the `alpha` and `beta` words. When there is not a specific version following the `gcloud` command, this means that the version is in the GA phase. The alpha and beta versions are not installed by default and it is necessary to run the `gcloud components install` command to use them.

Each of these phases has its own life cycle and recommendations. For example, GA indicates that the commands are stable and can be used without problems in production environments. In the event of any breaking changes, you will be informed in a timely manner through the official documentation channels.

Beta indicates that the commands work correctly but that they could still have some problems. Breaking changes could occur without announcements necessarily being made through the official channels, so although it is recommended to carry out concept tests or experiment with new GCP functionalities, its use is not recommended for production environments.

Alpha indicates that the commands are on an early release and that changes could occur on an ongoing basis without notice. This version is recommended for experimentation purposes only.

Then, there is the compute group, followed by the instance group.

Among the most used groups are the following:

- **Compute**: Commands related to the Compute Engine resource
- **IAM**: Commands related to Identity Access Management
- **Projects**: Commands related to project configuration
- **Container**: Commands related to Kubernetes

Some commands that require actions that could modify or remove resources within your Google Cloud project will request explicit confirmation from the user. When you want to ignore this confirmation, as in the case of a command that is executed in an automated workflow, the `--quiet` flag can be used. In cases where this confirmation does not require a binary response such as yes or no, the option that's defined by default will be used.

In this section, we reviewed the installation process of Cloud SDK, the main groups of commands, the order of hierarchy, and the syntax and recommendations on how to use the commands of the GCP SDK.

To learn about all the commands that can be used with the GCP SDK, please go to `https://cloud.google.com/sdk/docs/cheatsheet`.

# Using developer tooling

To develop applications in the cloud, it is necessary to orchestrate a set of technologies and tools that allow the code to be taken from an IDE to a production environment. GCP has a toolkit that facilitates and accelerates the development of applications in the cloud.

Among the best-known tools, we have the following:

- **Cloud Code**: A suite that allows you to develop applications with Kubernetes or Cloud Run clusters, thus facilitating application deployments and debugging

- **Cloud Build**: Allows you to construct pipelines for deploying and testing applications in different GCP environments

- **Container Registry**: A repository for Docker image storage

- **Artifact Registry**: A repository for storing artifacts

Cloud Code can be installed in an IDE of your choice, such as **IntelliJ** or **VSCode**, or can be used directly from your web browser through the Cloud Shell Editor IDE. You can use the **New Application** command to start developing applications using a base template for programming languages such as Python and Node.js. In addition, using the **Deploy to Cloud Run** command allows you to generate a Docker image, publish it to the Container Registry (GCP's image storage repository solution), and deploy the service directly to Cloud Run.

Cloud Build allows you to build integration flows and continuous deployment in a serverless way for applications that are developed in different programming languages such as Java, Go, and Node.js among others, and deploy resources within your GCP project, such as virtual machines on Compute Engine, serverless applications on containers such as Cloud Run, or clustered Kubernetes applications by storing created artifacts in Container Registry or Artifact Registry.

It is possible to choose individual steps within a workflow by using open source contributions from the Cloud Build team. Here, you can select from community contributions or create your own custom workflows.

Each step within a workflow is composed of a Docker image, which allows us to mix different combinations of steps to create our own workflow in the most personalized way possible.

Each of these workflows can be executed manually through `gcloud` commands or executed automatically; that is, they are triggered by some action from a source code repository such as Bitbucket, GitHub, or Cloud Source Repository (which is the source code storage and management solution for GCP).

The basic elements we need to construct a workflow in Cloud Build are as follows:

- The source code of the application, along with all the elements necessary for it to operate, stored in a source code repository, as mentioned previously.
- A Cloud Build configuration file in YAML or JSON format with all the necessary instructions

For more references on how to create the necessary configuration file to create a workflow in Cloud Build, please go to `https://cloud.google.com/cloud-build/docs/build-config`.

In this section, we learned about the main development tools available in GCP and how they can interact with each other to deploy applications in our GCP projects.

# Be sure that your application will work fine on the cloud with testing

The bigger our application gets, the more difficult it becomes to manually test it. This is why it's necessary to automate tests on applications – to speed up the time dedicated to this task and thus increase the speed of delivering value and new functionalities.

There are different types of test, but in this section, we will focus on the following:

- **Unit testing**: Tests that are performed on a particular component that performs a single action, to verify that the task is successful.

- **Integration testing**: Tests that are carried out between two components to verify that the connection between both components works correctly.

- **Load testing**: Tests that are performed on one or more components to determine the maximum call capacity that the application can support.

Each of these tests is important to ensure that our application functions properly, but some tests require greater implementation efforts and execution time, such as performance or load tests, though others such as unit tests require less effort. It is necessary to prioritize the number of tests to be implemented and executed for each type to optimize the benefit that's obtained.

We will review each of these tests in detail here:

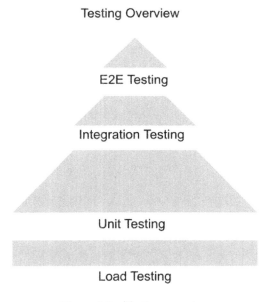

Figure 3.2 – Testing overview

# Unit testing

Unit tests are automated tests that ensure that a portion of the application code that executes a specific task returns an expected result. These tests generally consider executing classes or methods separately within the application:

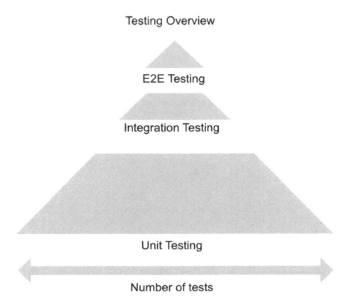

Figure 3.3 – Unit testing

As unit tests only involve testing a particular task, all the dependencies of this task must be replaced by mocks, which are objects that belong to the test frameworks that allow this activity to be carried out.

The more tasks that are performed in a unitary way within our application, the more security we will have when we add or modify existing functionalities without worrying about breaking the existing code. The amount of code that unit tests are defined for is called code coverage. The greater the code coverage, the greater the speed and confidence with which we will be able to deploy new functionalities in our application.

However, unit tests are not the only type of tests needed to verify that our application operates correctly. Just because the tasks work correctly when they're tested independently does not mean that they will work correctly when they are integrated with each other, so it is also necessary to perform what we call integration tests, to ensure that all our business flow works correctly.

# Integration testing

Integration tests enable us to verify that the tasks that were tested in the unit testing phase work correctly when they're joined together, ensuring that the combined operation of our activities delivers an expected result:

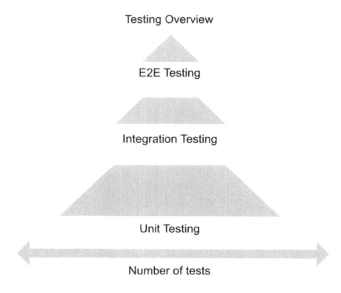

Figure 3.4 – Integration testing

To carry out integration tests, the same test framework that was used in the unit tests can be used, with the difference being that this time, we must take the dependencies of our execution into account; it will not be necessary to carry out integration mocks.

Although integration tests make it possible to ensure that the joint operation of different tasks is successful, their execution requires the use of greater resources and time, so it is recommended, unlike unit tests, to choose a set of the most critical and representative tasks of the application. This ensures that these tasks function correctly but at the same time avoid the integration testing process, thus becoming a bottleneck when we're deploying new functionality.

# End-to-end testing

**End-to-end** or **E2E** testing helps ensure that your application's business logic works properly without the need for manual testing. For this, it is necessary to put together a flow of activities that a particular user would carry out, and then verify that the result of this set of activities is as expected:

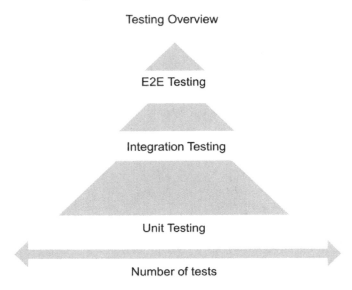

Figure 3.5 – E2E testing

To perform E2E tests, test frameworks such as **Selenium** can be used to automate user activities and thereby verify that what is shown on the screen is indeed the expected result. An example of an E2E test would be a user navigating a page of the application, selecting different items within a form, and verifying that these items are displayed correctly according to the user's selection.

These kinds of test require more time to carry out, in terms of development, implementation, and use of resources and execution, so unlike unit tests and integration tests, a set of such tests should be limited in size and focus on critical flows or those most representative of the application.

# Load testing

Load tests allow us to ensure that our application can support concurrent peaks of users without stopping working or presenting errors:

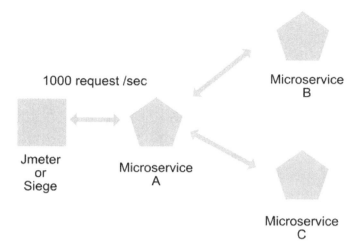

Figure 3.6 – Load testing

To carry out this type of test, it is necessary to simulate a user connecting simultaneously to our application with a load test framework such as **Jmeter** or **Siege**, where it is possible to specify the number of simultaneous users to be tested and the endpoint that they should be connected to.

Depending on the results of these tests, it will be necessary to increase the resources both in terms of the CPU or RAM of our instance (in case we only have one instance), or configure horizontal scaling policies to allow our application to generate multiple instances, and thus be capable of supporting the traffic that's generated by the number of concurrent users we are simulating.

It is always recommended that we carry out load tests on a recurring basis in order to understand how our system behaves in a general way, as well as to measure the effectiveness of our auto-scaling configurations to avoid unexpected behaviors.

# Improving your delivery speed with continuous integration and delivery pipelines

In the old days, when new functionality needed to be added to an application, it was necessary to perform a series of manual steps, such as downloading the source code, compiling and creating the artifact, running manual tests, reviewing security and code quality, and deploying the artifact on the servers.

Currently, thanks to the ease of provisioning resources in the cloud and the arrival of the DevOps culture in organizations, all these processes have been automated, which means that the time to deliver new functionalities to users has been reduced considerably. These automation processes are called continuous integration and delivery pipelines.

Continuous integration is where we automate tasks that take the source code of an application and carry out compilation, testing, and quality reviews in order to integrate changes with production branches.

Continuous delivery is an additional step of continuous integration that brings these changes into a productive environment with the prior approval of a technology team member.

Continuous deployment is the highest level of maturity in process automation. It allows us to directly deploy changes or new functionalities in productive applications without the need for the manual approval of a technology team member:

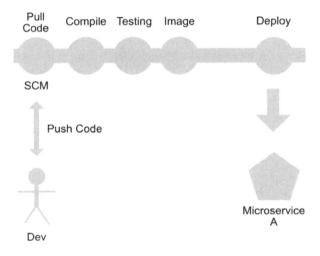

Figure 3.7 – CI/CD

Next, we will review the different tools and technologies that are necessary for building a continuous integration, delivery, or deployment flow.

# Source control management

In the old days, when you developed an application and wanted to have backups, different versions of the application were saved in different directories so that you could recover functional code in the face of certain types of errors. However, this way of managing source code was quite inefficient and for each change, it was necessary to save *all* the application code, which meant having the necessary storage to be able to make these backups:

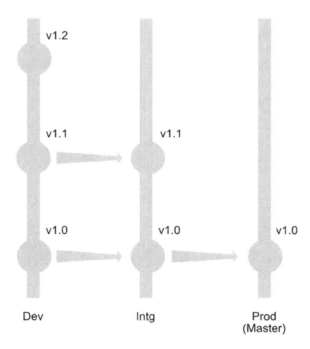

Figure 3.8 – Source control management

With the arrival of **Source Control Management (SCM)** tools, of which Git is the most well-known and most widely used example today, it is no longer necessary to store duplicate code to generate backups. Instead, it's possibly to only store the changes that are generated in our source code. This is obviously much more efficient in terms of storage.

In addition, the code is no longer stored in just one place but in a distributed way, both in a repository and on the computers of all the developers who are interacting with the application, which allows the backups of our application to be much more resilient. In addition, storing only the changes within our code allows us to understand what changes were made within our application, which means we can audit and accept or reject changes. Furthermore, we can maintain different branches with different versions of the code of our application, which is useful for keeping separate code that is in the development, testing, and production phases.

Within GCP, there is **Cloud Source Repositories (CSR)**, a service that allows us to store the source code of our applications directly in our projects. We can have unlimited repositories and mirror copies of GitHub or Bitbucket, extend search capabilities in the code, and diagnose problems and configuration. CSR can also have triggers integrated with Cloud Build to automate the deployment of new functionality in our applications.

Nowadays, the use of an SCM is essential. You should always consider having the source code of your application managed for the different development environments within your projects and organization.

## Creating secure container images from code

When you start implementing continuous integration flows, one of the many stages to consider is creating the container image that will later be deployed in a container service such as Google Kubernetes Engine or Cloud Run.

Generally, to create a container image, it is necessary to refer to a base operating system image, which can be found within the Dockerfile configuration file. It is very important that the image of the operating system that is being referenced within the Dockerfile is trusted; otherwise, there could be security problems in our application.

Here are some tips for creating your images safely:

- Always prefer images that use as few libraries as possible. The greater the number of libraries, the greater the risk of including a library that has some kind of vulnerability, so it is always recommended to choose Alpine-based versions and install the libraries that will be necessary to use in the application in a personalized way.

- Always create a dedicated user and group with the smallest number of permissions possible, following the principle of least privilege, in order to run the application and its processes in a way that reduces the attack surface.

- Always analyze your images with a vulnerability scanner to identify any open source image that is being used and that may be compromised early on. For this, GCP has the Container Analysis service, which delivers a list of vulnerabilities together with their severity, available solutions, and the name of the package that contains these vulnerabilities. This service can be used through the GCP SDK or through the Container Scanning API, which allows easy integration with integration and continuous deployment flows. For more details, visit the following link: `https://cloud.google.com/container-analysis/docs/get-image-vulnerabilities`.

- Always prefer images that have been certified to be from trusted partners. The security of our entire application could be compromised by uncertified images.

- Avoid pulling images that refer to the latest version. An image creator can constantly publish changes to this version while also exposing new vulnerabilities. To avoid this problem, choose a particular version and replicate this version in the GCP Container Registry service. By doing this, you can continue to use the image in a particular version without running the risk of the image being deleted. Note that it is necessary to constantly update to new versions once it has been verified that they do not have security vulnerabilities.

With the security measures we've discussed in this section, you can create more secure container images for your applications and thus reduce the attack surface that they are exposed to.

# Application modernization best practices

To use all the benefits that GCP offers, is it not enough just to move your monolithic application to the cloud. It is also necessary to perform refactoring processes to delegate the greatest amount of responsibility to self-managed cloud services, and also allow our application to have elasticity and automatic recovery capabilities.

To achieve this goal, in this section, we will review the steps we must follow to refactor a monolithic application to a modern architecture and microservices design pattern.

# Modern application design

In a design pattern oriented toward microservices, there are three fundamental elements that allow us to uncouple the responsibilities of the applications as much as possible, and thus reduce the amount of code to modify when it is necessary to make changes:

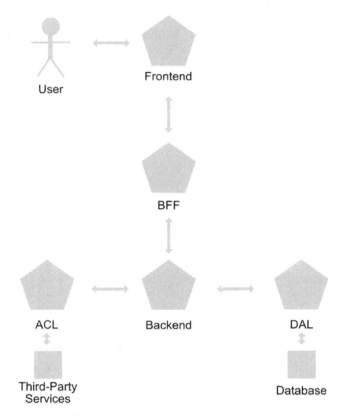

Figure 3.9 – Modern application design

**Backend for Frontend** (**BFF**) is a microservice that is responsible for making the services that our frontend application will need to perform its tasks available in a simplified way. Unlike applications that have been designed with a monolithic pattern, applications oriented toward microservices require us to orchestrate multiple calls to the microservice APIs to perform a single activity. The BFF is responsible for generating this transformation of a call from the frontend to the calls that are necessary in our backend. In this way, the developers of our frontend are only responsible for calling the BFF services they require. The BFF developers are responsible for orchestrating the microservices that are available in the backend layer, while the backend developers are responsible for each of the available microservices doing their job well.

The **Data Abstraction Layer** (**DAL**) is a microservice located between the data sources and the backend layer, thus making an abstraction of the data layer with the business logic layer. This allows greater flexibility when we make changes to the sources of data we are consuming. One of the most common examples of implementing a DAL is the implementation between a backend layer and a database. The DAL implements all the necessary libraries and dependencies, the credentials to be able to connect to the database, and all the necessary connection and exception control. It presents an agnostic API that is responsible for exposing basic operations such as Create, Read, Update, and Delete so that the backend layer can consume the database without needing to know how to make the connection, instead needing only to use the API methods to comply with the business logic that the layer was built for. In this way, when it is necessary to change the database, it will only be necessary to change the implementation of the connection in the DAL microservice; we don't need to change the connection in the services that consume the data.

The **Anticorruption Layer** (**ACL**) is a microservice that can be found between third-party services and the backend layer, allowing us to abstract the service provider that the business layer needs to consume. One of the most common examples of implementing an ACL is between the backend layer and a mailing service. The ACL implements all the necessary libraries and dependencies and consumes the credentials to connect to a mailing service provider. The ACL exposes an agnostic API that is made up of the minimum information necessary to send a notification, such as the recipient, subject, and body of the message. In this way, when it is necessary to change the email notification provider, it will only be necessary to change the code in the ACL microservice; the other microservices that used the ACL to send emails are unaffected.

# Refactoring a monolith to microservices

Before we begin transforming our monolithic application into a microservices application, it is important to remember that the more microservices there are, the harder it is to manage the operations, maintenance, and network connections. Refactoring a monolith to microservices will not always be the best option and this will depend exclusively on the number of people working on the project and the size of the application. In many cases, it is not even necessary to have a BFF, DAL, or ACL; it is enough just to have a monolithic application with a good software design that allows us to generate this same abstraction within our application to achieve very similar advantages. However, if you are facing a very large application that multiple people collaborate in, it is possible to exploit the advantages of an ecosystem of microservices. These include being able to decouple libraries, dependencies, and business logic from a single place, scaling only the part of our application that needs to use the most resources, and being able to separately deploy new functionalities in a small service without the need to deploy a large application:

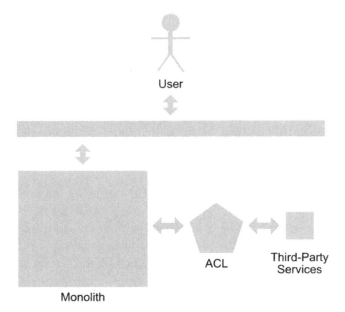

Figure 3.10 – Monolith to microservice

The first thing that is recommended is not to follow a big bang strategy, or rather not to move all our monolithic applications to microservices at once. On the contrary, select a particular task and migrate this task to a microservice that can be called from our monolithic application. In this way, we can experience this new design pattern in a safe way and without the chaos that could result from going immediately from a monolith to an ecosystem of microservices.

Another recommendation is to move a service that can be replaced by an ACL or DAL layer. In this way, we will be decoupling all the libraries and dependencies that are required either to consume a third-party service or to access a data source, thus reducing the dependencies and size of our monolith.

After moving the ACL and DAL layers, it is necessary to identify more complex business processes, decouple them from our monolith, create our own microservices, and thus continue with the reducing our monolith. This pattern is called *Strangler Fig*, and it was created by *Sam Newman*.

Among the recommendations to consider for carrying out the Strangler Fig strategy is to determine the different responsibilities that the monolith is carrying out, and then separate them into microservices. This task will be more or less complex, depending on how the software architecture of our monolith was designed. If the monolithic application is already correctly decoupled at the software architecture level, then moving to a microservices architecture will be simpler. However, if the application is poorly designed, for example because it contains classes coupled with each other, or if it fails to follow good software development practices such as **SOLID**, then the process of moving toward a microservices ecosystem will be more complex. Not only will it be necessary to move the code to another service, but we will also have to restructure the classes and methods to keep our application working.

Another recommendation is to start building a microservice in parallel with an existing functionality, thus implementing an interface within the monolith service. Then, once the microservice is complete, we must change the implementation of this interface so that it points to the new microservice.

But refactoring is not only about moving code from one place to another; it can also be about refactoring databases. Depending on the size of our application, it may also be necessary to redesign our database so that it can be part of this ecosystem of microservices. In theory, each microservice should have its own data source adapted to its own needs, which would mean completely refactoring our data sources. It might even be necessary to change the type of database, from a relational database to a NoSQL database, for example, with columnar and graph databases being other possible options. However, experience shows us that in cases like those mentioned here, when you have a very large application with large development teams, making this effort is sometimes worth it. In many cases, it is not necessary, however. Therefore, it is necessary to evaluate each case on its own merits before making a decision. We will consider which databases to use for each of our microservices in the third part of this book.

Carrying out a transformation from a monolithic application to a microservices ecosystem is a process that requires initial preparation and studying the application before proceeding. It is recommended that you start by individually moving small parts of the monolith and working through access to third-party services, databases, and business logic until you completely transform the application.

## Summary

In this chapter, we reviewed the basic configuration and tools necessary to start developing applications on GCP, and also looked at how to ensure that our deployments of new functionalities meet the basic quality conditions that ensure the serviceability of our applications. We also examined the difference between continuous integration, delivery, and deployment, as well as what their benefits are and what tools they use. Finally, we learned how to transform applications that have been designed according to monolithic patterns into modern microservices applications in GCP. In the next chapter you will learn how to use two serverless services to deploy your application in Google Cloud, App Engine and Cloud Functions.

# 4
# Using Cloud Functions and Google App Engine

One of the best ways to optimize the use of resources within our cloud application solutions is to use serverless services when possible, in order to only use resources when required and reduce the operational costs of infrastructure. For this, Google Cloud offers two computing solutions that allow us to meet this objective: Cloud Functions and App Engine.

In this chapter, you will learn about the following:

- The basics of Cloud Functions and App Engine
- The different types of Cloud Functions triggers and App Engine
- How to expose your services to the internet
- How to make a canary release strategy with A/B testing
- How to deploy an application in App Engine and Cloud Functions
- How to make your applications and services secure

# Technical requirements

Google Cloud SDK (a minimum of **version 317**) is required (`https://cloud.google.com/sdk`).

# Welcome to serverless applications

Serverless services are an excellent way of accelerating solution development and implementation processes within our solutions, but like many existing solutions in the cloud, they are not a silver bullet. You must be cautious when choosing which components within your solution can be implemented in this way in order to take full advantage of the benefits of using these services.

## What is serverless?

Before being able to evaluate the use of serverless services within our solution, it is necessary to understand what serverless really means. The serverless concept does not really mean that our solutions are not implemented in servers, but that we do not have to worry about the operation of these servers, and thus we can focus on delivering value by building new features in our application in a much more optimal way.

## Advantages and disadvantages of serverless applications

Serverless applications are not a silver bullet. They have both advantages and disadvantages, which we will consider in this section.

Among the advantages of serverless applications is the delegation of responsibility for the operation of the infrastructure and maintenance of the operating system of our environment. The consequent reduction of time dedicated to this type of activity transforms into a cost reduction.

In addition, serverless applications have the possibility of being scaled horizontally, allowing considerable traffic peaks to be supported without the need for major configuration work by developers. However, this advantage can also be transformed into a disadvantage, of not being able to control, in some cases, the limit quotas for the use of these services. This can expose us to very large charges in the event that we have made an error in the coding of our applications and their use of resources. Therefore, it is recommended to test serverless solutions very well before deploying them in production environments.

On the other hand, serverless applications can be triggered by events, which allows resources to be used for only as long as necessary, thereby optimizing the resource consumption of our cloud infrastructure.

In addition to the advantages mentioned, not having to worry about operations allows you to focus your efforts on development, accelerating the generation of value by the development team.

Similarly, a cloud-native approach to code frees developers from worrying about tasks related to the operation of the infrastructure, enabling them to focus on the creation of new functionalities and meeting the needs of the client.

However, while the ability to trigger by event is a great advantage, it is not always the best solution for our workloads. For example, if we have a workload that needs to be executed for extended periods of time. A solution implemented in a serverless environment would not be the best alternative in that case, since apart from a charge for use, there are limits to the maximum time that a process can be running. Hence it is always recommended to read the documentation to understand whether our workload can be adapted to the maximum execution time of the solution, or whether it will be necessary to select another solution.

# Event-based applications

Event-oriented architectures consist of solutions optimized to process actions generated by other systems. Before the arrival of serverless solutions, the only option to be able to process an event in an event-oriented solution was to have a server on 24/7 in order to receive the event and thus be able to process it. Now, fortunately, it is possible to take advantage of serverless services by initializing computing capacity for only the time that is necessary and thus not wasting resources by keeping a server on 24/7:

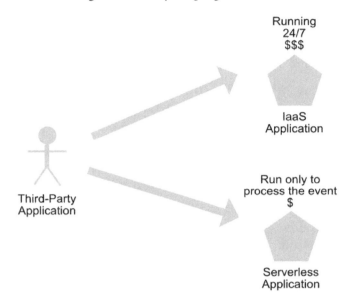

Figure 4.1 – Event-based applications

# What is Google App Engine?

Google App Engine is one of the first cloud solutions that Google launched, in *2008*. It consists of a multipurpose serverless platform that allows the scaling of applications horizontally without the need to manage infrastructure, server configurations, or configuration settings. It also allows you to use the most popular programming languages, such as **Node.js**, **Java**, **Ruby**, **C#**, **Go**, **Python**, or **PHP**.

The use of Google App Engine is recommended if you wish to obtain the benefits of serverless applications in complex workloads, involving multiple dependencies, classes, and functions within the application code.

Google App Engine is a single regional resource, which means that it has high availability by default. We can have just one instance of App Engine per project, unlike Cloud Functions where it is possible to have more than one instance in a single project.

In addition to the region, for App Engine it is necessary to select an environment type, which can be standard or flexible.

After the initial configuration of App Engine, it is possible to deploy our application and start using the features that we will see in the next section.

# Introducing Google Cloud Functions

Google Cloud Functions is a serverless, lightweight, asynchronous, and event-driven solution that allows you to run specific single-purpose processes using the open source **Framework as a Service (FaaS)** framework and programming languages such as Python, Node.js, Java, and Go. It also has direct integrations with other Google services such as Cloud Storage, Pub/Sub, and Firestore without the need for additional configurations.

Google Cloud Functions is recommended for event processing, service integration, real-time data processing, virtual assistants, image, video, and natural language processing, among other solutions that require the execution of processes quickly and in a unified manner.

Each cloud function is in a region, which means that the resource is regional. It also has a URL to be invoked, composed of the name of the region plus the project ID and the name of the function. It has from 256 MiB to 4 GiB of allocated memory, a timeout configuration of up to 9 minutes, and the option to select the maximum number of instances running concurrently in order to control resource usage quotas.

It is also possible to add environment variables that can be consumed at runtime to parameterize values between the different environments that we may have, such as development, integration, and production.

With regard to networks and connections, it is possible to allow traffic access from the internet, only within a **Virtual Private Cloud** (**VPC**) or a hybrid possibility by using a Cloud load balancer for the inbound traffic. For outbound traffic, calls to the internet are allowed by default, but if it is necessary to make calls within resources that are in a VPC, it is necessary to create a VPC connector and indicate whether the outbound traffic will be sent in its entirety by the VPC connector or whether only calls to private IPs will be delivered to the connector, in the event that we have calls both to the internet and to our private network.

Finally, with regard to security, our cloud function is configured by default with a service account associated with App Engine that has Editor permissions, but keeping the default settings is not a good practice. Therefore, it is recommended to create a service account with the necessary permissions for the execution of the cloud function in order to comply with the good security practices of the principle of least privilege.

# Different flavors for different situations

Both Google App Engine and Cloud Functions have different options for the different workloads that we may wish to implement. In this section, we will review the different options and consider when to use each one.

## HTTP functions

HTTP functions are functions that can trigger process executions through HTTP calls, such as calls from a backend service to a cloud function. By default, and for security reasons, when a cloud function is deployed, it requires authentication from the consumer. To avoid this type of behavior, a cloud function can be deployed from the GCP console by selecting the **Allow unauthenticated invocations** option or by adding the allow-unauthenticated flag if the Google Cloud SDK is used. It is important to note that only cloud functions that act as public APIs should allow calls without authentication; the other APIs should always have both authentication and authorization from the consumer.

To be able to make a call to a public cloud function, just make an HTTP call from a client such as curl or Postman of type GET or POST to the URL available in the **Trigger** section at the time of creating the function or already in the deployed instance.

If the cloud function requires authentication from the consumer and the consumer is within the GCP project, it is necessary to create a service account with the roles/cloudfunctions.invoker role and use it to make an authenticated call. If a call is made without performing the authentication process, the cloud function will return an error of type Forbidden and a status code of 403. If the consumer is outside the GCP project, it is necessary to create a .json key of the service account and deliver it to the consumer so that they can perform the authentication process programmatically.

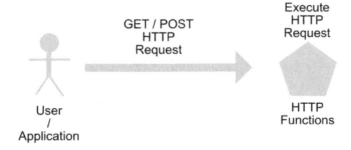

Figure 4.2 – HTTP functions

# Background functions

Background functions are functions that, unlike HTTP functions triggered by an HTTP call, are not exposed to the internet and can only be activated through events such as the creation of a file in Cloud Storage, the arrival of a message in a Pub/Sub topic, and modifying a document in Firestore. In the following section, we review in detail each type of trigger available for background cloud functions.

# Triggering cloud functions from Cloud Storage

Background functions triggered by Cloud Storage events can respond to different types of events generated by actions performed on files within a particular bucket. The events are implemented through Pub/Sub notifications for Cloud Storage and are sent to the function in JSON format.

Among the events available to trigger execution processes in background functions are the following:

- `Google.storage.object.finalize`: Triggered when a file is created or overwritten in a particular bucket.

- `Google.storage.object.delete`: Triggered when a file is deleted or overwritten in a particular bucket. For versioned files, it is activated when a version of the file is removed.

- `Google.storage.object.archive`: Triggered when a versioned file is deleted or archived.

- `Google.storage.object.metadataUpdate`: Activated when the metadata of a file is modified:

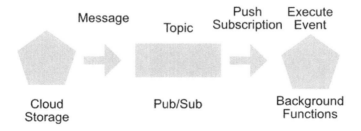

Figure 4.3 – Cloud Storage functions

# Triggering cloud functions from Pub/Sub

Background functions triggered by Pub/Sub events can respond to messages on a particular topic.

Unlike Cloud Storage event-triggered background functions, there is only one type of event called `google.pubsub.topic.publish` that fires when a message is posted to a specific Pub/Sub topic:

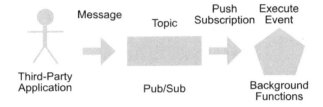

Figure 4.4 – Pub/Sub functions

# Triggering cloud functions from Firestore

Background functions triggered by Firestore events can respond to actions performed at the document level in the GCP NoSQL database.

Among the events available to trigger execution processes in background functions are the following:

- `Providers/cloudfirestore/eventTypes/document.create`: Activated when a document is created

- `Providers/cloudfirestore/eventTypes/document.update`: Activated when a document is updated

- `Providers/cloudfirestore/eventTypes/document.delete`: Activated when a document is deleted

- `Providers/cloudfirestore/eventTypes/document.write`: Activated when a document is created, updated, or deleted:

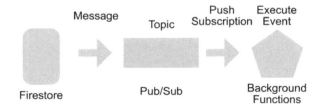

Figure 4.5 – Firestore functions

# Terminating HTTP functions

Every time tasks are executed in the background within HTTP functions (such as an asynchronous call to an external service) it is necessary to wait for the tasks to be executed before completing the execution of the function. For this it is necessary to always return an HTTP response, otherwise, our cloud function could continue executing until it is finished by timeout. This would cause unexpected behaviors and the use of resources for longer than required:

Figure 4.6 – Terminating HTTP functions

# Terminating background cloud functions

As with HTTP functions, for background functions, it is also necessary to wait for these tasks to be executed before ending the execution of the function. To control when a function can end its execution in a background function, there are two alternatives:

- Return a promise that is resolved when the tasks executing in the background finish (either with success or with error).

- Execute the callback argument in a function of the callback type after the tasks executing in the background finish (either successfully or with error).

In this way, we ensure that our processes can always be completed without being interrupted by the end of the execution of our function, and in addition, we optimize the use of Cloud Functions resources:

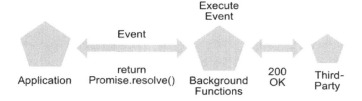

Figure 4.7 – Terminating background functions

# App Engine standard environment

If your application needs to support large peaks of users in an unpredictable way, at an accelerated scaling speed, and requiring very low-cost consumption (or even taking advantage of the free GCP tier), the App Engine standard environment is the right option.

It is important to note that, unlike the flexible version, the App Engine standard environment supports specific versions of programming languages, so if your application requires a particular version that is not available, it is necessary to use the flexible version.

The programming languages and versions available are as follows:

- Python (a minimum of **version 2.7**)
- Java (a minimum of **version 8**)
- Node.js (a minimum of **version 8**)
- PHP (a minimum of **version 5.5**)
- Ruby (a minimum of **version 2.5**)
- Go (a minimum of **version 1.11**)

Other advantages of the standard version of App Engine are the startup speed of the instances, which is in the order of seconds, and the possibility of scaling to zero, allowing the saving of resources when there is no traffic to the application, because of a pricing model based on instance usage per hour.

If your workload requires running processes in the background, debugging via SSH, modifying the runtime, or using WebSocket, then you should consider using the flexible App Engine option.

# App Engine flexible environment

If your application has a constant and predictable flow of users, or if it is possible to plan a gradual escalation and the application is deployed in Docker containers, then an App Engine flexible environment is the right choice.

Also, if your application requires a specific version of a programming language such as Python, Java, Node.js, Go, Ruby, PHP, or .NET, or depends on frameworks that include native code, then again, the flexible version of App Engine allows these needs to be satisfied.

Flexible App Engine allows processes to run in the background, as well as debugging via SSH, modification to the runtime, and the use of WebSocket.

If the workload requires a deployment speed in the order of seconds, scaling to zero, and having pricing oriented to the use of the instances, you should evaluate the use of the App Engine standard option.

# Exposing your services to the internet

One of the objectives when developing our application is that it can be consumed by end users, and in most cases (except for some corporate applications), that means that our application has to be exposed to the internet.

In this section, we will review how to expose our applications to the internet, deployed in both Cloud Functions and App Engine, in order to make functionalities available to our users.

## Google App Engine invoked via HTTP

In order to expose services deployed in App Engine, it is necessary to create a web service that allows us to set up an HTTP server in our application. To achieve this, depending on the programming language we use, we can use a framework that facilitates this task, such as the Express framework in the case of using Node.js. It is important to note that App Engine automatically selects the port through which our service will be exposed, therefore when coding our web server, it is necessary to consider the use of the port environment variable in order for App Engine to make the port available to use and allow our application to consume the port information.

After creating our web server and carrying out the corresponding coding, it is necessary to create the app.yaml configuration file in order to indicate to App Engine which runtime environment we want to use, the type of instance, and the environment variables at the level configuration and command configuration that allow our application to receive HTTP calls.

To configure this objective, it is necessary to add the runtime parameter indicating the runtime environment that we will use, and the service parameter with a unique name in order to be able to handle different versions of our service and thus be able to carry out deployment strategies such as canary release that we'll see later in this chapter. Also, in the case of not having a file with the necessary commands to start the web server, as would be the case of the package.json file if we were using Node.js, it is necessary to add the command that starts the web server in the entrypoint section.

And finally, to be able to make a call about our service, it is necessary to use a client that makes HTTP calls and enter the URL that the service gives us at the time of deployment with the `gcloud app deploy` command.

For more information on how to configure the `app.yaml` configuration file, you can check the following link in the official documentation: `https://cloud.google.com/appengine/docs/standard/nodejs/config/appref`.

## Cloud functions invoked via HTTP

Unlike App Engine, exposing our services through Cloud Functions requires no additional configuration. It is only necessary to indicate when creating the resource whether the endpoint generated by our function will require authentication or whether the **Allow unauthenticated invocations** option is not selected. The security aspects and good practices related to authenticated and unauthenticated calls on services deployed in Cloud Functions will be reviewed in the next section.

# Deployment and security considerations

When deploying our applications in serverless services such as Cloud Functions or App Engine, it is important to consider factors such as location and good security practices, in order to improve the user experience, reduce costs, and avoid incidents related to the poor configuration of security policies.

In this section, we will review what aspects to take care of to avoid having such problems when our applications are deployed in the cloud.

## Location considerations

Both Cloud Functions and App Engine are regional services, so it is necessary to consider in which region we are going to deploy our application so as to reduce latencies between our application and its users and/or other services that it will consume or be consumed by. If we deploy our service in a different region than the one where it is located, we will have latency problems and could also have cost increases due to the use of bandwidth between regions. This is why it is important to always check that both Cloud Functions and App Engine are in the same region as our other resources:

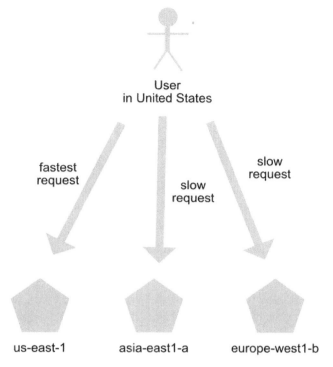

User
in United States

fastest
request

slow
request

slow
request

us-east-1          asia-east1-a          europe-west1-b

Figure 4.8 – Location considerations

# Securing cloud functions

Cloud functions of the trigger HTTP invocation type, unlike those of the background functions type, are exposed to the internet, so it is necessary to evaluate the type of security to apply to this resource. If the functionality of the service requires it to be of a public type (such as the display of information from a combo-box on a form on a public web page) the cloud function should have the **Allow unauthenticated invocations** option enabled so that any user visiting the website can access the information without having to log in. However, having a serverless resource exposed to the internet without the need for authentication involves other considerations, such as correctly configuring the use of memory allocated. The configuration might involve selecting the amount of memory necessary to perform the execution, selecting the maximum expected execution time before timeout, and selecting the maximum number of instances that the application should scale to. In that way, we can avoid the abuse of resource consumption by malicious users.

If our application requires that users or services be authenticated in order to consume it, it will be necessary to deselect the **Allow unauthenticated invocations** option and create a service account that has the `roles/cloudfunctions.invoker` role to enable authenticated calls to our application.

Also, if our cloud function is invoked only by services that are within a VPC of our project, it is possible to reduce the attack surface by restricting the ingress settings in the **Connections / Ingress** settings section when creating our function by selecting the **Allow internal traffic only option**, to allow calls only from applications that are in our private network and not from *any* internet user.

Another security measure we can take to protect our cloud function is to limit the outbound traffic in the **Connections / Egress** settings section, thereby preventing information from being sent to third-party services.

Finally, it is very important to remember that although cloud functions have the ability to configure environment variables for use at runtime, these variables should only be used for non-sensitive data. If sensitive data is required in the function, such as keys or a password, it is necessary to use the GCP Secret Manager service, which is a key vault that allows us to store secrets safely for consumption by our applications.

## Securing App Engine

To ensure that our application on App Engine is exposed safely to the internet, it is possible to follow good security practices and, in conjunction with security services provided by GCP such as Security Scanner, protect our application proactively by identifying possible vulnerabilities.

One of the first things when invoking services through HTTP calls is to ensure that the communication between the user or service with our application is done safely. To achieve this goal, it is possible to directly use the default domains of the `appspot.com` type or configure custom domains using the SSL certificates functionality included in App Engine to configure our certificates.

Another possible security measure is the use of the App Engine firewall, which allows us to limit access to our resources by configuring specific IP ranges. This functionality is useful when we want to limit access to our application from a specific network where other applications of ours are located within the organization, or to block an IP address that may be carrying out malign acts such as attacks on our application.

Like Cloud Functions, App Engine also offers the possibility of configuring the ingress traffic that we have, to accept traffic from the internet, or only allow traffic from a private network within our GCP project.

Finally, if we want to proactively perform analysis on our applications deployed on App Engine, it is possible to use the Cloud Security Scanner service to analyze the exposed URLs of our application by generating inputs and thus simulating the behavior of possible users, in order to detect vulnerabilities and take action on them.

# How to make a canary release strategy with A/B testing

One of the strategies used when you want to release functionality without running the risk that an error in the new functionality interrupts the application is to expose the functionality to a small group of users in the live environment. Then, you observe its behavior and determine whether the behavior is as expected. If an error is detected, the previous functionality is simply exposed again to all users by reverting to the previous version. Otherwise, if its behavior is correct, the new functionality is exposed to more and more users until it reaches 100% of users. This is called the canary release strategy:

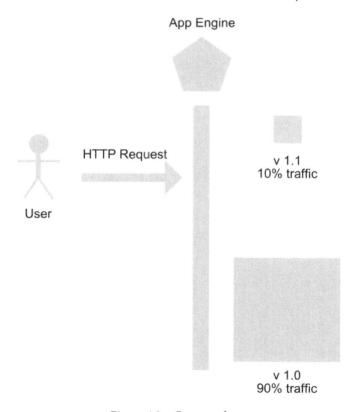

Figure 4.9 – Canary release

# Static versus dynamic data considerations

When implementing the canary release strategy, it is important to understand the type of data that will be exposed by our new service, in order to control possible version update problems that may occur due to external factors.

An example of this is the exposure of static data versus dynamic data. When exposing dynamic data, generally exposing a REST API service directly is enough to perform this strategy without considering external factors.

To avoid any kind of problems in the consumption of our dynamic data, it is recommended to configure the **Cache Control** and **Expires** headers in order to inform the proxy that this content is dynamic and thus avoid cache update problems.

By exposing static data such as images, videos, or files typical of a frontend application (such as a .css file), we expose ourselves to the problem of cache control in a more direct way. This can be detrimental to our canary strategy release, since the static content may not be shown in an updated way to the user, preventing us from carrying out our strategy correctly.

In this case, it is recommended to change the URL of the static resource in order to prevent the browser from obtaining a version that is in the cache:

..../image94753.png

v 1.1
10% traffic

..../image23474.png

v 1.0
90% traffic

Figure 4.10 – Static content

# Using traffic splitting in App Engine

One way to implement the canary release strategy using GCP's serverless solutions is to use App Engine's traffic splitting feature. This allows traffic to be divided between different versions of the application, in order to verify the correct operation of new functionality without putting at risk the total availability of the application in live environments.

To use this feature, it is important that the URL of the service is exposed to the internet without indicating a specific version, otherwise, the request will go directly to the selected version.

We can split the incoming traffic to our application in two ways: separating at the IP level and separating at the cookie level. If we separate our traffic at the IP level, we may find problems such as users having dynamic IP addresses, which prevents the traffic splitting functionality from being able to correctly identify which version of the application to refer the user to. In addition, if you want to apply the canary release strategy to communication between applications, it is recommended that you use the cookie splitting method, because the IP method could result in reaching only one version of the functionality:

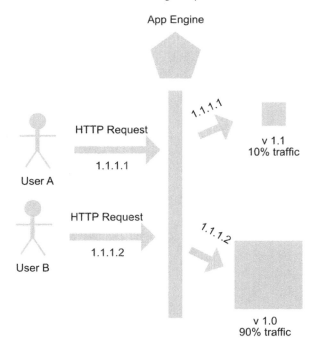

Figure 4.11 – IP-based traffic splitting

If we use the cookie splitting method, then the application, instead of checking which IP the request comes from, will check a cookie called Google Application ID (GOOGAPPUID). If this cookie already exists, the existing value will be used, otherwise, the received request will be routed to one of the alternative available versions. The use of this method allows for the much more precise separation of traffic than the method of separation by IPs. However, it too has its problems when making calls from a desktop or mobile application, where it will be necessary to manage cookies manually.

In addition, although cookie splitting is the recommended option for managing internal traffic between applications, it is necessary to carry out a manual process of sending the cookie between the services that call each other in order to be consistent in the use of the selected version:

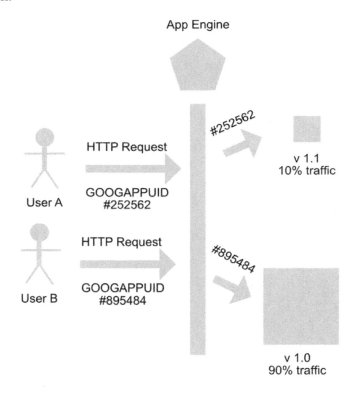

Figure 4.12 – Cookie-based traffic splitting

# Summary

In this chapter, we've reviewed what serverless is, we've looked at the basics of Cloud Functions and App Engine with the different types of triggers available, and we've outlined how to expose these services to the internet. We've also learned how to carry out A/B testing to simulate a canary release deployment in App Engine, and how to make your applications and services more secure. In the next chapter, you will learn more about virtual machines and containers, using GCP computing services such as Google Compute Engine and Cloud Run.

# 5

# Virtual Machines and Container Applications on Google Cloud Platform

In this chapter, you will learn how to use the different services offered by **Google Cloud Platform (GCP)** to deploy VMs and container applications using Compute Engine, **Google Kubernetes Engine (GKE)**, and Cloud Run. You will also learn how to expose and deploy applications in those services.

In this chapter, you will learn about the following:

- Introduction to Docker and Kubernetes
- How to use virtual machines on GCP
- Forgetting the complexity of managing a Kubernetes cluster with GKE and Cloud Run
- The full deployment life cycle of an application on Google Compute Engine
- The full deployment life cycle of an application on Google Kubernetes Engine and Cloud Run

# Technical requirements

In this chapter we are going to interact with Google Cloud services and with the Kubernetes API. Therefore you will need to install the following tools:

- Google Cloud SDK **317** or later: `https://cloud.google.com/sdk`
- `kubectl` **1.16.13** or later: `https://kubernetes.io/docs/tasks/tools/install-kubectl/`

# Introduction to Docker and Kubernetes

Before starting to explore the world of applications deployed in IaaS and CaaS services, it is worth familiarizing ourselves with some basic concepts in order to understand how the different technologies interact in an ecosystem of microservices in the cloud. Thus, we will start by reviewing what containers and Docker container images are, and what Kubernetes is.

## What is Docker?

Docker is a set of platforms and services that allow us, through the virtualization of the operating system, to decouple the dependency of applications to a particular infrastructure. We are able to execute our applications through units called containers, which encapsulate the entire application, together with the necessary dependencies, so that the applications can function properly in any environment.

## What are containers and Docker container images?

A container is a unit of software that encapsulates all the code and dependencies necessary for an application to function in different environments.

A Docker container image is an encapsulated unit that contains everything necessary to run an application independently, such as the code and libraries of a container, but also the runtime, tools, and system libraries, as well as the necessary configurations.

In addition, the use of containers allows the use of system resources to be optimized, and accelerates the deployment of applications and porting of applications from one environment to another in a simple way, without incurring the typical problems related to environment configurations.

# What is Kubernetes?

Kubernetes is an open source container orchestration system created in order to facilitate and automate application deployment, autoscaling, and management.

Among the most important features that Kubernetes offers are the following:

- **Automated rollouts and rollbacks**: Deploy new versions of your applications and revert to a previous version in the event of errors.

- **Service topology**: Route traffic to endpoints near the client.

- **Secret and configuration management**: Keep secrets and configuration secure inside the cluster.

- **Batch execution**: Create batch jobs and ensure that a specified number of them successfully terminate.

- **Horizontal scaling**: Allow your workloads to support traffic peaks by creating autos caling policies.

- **Service discovery and load balancing**: Expose workloads in an easy way through services.

- **Storage orchestration**: Allow users to mount a storage system of choice.

- **Self-healing**: Configure policies to automatically restart workloads in the event of failures.

Within GCP, there is the GKE service, a self-managed Kubernetes solution that allows us to use all the advantages mentioned without the need to worry about the operation of the infrastructure. In the following sections, we will go into detail about this GCP service.

If you want to know more about Kubernetes, you can check the official documentation at https://kubernetes.io/.

You can also get hands-on experience by following this "hello world" app tutorial from the official Google Cloud tutorials documentation: `https://cloud.google.com/kubernetes-engine/docs/tutorials/hello-app`.

# Clusters, nodes, and pods in Kubernetes

To understand the operation of a Kubernetes cluster, it is necessary to understand at a general level the elements that compose it:

- **Clusters**: Sets of compute instances managed by Kubernetes
- **Nodes**: Compute instances that execute tasks required by Kubernetes
- **Pods**: Units within a node that can contain one or more containers with shared storage and network resources

In order to deploy a pod within a Kubernetes cluster, it is necessary to create a definition of type deployment in a YAML file where you will find all the necessary configuration information such as the name, number of replicas, metadata, the containers, and their associated images.

After creating the definition file, it is necessary to upload this file to the cluster's master server so that Kubernetes can execute this task on any of the available nodes, depending on the node's resource availability.

In later sections of this chapter, we will review in detail how to deploy an application to a Kubernetes cluster:

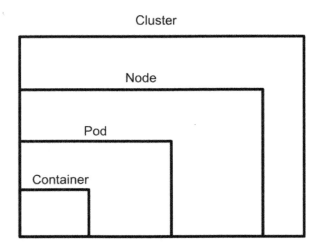

Figure 5.1 – Clusters, nodes, and pods

# How to use virtual machines on GCP

VMs are the basis of all the infrastructure we have in the cloud. Hence, although we increasingly use self-managed or serverless services, we need to know about the fundamentals of VMs in order to understand the infrastructure we use to deploy our applications. In this section, we will review how to create and manage a VM in order to create environments for our applications in the cloud.

## Google Compute Engine fundamentals

**Google Compute Engine** or **GCE** is the VM solution that GCP offers us.

Among the possibilities that GCE provides for the creation of VMs are the following:

- The selection of the region and zone of the instance
- The creation of labels to organize the instances
- The selection of the machine type considering the virtual CPU and memory
- Boot disk selection for both Linux and Windows
- Service account configuration
- Scope configuration to allow access to GCP APIs
- Enabling firewall rules for HTTP and HTTPS traffic

A VM is a zonal resource, which means that to create a particular instance, you have to select a specific region and zone. If you want to have a service that offers high availability to users, it is necessary to create instances in more than one area to avoid the failure of a particular area causing service unavailability.

GCE also has different default machine types for general-purpose, compute-optimized, memory-optimized, and GPU-oriented workloads. If none of these default options satisfies the needs of the workload, it is possible to select the **Custom** option so that the number of cores and memory can be specified manually.

Also, depending on the needs we have, we can select between different images, such as CentOS, Debian, Fedora, Red Hat, SQL Server, SUSE, Ubuntu, and Windows Server. If none of these images meets the needs of our workload, it is possible to select an existing container image in a repository to use as a custom image.

Regarding security, in GCE we can use a default service account with **Editor** permissions or we can select a custom service account, which is the recommended option in order to comply with the principle of least privilege. On the other hand, access scopes are a legacy option to select which access permissions to the GCP APIs our instance has. A good practice is to select full **Access Scope** access to the instance and restrict permissions through the custom service account, based on the principle of least privilege.

Finally, although it is possible to carry out this type of security configuration directly from the **Firewall** section of GCE, it is possible to select, by means of a checkbox during the creation of a VM, whether or not to enable HTTP and HTTPS traffic access to our instance:

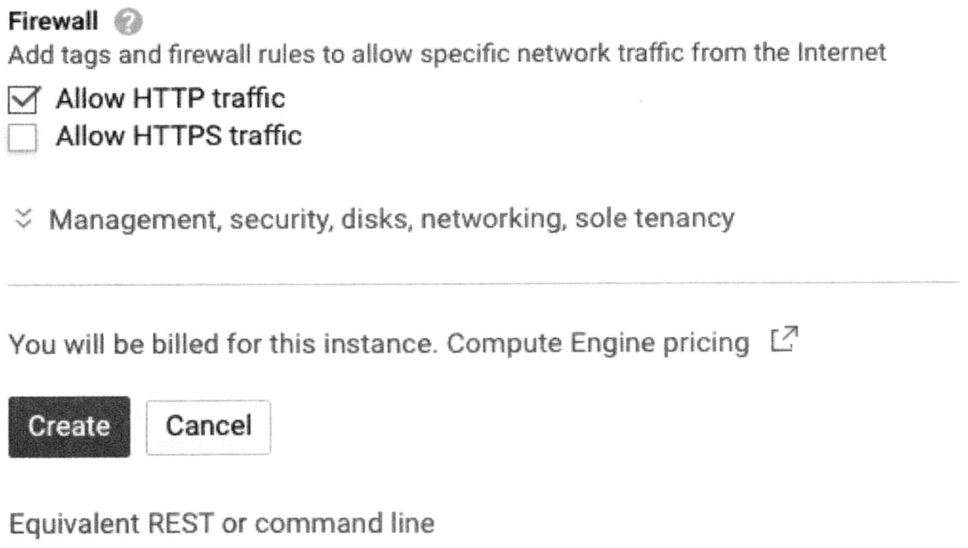

**Firewall** ❓
Add tags and firewall rules to allow specific network traffic from the Internet

☑ Allow HTTP traffic
☐ Allow HTTPS traffic

⌄ Management, security, disks, networking, sole tenancy

You will be billed for this instance. Compute Engine pricing ↗

Create    Cancel

Equivalent REST or command line

Figure 5.2 – Security configuration

If you want to know more about GCE, you can check the official documentation at this link: `https://cloud.google.com/compute/docs`.

## Managing service accounts for VMs

A GCE VM instance can be configured to use a single service account, but that service account can be used by many VM instances. However, bear in mind that any change in the permissions to the service account used will affect all the VMs that use it. It is a best practice that each VM instance has its own service account with only the necessary permissions. In cases where the instances have the same workload, it is OK to use the same service account.

Note that, unlike other GCP services, in GCE the permissions of both the access scope (legacy security service) and the service account (Cloud IAM) must match in order to execute the requested action. The best practice in this particular case is to leave the access scope with the highest number of privileges and limit permissions through the service account and Cloud IAM.

Once the service account has been configured, all you have to do is integrate Google Cloud services with your application using the Google Cloud client libraries (for example, if you need to use Cloud Storage, you can check the following link to find a client library for the programming language you are using in your application: `https://cloud.google.com/storage/docs/reference/libraries`). The client library will automatically identify the service account and carry out the authentication process. This is possible because the VM exposes the path of the service account through the `GOOGLE_APPLICATIONS_CREDENTIALS` environment variable, which the library uses to automatically carry out authentication. Also, by using a command from the GCP SDK we can authenticate ourselves and perform actions against the GCP services.

In the event that we have to perform authentication manually, either because the available libraries do not have any method that we need to use or because we are using a programming language not available in the existing libraries, we must perform the following steps:

1. Obtain an `"access token"` by making an `HTTP GET` call with the `"Metadata-Flavor: Google"` header to the following URL: `http://metadata.google.internal/computeMetadata/v1/instance/service-accounts/default/token`.

2. Call the API of the selected service sent `access_token` with the following header: `"Authorization": "Bearer [ACCESS_TOKEN]"`.

In this way, it will be possible to make authenticated calls from VMs in GCP.

# Bootstrapping applications

If we want to deploy our application in a VM instance, it is necessary to execute one or more initial commands before our application is able to receive requests from users or other applications. This is why GCE allows the configuration of startup scripts, which are scripts that can be executed when starting an instance in order to automate processes that are required for our application to be in an available state.

Although this option is very useful for situations where we have a single instance, in other cases, it is essential, such as when we want to configure instances that need to automatically scale horizontally. Otherwise, it would not be possible to manually execute these scripts for each instance created under the load balancer.

A startup script can be configured directly in the **Automation** section of GCE when creating a GCE instance or passed through as a reference to a script stored in a Cloud Storage bucket. For the configuration of startup scripts, it is necessary to have the `compute.instances.setMetadata permission`. In the case of configuration using a Cloud Storage bucket, the instance also needs to have permission to access the specific bucket:

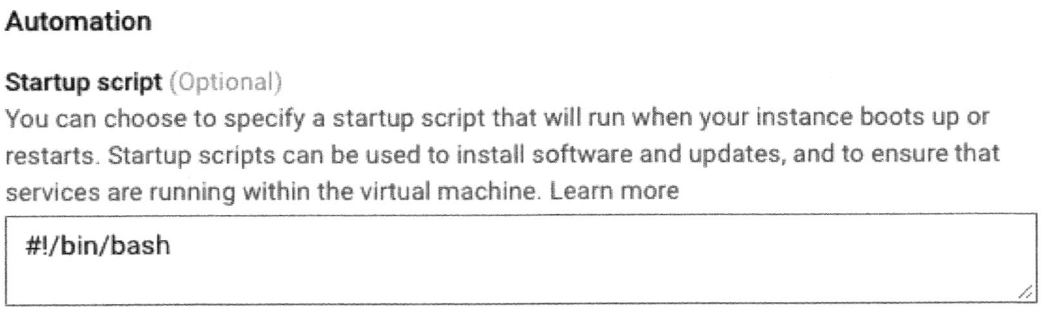

**Automation**

**Startup script** (Optional)
You can choose to specify a startup script that will run when your instance boots up or restarts. Startup scripts can be used to install software and updates, and to ensure that services are running within the virtual machine. Learn more

```
#!/bin/bash
```

Figure 5.3 – Automation configuration

As a last tip, it is important to consider that these scripts will be executed every time the instance is started, so it is essential to consider that our startup script is idempotent, to avoid execution ending in partial or inconsistent states.

# Managing Compute Engine VM images

To create a VM instance in GCE, it is necessary to select one of the public images available from Google or select one of the custom images within your project. The use of public and personalized images has no cost. However, in the case of personalized images, there may be charges related to the storage of the image in the project. In addition, for some images, there may be costs related to the use of licenses.

By default, disks are created the same size as the selected images, so if it is necessary to have a larger boot disk, it is necessary to resize it.

With regard to security issues, Google frequently updates public images in order to solve any critical vulnerabilities found. Updated images are generally posted on a monthly basis. Also, all images in GCE are encrypted by default, using GCP keys. If necessary, it is possible to use your own encryption keys to encrypt an image.

As a good practice, the creation of custom images is recommended when startup scripts require a lot of warming up time, thus allowing an acceleration of application readiness, and in addition, reducing dependencies on external components and thus reducing points of failure at instance startup.

If you want to automate the process of creating custom images, it is possible to use tools such as Packer to create integration with Jenkins or Spinnaker (solutions that allow us to create integration and continuous deployment flows).

Finally, in order to facilitate image management, it is possible to mark images with three different states:

- **DEPRECATED** – Images that can still be used, but there will be a warning at the time of execution

- **OBSOLETE** – Images that should not be executed either by users or by automated processes

- **DELETED** – Images that have already been deleted or are marked to be deleted in the future

These labels indicate to the responsible teams which images are close to ending their life cycle, enabling them to perform appropriate actions to avoid future support issues. It is also possible to include the validation of these labels in our automated integration and continuous deployment flows in order to preclude the use of particular images.

# Reading instance metadata to obtain application configuration

The metadata of a VM instance created in GCE is very important for process automation as it allows us to obtain data such as the hostname, instance ID, custom metadata, and information about the service account that the particular instance has configured. This can be used in automated scripts, such as the startup script, which is executed every time an instance is started. The metadata can be obtained from the instance in the form of key-value pairs without the need for any additional authorization step.

To obtain the metadata of an instance, it is necessary to have the following permissions:

- `compute.instances.setMetadata`

- `compute.projects-setCommonInstancesMetadata`

- `compute.projects.get`

- `compute.instances.get`

Among the most common attributes that are normally used, we can find the following:

- `project-id`: The project ID
- `hostname`: The hostname of the instance
- `name`: The instance name
- `machine-type`: The machine type of the instance, in the following format: `projects/projectnum/machineTypes/machine-type`
- `tags`: The tags of the instance
- `zone`: The zone where the instance runs, in the following format: `projects/projectnum/zones/zone`

To obtain the metadata from an instance created in GCE, just make a query using the `Metadata-Flavor` header: Navigate to the following URL: `http://metadata.google.internal/computeMetadata/v1/` or `http://metadata.google.internal/computeMetadata/v1/instance/` and include the resource you want to consult. For example, if we want to consult the area where the instance is located, the URL to consult should be `http://metadata.google.internal/computeMetadata/v1/instance/zone`.

To understand all the query options that can be performed to obtain metadata, you can consult the official GCP documentation at the following link: `https://cloud.google.com/compute/docs/storing-retrieving-metadata`.

If you want to configure custom metadata, it can be done when creating the instance, in the **Metadata** section, including it in key/value format.

It is important to clarify that there are two types of metadata, one that can be configured at the instance level, called instance metadata, and another that can be configured at the project level, called project-wide custom metadata. The project-wide custom metadata should be used only for information that can be obtained by any of the existing entities according to the security policies defined by the organization. The instance-level metadata is adequate for information that can only be accessed at the level of a particular instance according to the security policies defined by the organization.

# Forgetting the complexity of managing a Kubernetes cluster with GKE and Cloud Run

Kubernetes is a container orchestrator that greatly facilitates the management and operation of our applications, especially when we are faced with an ecosystem of microservices that require constant updates and that scale independently. However, the initial setup and installation of a Kubernetes cluster can be a demanding and complex process.

Fortunately, most cloud providers offer self-managed alternatives, so that we don't have to worry about the installation and operation of Kubernetes clusters. Here, GCP is not an exception, offering us GKE.

In addition, GCP offers an even easier and faster version to start experimenting with containerized applications called Cloud Run. This is implemented in an abstraction layer on Kubernetes called **Knative**, and it allows us to take advantage of totally serverless capabilities, making our applications scale horizontally in a completely automatic way and consuming only the resources we use.

In this section, we will review in greater depth both GKE and Cloud Run. We will look at their characteristics and see how which one we should select depends on the needs of our workload.

## GKE fundamentals

GKE is a GCP service that allows us to create a Kubernetes cluster in a totally self-managed way, reducing the time and costs of the operation. It also allows us to create clusters in different zones and regions in order to create applications with high availability, secure our applications through proactive reviews of vulnerabilities to the container images that we use, and gives us the possibility of integrating with monitoring tools such as Cloud Monitoring for an e2e review.

In relation to the autoscaling of our applications, it is possible to configure policies based on the use of CPU or custom metrics to allow scaling horizontally and also the dynamic adjustment of the CPU and memory of our pods to allow vertical scaling. GKE can also be configured to scale the number of nodes available in the cluster, providing more resources for the deployment of our application instances.

GCP also allows applications to install directly in our Kubernetes cluster using Google Cloud Marketplace, where you can find solutions to be installed directly into your environments, thus accelerating the development or configuration of third-party applications.

If you want to know more about GKE, you can check the official documentation, available at `https://cloud.google.com/kubernetes-engine/docs`.

## Cloud Run fundamentals

Cloud Run is a service that allows us to deploy our applications packaged in containers developed in the programming language of our liking in a totally serverless and self-managed environment. This allows flawless integration with GCP development tools such as Cloud Build, Cloud Code, and Google Container Registry. Being a serverless service, Cloud Run only charges us for our actual consumption, measured at a precision level of 100 milliseconds. This means that if we do not use the service (or if no user or system makes calls to our application), then we are not charged anything.

Being a regional service, by default, our application has high availability since it is replicated automatically in multiple zones.

Cloud Run also allows us to have fully automatic HTTPS endpoints, allowing the integration of our applications in a secure way with Cloud Storage, Pub/Sub, or any of our own or third-party services.

Speaking of security and network features, Google Cloud offers the option of creating a serverless **network endpoint group (NEG)** to represent a Cloud Run service or group of services that share the same URL pattern. This allows the implementation of an HTTP(S) load balancer over Cloud Run, thus enabling the receipt of requests over IPv4 and IPv6. It also enables integration with Cloud Armor, which allows us to protect our services from DDoS attacks and provide security through a **Web Application Firewall (WAF)**.

If you want to know more about Cloud Run, you can check the official documentation here: `https://cloud.google.com/run/docs`.

## Configuring Kubernetes namespaces

A namespace is a way to organize objects within your Kubernetes cluster, such as pods, deployments, and services. By default, when creating a cluster, there is a namespace called `default`. There are also other namespaces, such as `kube-system` and `kube-public`, which are for objects used specifically for Kubernetes and GKE. For demos and proofs of concept, there is no problem in using the default namespace, but for live projects, it is important to have all our objects organized within the cluster, to facilitate administration and technical staff access to objects, and to increase the performance of Kubernetes APIs.

When creating any object within a namespace using the kubectl apply command, it is necessary to add the -namespace flag in order to indicate to Kubernetes where we want the object to be created. If we do not add this flag, it is necessary to add the namespace name to the object definition metadata. If we don't add the flag or the metadata in the object definition, it will be created in the default namespace:

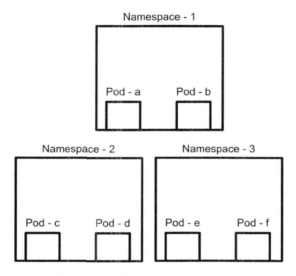

Figure 5.4 – Kubernetes namespaces

# Pod life cycle and resource configuration

Pods are components that are designed to run tasks temporarily, they do not exist indefinitely, and when they end their life cycle they can no longer be started again unless a completely new instance is created. Instead of being repaired, in the event of a problem, pods are deleted and recreated. In order to know at what point in the life cycle our pod is, it is possible to consult the status attribute through the PodStatus API. This can tell us the current status in terms of one of the following:

- Pending: The pod was already created within the cluster, but one or more of the containers within the pod is not yet running.

- Running: The pod and all its containers have already been created and at least one container is already running.

- Succeeded: All the containers inside the pod finished successfully.

- Failed: At least one container inside the pod failed.

- Unknown: The pod status cannot be determined.

When a pod starts up, it requests a previously configured amount of CPU and memory from Kubernetes depending on the needs of our workload, to allow Kubernetes to determine which node within the cluster has enough resources to allow the execution of the pod. As long as the amount of CPU and memory required to run the pod does not exist, the pod will not run.

Among the good practices to consider in the allocation of resources to a pod is to replace the default values for the CPU and assign a value to the memory so that our application can function correctly and use the resources offered by the device nodes within the cluster optimally. It is also important to consider that setting very low values for the CPU and memory could cause the creation of many pods and reduce performance. On the other hand, setting very high values for the CPU and memory could mean that pods cannot be executed and may cause problems with node scaling as a result of pod requirements.

Finally, in addition to the amount of resources that a pod can request from Kubernetes, there is the configuration of resource limits, which allows us to indicate the maximum CPU and memory resource that a pod can use once it is already running on a particular node. The limit value must always be equal to or greater than the request value previously configured.

# Managing Kubernetes RBAC and Google Cloud IAM relationships

The GKE solution, being a Kubernetes implementation within GCP, has two identity and role management controls, Cloud IAM and Kubernetes RBAC. Cloud IAM is part of Google Cloud and takes care of identity and role management on the GKE solution (GKE-related APIs) and all clusters within the project. Kubernetes RBAC is part of Kubernetes itself and takes care specifically of a particular Kubernetes cluster along with the namespaces and resources found within.

following are the main roles for GKE in Cloud IAM:

- **Kubernetes Engine Admin**: Provides full access for managing both clusters and Kubernetes object APIs within the project

- **Kubernetes Engine Cluster Admin**: Provides access to manage clusters within the project

- **Kubernetes Engine Developer**: Provides access to the Kubernetes object APIs within the project

- **Kubernetes Engine Viewer**: Provides read-only access to GKE resources within the project

If we talk about Kubernetes RBAC, we find the following main roles:

- **Cluster-admin**: Gives superuser access to execute any action on any resource on the cluster

- **Admin**: Provides read and write access to the selected namespace

- **Edit**: Provides read and write access to the selected namespace without the ability to edit role assignments

- **View**: Provides read access for most objects within the namespace

Although some Cloud IAM roles have similar names to the Kubernetes RBAC roles, it is important to remember, as we mentioned earlier, that they are different roles and that both must be configured for both the administration of the GKE service (Cloud IAM managing GKE API permissions) and the clusters (Kubernetes RBAC managing the cluster permissions itself) within our project, and the administration within the namespaces within our cluster together with its resources.

As a matter of good security practices, and following the principle of least privilege, it is recommended that you configure read permissions on Cloud IAM using the Kubernetes Engine Viewer role and on Kubernetes RBAC, configure more granular settings by granting permissions to namespaces that particular technical staff require to access the cluster.

# The full deployment life cycle of an application on Google Compute Engine

Now that we understand the fundamental concepts and characteristics of a VM created using GCE, we can review how to deploy an application together with the components needed to consume its services.

# Installing an application in a virtual machine

To install an application in a VM, simply connect remotely via SSH or Windows Remote Desktop to the VM and carry out the installation as you would do in a local environment. This procedure is called application deployment in a simple instance.

But what happens when you want to perform an installation in a group of self-managed VMs that have the possibility of scaling horizontally using scale out (creating new instances) or scale in (eliminating previously created instances)? In this case, our installation strategy of connecting to the particular instance is not feasible. Instead, it is necessary to run an automated installation script, create an instance template that uses this script through a startup script, create a group of self-managed instances that use the instance template, and expose this group under a load balancer that allows us to expose our services to the internet.

We will review each of these activities in detail as follows.

# Creating an instance template

An instance template allows us to create and save a configuration of all the elements that we would like a VM created in GCE to have, such as the type of machine, boot disk image, and startup scripts. This template could then be used by a group of self-managed instances, which would thus be able to use autoscaling policies.

To create an instance template, we can go to the **Instance template** section or use the gcloud command through the Google Cloud SDK.

In this case, we will show an example using the gcloud command:

```
gcloud compute instance-templates create my-instance-template \
    --machine-type n1-standard-1 \
    --image-family debian-9 \
    --image-project debian-cloud \
    --boot-disk-size 250GB
    --startup-script-url=URL_TO_STARTUP_SCRIPT
```

Here, URL_TO_STARTUP_SCRIPT is the URL where the automated script for the installation of our application is stored. It is generally recommended to leave this script in a Cloud Storage bucket.

(For more information about the different options available to create an instance template, consult the initial documentation at https://cloud.google.com/sdk/gcloud/reference/compute/instance-templates/create.)

In this way, we will already have our instance template together with our startup script ready to be used in a group of self-managed instances:

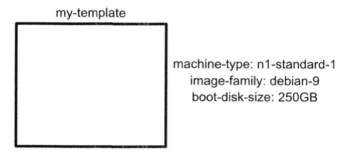

Figure 5.5 – Instance templates

# Creating a managed instance group

A group of self-managed instances is a group of VMs created in GCE by means of an instance template that can be managed in one place, allowing you to configure high availability and auto-staking policies under a load balancer.

To create an instance template, we can go to the managed **Instance groups** section or use the gcloud command through the Google Cloud SDK.

In this case, we will show an example using the gcloud command:

```
gcloud compute instance-groups managed create my-instance-
group\
    --size SIZE \
    --template INSTANCE_TEMPLATE \
    --zone ZONE
```

Here is a breakdown:

- SIZE is the number of instances the self-managed instance group will have.

- INSTANCE_TEMPLATE is the name of the instance template that has the configuration of the VMs and the startup script.

- ZONE is the area where group instances will be created.

In this way, we will have created the self-managed group of instances ready to be used by the load balancer that will expose our application to the internet:

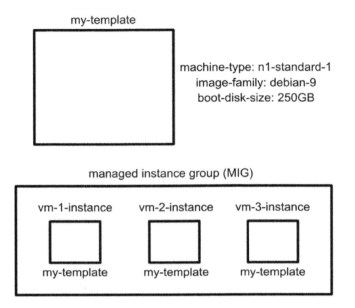

Figure 5.6 – Managed instance groups

# Configuring a load balancer

In order to use a load balancer that exposes our application to the internet, it is first necessary to create a backend based on a group of self-managed instances.

To create a backend, we can go to the **Load balancing** section or use the gcloud command through the Google Cloud SDK.

In this case, we will show an example using the gcloud command:

```
gcloud compute backend-services add-backend my-backend \
        --instance-group=INSTANCE_GROUP \
        [--instance-group-region=INSTANCE_GROUP_REGION |
--instance-group-zone=INSTANCE_GROUP_ZONE] \
        --balancing-mode=UTILIZATION
        --max-utilization=MAX_UTILIZATION
```

Here's a breakdown:

- `INSTANCE_GROUP` is the name of the previously created instance group.
- `INSTANCE_GROUP_REGION` is the region where the instance group is configured.
- `INSTANCE_GROUP_ZONE` is the one where the instance group is configured.
- `MAX_UTILIZATION` is a fraction between `0.1` and `1.0` that indicates the maximum utilization of the instances that the balancer will allow before diverting the traffic to another instance.

Once our backend is created, we go to the **Load Balancer** section of the GCP console and select **Create load balancer**. Then we select **Start configuration in HTTP(S) Load Balancing** and select the **From Internet to my VMs** option.

Once on the configuration screen of our load balancer, we go to **Backend configuration** and select the previously created backend.

In the **Host and path rules** and **Frontend** configuration sections, we do not make any changes.

Finally, we click on **Create**.

Having already created our load balancer, we can use the IP of the balancer to be able to consume our service from a group of VMs created in GCE:

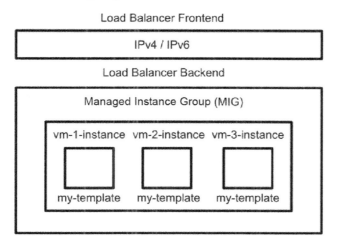

Figure 5.7 – Load balancer

## Hands-on tutorials in Google Compute Engine

If you want to get more hands-on experience using GCE, you can refer to the following tutorial on the official documentation of Google Cloud:

- Running a basic Apache web server: `https://cloud.google.com/compute/docs/tutorials/basic-webserver-apache`

- Deploying an ASP.NET app to your VM instance: `https://cloud.google.com/compute/docs/quickstart-windows`

# The full deployment life cycle of an application on Google Kubernetes Engine and Cloud Run

Now that we have reviewed the basic concepts of Kubernetes, GKE, and Cloud Run, it is possible to explore the steps needed to deploy an application and how to expose it to the internet to be consumed by either users or other applications.

## Building a container image using Cloud Build

The first thing we need to do to deploy an application in a cluster created in GKE or in Cloud Run is to create an image of a container of our application. For this, our application must have previously created its Dockerfile. By having the Google SDK installed in our local environment or by using Cloud Shell, we can use Cloud Build to generate our image and upload it directly to the GCP image repository called Google Container Registry.

To build the image, we use the following command, assuming that we are at the root of the project where the Dockerfile is located:

```
gcloud build submit -tag gcr.io/PROJECT_ID/IMAGE_NAME
```

The parameters used mean the following:

- `PROJECT_ID` is the GCP project ID.

- `IMAGE_NAME` is the name of the image.

In this way, we will have created from an application together with its Dockerfile a container image stored in a Google Container Registry repository within our GCP project. This is a fundamental task required in order to continue with the deployment of our application in both GKE and Cloud Run.

# Defining workload specifications

If we want to deploy our application in a Kubernetes cluster, there are four types of workload we can select:

- **Stateless applications**: Non-stateful workloads and no persistent data storage. All information related to users and their status is stored on the client side. To create a workload of this type, the `Deployment` type object is used.

- **Stateful applications**: Workloads that require their state to be saved or persistent. This is done using lingering volume objects within the cluster. To create a stateful type workload, the `ScalefulSet` type object is used.

- **Batch jobs**: Workloads that represent tasks of finite duration that are independent and that can be performed in parallel. To create a workload of the batch job type, the object of type `Job` is used.

- **Daemons**: Workloads that run continuously across the cluster without the need for user intervention. The `DaemonSet` type object is used to create a workload of the daemon type.

# Deploying a containerized application to GKE

To deploy an application in a Kubernetes cluster managed by GKE, it is possible to use Cloud Build together with **gke-deploy builder** (the tool recommended by Google to deploy applications in Kubernetes) to use a container image previously saved in Google Container Registry and deploy it to the GKE cluster.

The first thing to do is to make sure that the service account used by Cloud Build in the project has the Kubernetes Engine Developer role, to allow Cloud Build to run the deployment actions within the GKE cluster. After assigning the role, it is necessary to create two configuration files: a build configuration file for Cloud Build and another file corresponding to the Kubernetes resource file.

Our configuration file for Cloud Build should look like this, referencing the `gke-deploy` image:

```
{
    "steps": [
      {
        "name": "gcr.io/cloud-builders/gke-deploy",
        "args": [
          "run",
          "--filename=kubernetes-resource-file",
```

```
        "--location=location",
        "--cluster=cluster"
    ]
  }
 ]
}
```

The parameters used mean the following:

- `kubernetes-resource-file` is the path of the file that contains the definition of the deployment of our application for Kubernetes.

- `location` is the region and area where our cluster is located.

- `cluster` is the name of the cluster where we will deploy our application.

Our Kubernetes resource file with the minimum configurations to be able to deploy an application will look as follows:

```yaml
apiVersion: "apps/v1"
kind: "Deployment"
metadata:
  name: "your-application"
  namespace: "default"
  labels:
    app: "your-application"
spec:
  replicas: 3
  selector:
    matchLabels:
      app: "your-application"
  template:
    metadata:
      labels:
        app: "your-application"
    spec:
      containers:
      - name: "your-container"
        image: " YOUR_IMAGE "
---
```

```
apiVersion: "v1"
kind: "Service"
metadata:
  name: "your-service"
  namespace: "default"
  labels:
    app: "your-application"
spec:
  ports:
  - protocol: "TCP"
    port: 80
  selector:
    app: "your-application"
  type: "LoadBalancer"
  loadBalancerIP: ""
```

Here, YOUR_IMAGE is the path to the image of your application in Google Container Registry.

Finally, to deploy the application in the GKE cluster, it is necessary to execute the following command:

```
gcloud build submit -project=PROJECT_ID -config BUILD_CONFIG
```

The parameters used mean the following:

- PROJECT_ID corresponds to the GCP project ID.
- BUILD_CONFIG corresponds to the name of the build configuration file for Cloud Build.

Finally, to consume our service, simply enter the cluster in the **Kubernetes Engine** section in the GCP console and go to the **Services & Ingress** section to obtain the IP of the endpoint of our service under the name of your service.

In this section, we have exposed our service to the internet using the **External Load Balancer** type. There are also two other ways of exposing our services that can be used, **NodePort** and **ClusterIP**:

- **ClusterIP**: Used when we want to consume our service only within the cluster, without exposure to the internet.

- **NodePort**: In addition to being able to access our service within the cluster, we can obtain access through the external IP of the node where our service is located.

For more information about the different types of exposure in Kubernetes, you can refer to the official documentation at `https://kubernetes.io/docs/concepts/` `services-networking/service/#publishing-services-service-types`.

In this way, we will be able to deploy our application in a Kubernetes cluster managed by GKE and be able to consume our services exposed to the internet:

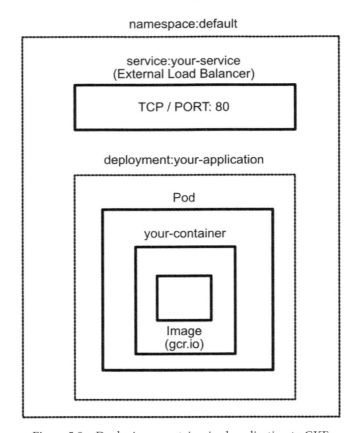

Figure 5.8 – Deploying a containerized application to GKE

# Deploying a containerized application to Cloud Run

One of the biggest advantages of Cloud Run, apart from it being a serverless service, is the ease of deploying applications if your images are already stored in a repository such as Google Container Registry. To deploy an application in Cloud Run, just execute the following command:

```
gcloud run deploy --image gcr.io/PROJECT_ID/IMAGE_NAME
--platform managed
```

The parameters used mean the following:

- `PROJECT_ID` is the GCP project ID.

- `IMAGE_NAME` is the name of the image.

- `--platform managed` is a flag that indicates that the application will be deployed in a managed environment.

When executing this command, it is necessary to enter both the name of the service and the region where the service will be deployed, since Cloud Run is a regional-type service. In addition, depending on the needs of the service, it is possible to indicate whether or not it requires authentication to be consumed.

Once application deployment is completed, the URL on which to consume the service will be displayed. If the service was configured to be consumed without authentication, just make an HTTP call to the service. Otherwise, if the service was configured to forbid unauthenticated calls, it is necessary to make a call to the service using a service account that has the `roles/run.invoker` role.

Cloud Run, unlike services deployed in GKE, is intended only for stateless workloads, because the execution of the process is triggered by events. You, therefore, pay only for the CPU, memory, and networks consumed during the execution of the request.

# Hands-on tutorials in Cloud Run

If you want to get more hands-on experience using GKE and Cloud Run, you can refer to the following tutorial on the official Google Cloud documentation:

- **Cloud Run Quickstart**: `https://cloud.google.com/run/docs/quickstarts`

- **GKE how-to**: `https://cloud.google.com/kubernetes-engine/docs/how-to`

# Summary

In this chapter, we've learned the fundamentals of containers and Kubernetes, and how to create, use, and deploy applications on Compute Engine in GCP. We've also reviewed what GKE and Cloud Run are and when to use them. In addition, we've learned how to deploy services in a secure way following best practices, and how to configure high availability, autoscaling, and deployment strategies on container-based applications.

In the next chapter, we will learn about the importance of API management in our applications.

# 6
# Managing APIs on Google Cloud Platform

In this chapter, you will learn how to implement, expose, manage, and secure APIs deployed on Google Cloud Platform using three different runtimes technologies such as **FaaS** with Cloud Functions, **Platform as a Service (PaaS)** with Google App Engine, and **Container as a Service (CaaS)** with **Google Kubernetes Engine (GKE)**. You will also learn the basics and best practices to design and implement an application programming interface **API**. In this chapter, we will cover the following topics:

- The basics before implementing an API management solution in Google Cloud
- How to protect your APIs using Cloud Endpoints on your deployments
- Discovering the enterprise API management world with Apigee
- Securing and managing your serverless workloads with the new Cloud API Gateway
- API development best practices

# Technical requirements

- **Google Cloud SDK 317** or later: `https://cloud.google.com/sdk`.

- An **Apigee** account: `https://login.apigee.com/sign_up`.

# The basics before implementing an API management solution in Google Cloud

Before starting to implement an API management solution in our Google Cloud project, it is important to understand some basic concepts about the development of related services, for example, what an API really is, how it differs from a service, what points make up an API management solution, and what tools are available to help us.

In this section, we will review all the basic concepts necessary to understand to implement an API management solution in the cloud.

## APIs

An **Application Programming Interface** (**API**) is a specification that indicates how different services should interact within a solution, thus allowing their integration and reuse. Although the concept of an API is generally used to refer to services, it is important to say that the concept of an API refers exclusively to the way in which the service should be interacted with (for example, the specification of the request and response) and not to the service itself (the business logic).

In simple words, APIs are the way software talks to other software, keeping industries and ecosystems glued together. They enable the business to rapidly expand into new contexts or adapt to meet changing user needs and preferences with agility.

Because the development of services within an organization can be a complex task, due to the amount of business knowledge that must be mastered, more and more organizations are publishing their services within their organizations. This enables them to reuse what they develop to the maximum extent, and thus it accelerates the creation and deployment of new applications.

As the publication of services within an organization is a task that, depending on the number of services, can become increasingly complex, there is the concept of API management, which we will review as follows.

# API management

The concept of API management refers to the ability to manage services within the organization in order to consider them as a business asset, allowing the exposure of these services in a documented, secure, and scalable way. Among the points to consider for the correct management of services are the following:

- **Service design**: Reflect business concepts in the design of services.

- **Documentation**: The existence of clear documentation for the consumption of the service by third parties.

- **Publication**: The exposure of existing services through a developer portal in order to be easily located and consulted.

- **Security**: Management of the authentication and authorization of users on the services, plus the audit log of the activities carried out.

- **Analytics**: Identification of which services are consumed and in what way.

- **Scalability**: The ability to serve large numbers of requests on demand.

We will describe some useful concepts and tools that cover the preceding points.

# The most common authentication methods

In order to protect our published services and prevent any user or application from having access to them, it is necessary to consider authentication methods that allow us to verify who is trying to consume the services and determine whether they have permission to perform an action.

In this section, we will review some of the most popular service authentication methods:

- **Basic auth**: An authentication method in which a username and password sent in the header of the request is provided, in Base64 format, in order to perform the verification.

- **Bearer auth**: An authentication method that involves the use of security tokens called bearer tokens, previously generated by a certificate authority (commonly a server) and sent in the header of the request to perform the verification.

- **API keys**: An authentication method based on the initial generation of a key for the consumer, which is used in subsequent calls in order to perform the verification.

- **OAuth 2**: A security standard that allows a particular user to deliver the corresponding permissions on a service to an application (either from the organization or from third parties) without the need to share their username and password. This process is called delegated authorization, and is based on obtaining and sending an access token in each request for verification and a refresh token to obtain a new access token when it expires. OAuth 2 is designed for authorization only, but is the basis for OpenID usage.

- **OpenID**: An authentication method that works on OAuth 2 where, in addition to providing authorization information for the consumption of services through an access token, information about the identity of the owner of the resources or the user is provided through an ID token delivered by an identity provider in **JSON Web Token (JWT)** format.

## OpenAPI Specification

The OpenAPI Specification is a description format for APIs written in both YAML and JSON that allows a description of the following characteristics:

- **Endpoints**: Information about the available resources and what operations can be performed on them based on the available HTTP verbs (GET, POST, PUT, DELETE)

- **Operational parameters**: Information about the input and output for the consumption of each endpoint

- **Authentication methods**: Ways in which it is possible to authenticate with services such as basic auth, OAuth 2.0, and OpenID Connect

- **Contact information**: Information such as the contact details of the creators, terms of use, and license conditions

As it is a standard format for the description of services, most cloud providers have tools within their API management offering that allow this specification to be read and the corresponding documentation for each service to be generated.

However, in some cases, such as when developing locally, it is very useful to have tools that allow us to view the relevant service documentation and carry out tests simulating a payload based on the documentation. Two tools for this that can be very useful are **Swagger UI** and **Swagger Editor**.

# Swagger UI

Swagger UI is a library that allows developers to quickly and easily implement a visualization panel on their services that are already documented through the OpenAPI Specification:

Figure 6.1 – Swagger UI

# Swagger Editor

**Swagger Editor** is a free service available via https://editor.swagger.io/ that allows us to quickly view API specifications created in OpenAPI in a graphical way that is more readily understood by developers:

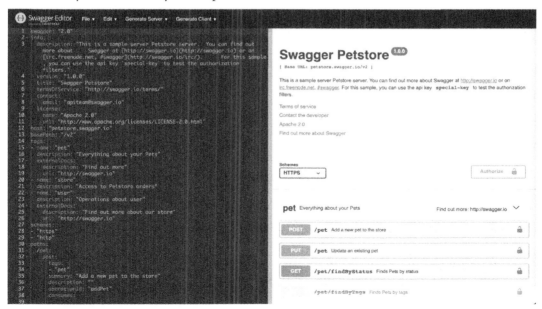

Figure 6.2 – Swagger Editor

# How to protect your APIs using Cloud Endpoints on your deployments

Cloud Endpoints is an API management system offered by Google Cloud for the protection, monitoring, analysis, and control of quotas on our services, using the same service as Google does for its own services.

Cloud Endpoints works through an **Extensible Service Provider** (**ESP**) to deliver API management functionalities to your services.

Depending on the communication protocol that your service uses and where it is hosted, there are three Cloud Endpoints options:

- **Cloud Endpoints for OpenAPI**: A Cloud Endpoints solution that works with the OpenAPI API description specification.

- **Cloud Endpoints for gRPC**: A Cloud Endpoints solution that works with the open source RPC framework developed by Google for high-performance connections, allowing calls between methods of different servers as if they were local objects, facilitating the development of distributed applications.

- **Cloud Endpoints Frameworks**: A specific web framework for applications deployed in App Engine in its standard version for the **Python 2.7** and **Java 8** programming languages, allowing the creation of REST APIs in your application.

Next, we will review in detail the steps required to implement a Cloud Endpoints solution in a Kubernetes cluster using the Cloud Endpoints solution for OpenAPI.

## ESP implementation for Cloud Endpoints

In order to deploy Cloud Endpoints to a service deployed in a GKE-managed Kubernetes cluster, it is necessary to deploy the service specification on Cloud Endpoints using OpenAPI and use an **ESP**. An ESP is an NGINX-based proxy that is implemented in front of our services in order to intercept calls and provide API management features.

If you want to learn more about the NGINX proxy, you can visit this site: `https://www.nginx.com/resources/wiki/`.

In the case of a service deployed in GKE, ESP can be deployed in the same Pod as the service, in a container called endpoints, referring to the open source image available in the **Google Container Registry** repository. To carry out the ESP implementation, it is necessary to add an ESP container with the following characteristics to the Pod's deployment manifest:

```
- name: endpoints
    resources:
      limits:
        cpu: CPU_LIMIT
      requests:
        cpu: CPU_REQUEST
    image: gcr.io/endpoints-release/endpoints-runtime:1.32.0
    args:
    - --http_port=EXPOSE_PORT
    - --backend=127.0.0.1:BACKEND_PORT
    - --service=SERVICE_NAME.endpoints.PROJECT_ID.cloud.goog
    - --rollout_strategy=managed
    - --cors_preset=basic
    - -z=healthz
    readinessProbe:
      httpGet:
        path: /healthz
        port: EXPOSE_PORT
    ports:
      - containerPort: EXPOSE_PORT
```

Here, we have the following:

- CPU_LIMIT: CPU limit for the ESP container
- CPU_REQUEST: CPU requested for the ESP container
- EXPOSE_PORT: The port through which ESP is exposed within the cluster
- BACKEND_PORT: The port through which the service is exposed within the cluster

- SERVICE_NAME: The name of the service deployed in Cloud Endpoints (which we will create in the next section)
- PROJECT_ID: The ID of the Google Cloud project where the Cloud Endpoints service is deployed

With this configuration, we will allow calls made to the service to go through the ESP initially, which will communicate with the service deployed in Cloud Endpoints and verify that the user or application has the necessary permissions to consume the service:

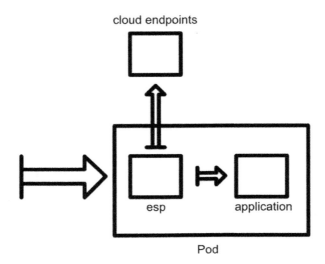

Figure 6.3 – ESP

Next, we will review in detail how to deploy the service specification in Cloud Endpoints so that it can be consulted by ESP.

## OpenAPI configuration for Cloud Endpoints

For ESP to verify whether the request made by a user or application complies with the service specification, check whether it has the permissions to perform the query, and also register each of these requests to perform analytics, it is necessary to deploy the service specification in OpenAPI format on Cloud Endpoints.

To deploy the specification, you must first create an openapi.yaml file that contains at least the following information about the service to be deployed:

```
swagger: "2.0"
info:
  title: "My Service"
```

```
        description: "This is the description of the service."
        version: "1.0.0"
    host: "SERVICE_NAME.YOUR-PROJECT-ID.appspot.com"
    schemes:
      - "https"
    paths:
      "/myService":
        get:
          description: "This is the description of the
endpoint."
          operationId: "myServiceName"
          parameters:
            -
              name: parameterName
              in: query
              required: true
              type: string
          responses:
            200:
              description: "Success."
              schema:
                type: string
            400:
              description: "The resource is invalid or
missing."
```

Here, we have the following:

- Swagger: OpenAPI version
- Title: The title of the service (informative)
- Description: A description of the service (informative)
- Version: The version of the service to be deployed
- Host: The name of the service plus the ID of the project
- Schemes: Supports HTTP and HTTPS
- Paths: A description of the service endpoints

Furthermore, to protect a particular service or endpoint, it is necessary to add the security specification to the document. This example shows how we would protect the services through the `apiKey` method:

```
securityDefinitions:
  security_method:
    type: "apiKey"
    name: "key"
    in: "query"
```

Finally, to indicate that the service endpoints are going to be protected by the `apiKey` security method, we have to add the following specification to the selected endpoints:

```
paths:
  "/myService":
get:
    description: "This is the description of the endpoint."
    operationId: "myServiceName"
    security:
    - security_method: []
```

If you want to protect all the endpoints of the service, you can add the previous specification at the top level of the document.

To protect the services through an OAuth-type authentication method, add the following security declaration:

```
securityDefinitions:
  security_method:
    authorizationUrl: ""
    flow: "implicit"
    type: "oauth2"
    x-google-issuer: "SA_EMAIL_ADDRESS"
    x-google-jwks_uri: "https://www.googleapis.com/robot/v1/
metadata/x509/SA_EMAIL_ADDRESS"
```

Here, SA_EMAIL_ADDRESS is the email address of the service account that will be used to authenticate with the services.

Once the service specification document has been completed, it is necessary to validate the document and deploy it to Cloud Endpoints. For this, it is possible to use the Google Cloud SDK.

In order to validate the document, we can use the following command:

```
gcloud endpoints services deploy [YOUR_OPENAPI_DOCUMENT]
--validate-only
```

Here, YOUR_OPENAPI_DOCUMENT is the path to the OpenAPI service specification document.

If the document is valid, it is possible to perform the deployment using the following command:

```
gcloud endpoints services deploy [YOUR_OPENAPI_DOCUMENT]
```

In this way, we can have the specification of our service in Cloud Endpoints so that it can be consumed by the ESP that is acting as a proxy to grant the API management functionalities.

# Discovering the enterprise API management world with Apigee

**Apigee**, that is, **API Gateway Enterprise Edition**, is an API platform product, acquired by Google in 2016, that allows us to manage and protect our services.

In this section, we will review in detail how to implement the Apigee API management solution on a service deployed in Google Cloud.

## Deploying a serverless API using Cloud Functions

The first thing we have to do before implementing the Apigee solution is to have an API to work on. In this case, we will deploy an API in Cloud Functions, to demonstrate how to protect a serverless service through Apigee.

For this example, we will deploy a cloud function with a trigger of the HTTP type that, by making a call of the GET type, will obtain the words Dog Resource to simulate obtaining the resource. In a real scenario, this service would return a list of the corresponding resources.

To deploy the cloud function of this example, we will use the following code:

```
exports.getDogs = (req, res) => {
  res.send('Dog Resource');
};
```

Once the cloud function is deployed, it is important to save the trigger URL that will allow calls to be made to the service. For this, we can go to the **Trigger** section of Cloud Functions and save the URL of the HTTP trigger.

Having already deployed our test service, we can proceed to create our proxy within Apigee and make the connections needed to consume our service in Cloud Functions.

# Implementing an API management solution with Apigee

Once our service is created, we have to create an account at `https://login.apigee.com/sign_up`.

Although Apigee is a paid service, there is the possibility of opting for a free trial to carry out tests.

Once our account is created, we must log in to `https://login.apigee.com/login` and create the proxy that will intercept calls made to our service. For this, it is necessary to access the **Proxy API** section and select the **+ Proxy | Reverse Proxy** option.

Being in the **Reverse Proxy** section, we have to create our proxy with the following information:

- **Proxy Name**: The name that the proxy will have
- **Proxy Base Path**: The base path through which the service will be consumed (it is recommended that it be a self-explanatory name)
- **Existing API**: The URL of our service (in this case, the URL of the HTTP trigger of our cloud function)

Having configured our proxy, we can proceed to click on the **Next** button.

In the **Policies** section, select the **API Key** option, in order to protect our service through the `apiKey` authentication method, and then click **Next**. (If we need an API without authentication, we can select the pass-through option.)

In the **Virtual Hosts** section, leave the default configuration and click **Next**.

Finally, in the **Summary** tab, select the **test** environment option in the **Optional Deployment** section and click on **Create and Deploy**. This ensures that our proxy is ready to intercept the calls that come to our service.

## Adding policies

In order to make our API effectively verify the API key delivered by the user or application that consumes the service, it is necessary to create a policy that performs this action. For this, we have to go to the **API Proxy** section, select the proxy created in the previous section, and select the **Develop** tab. In the **Proxy Endpoints** section, we have to select **Preflow**, which means that we will apply this validation logic before sending the traffic to our service in Cloud Functions.

Within the policies to be configured in the preflow, it is possible to select options for controlling calls per second, such as the Spike Arrest policy and quota management, among others, to be applied before referring traffic to our services. In this case, we will select the **Verify API Key** policy and keep the name and display name parameters as the default.

In order to later test our service, we must edit the current CORS policy by going to the **Target Endpoints** section and selecting **Preflow**. Then, in the **Access-Control-Allow-Header** tag of the XML configuration, add **apikey** within the available options.

In this way, we create a policy within our proxy to validate that the consumer of our service has a valid API key.

Next, we will proceed to create an *API product* in order to be able to assign an API key to a particular service.

## Creating an API product

An API product allows us to protect the services that we expose in our API management solution based on the proxies that we have configured in Apigee. In this particular case, we will create an API product to protect the proxy created in the previous section.

In order to create an API product, we have to go to the **Publish** section and then select **API Products | + API Product**.

Then, create an API product with the following information:

- **Name**: Product name.
- **Display name**: Friendly product name.
- **Environment**: Test.

- **Access**: Public.

- **Automatically approve Access request**: Selected.

- **Quota**: Request frequency that the API will allow.

- **API Proxies**: Select the proxy created in the *Implementing an API management solution with Apigee* section.

Once the configurations have been set, click on the **Save** button.

Having created our API product, we can proceed to create the last necessary component, a developer app that will allow us to associate our credentials with the consumption of our service.

# Creating a developer app

The creation of a developer app will allow us to associate credentials for the consumption of our service.

In order to create a developer app, we have to go to the **Publish** section and select **Apps**.

Then, create an app with the following information:

- **Name**: The name of the app.

- **Display Name**: A friendly name of the app.

- **Company / Developer**: The developer.

- **Developer**: Use the account that appears by default.

- **Callback URL**: Leave blank.

- **Notes**: Leave blank.

In the **Credentials** section, we add the API product created in the *Creating an API product* section and then click **Create**.

Finally, to be able to consume our API, obtain the API key from the **Credentials | Key** section by pressing the **Show** button.

Now that we have our API key, we can proceed to consume our service.

To consume our service through Apigee, we have to make a call to the following URL:

```
https://ENVIRONMENT_SUBDOMAIN.apigee.net/PROXY_NAME/ENDPOINT_
NAME?apiKey=API_KEY.
```

Here, we have the following:

- ENVIRONMENT_SUBDOMAIN is the name of the test environment subdomain delivered by Apigee (which can be obtained from the proxy created in the *Implementing an API management solution with Apigee section*).

- PROXY_NAME is the proxy name (created in the *Implementing an API management solution with Apigee* section).

- ENDPOINT_NAME is the name of the endpoint exposed by our service in Cloud Functions (in this case, it would be getDogs).

- API_KEY is the API key obtained in the creation of the developer app.

In this way, we can consume our service protected by Apigee. If we wanted to consume another endpoint, we would simply have to replace the name entered in ENDPOINT_NAME, and if we wanted to consume our service exposed in another previously created environment, we would have to replace the ENVIRONMENT_SUBDOMAIN value.

# Securing and managing your serverless workloads with the new Cloud API Gateway

API Gateway is a fully self-managed API management service with high performance and scalability from Google Cloud. It does not need any type of additional implementation such as proxies or ESP. API Gateway also provides the easy consumption of services for developers, protection of services, and tools for monitoring, alerts, logging, and tracing.

In this section, we will review in detail how to implement an API management solution made in API Gateway on serverless components.

## Deploying a serverless API using Cloud Functions

The first thing we have to do before implementing the API Gateway solution is to have an API to work on. In this case, we will deploy an API in Cloud Functions to demonstrate how to protect a serverless service using API Gateway.

For this particular example, we will deploy a cloud function with a trigger of the HTTP type and a GET call to which we will return the words Dog Resource to simulate obtaining a resource. In a real scenario, this service would return a list of the corresponding resources.

To deploy the cloud function of this example, we will use the following code:

```
exports.getDogs = (req, res) => {
  res.send('Dog Resource');
};
```

Once the cloud function is deployed, it is important to save the trigger URL that will allow calls to be made to the service. For this, we can go to the **Trigger** section of Cloud Functions and save the URL of the HTTP trigger.

Having already deployed our test service, we can proceed to implement our API in API Gateway and make the connections that enable our service to be consumed in Cloud Functions.

## Creating an API in API Gateway

To create our API in API Gateway, we will use Google Cloud SDK and the following command:

```
gcloud api-gateway apis create API_NAME --project=PROJECT_ID
```

Here, we have the following:

- API_NAME is the name of the API.
- PROJECT_ID is the ID of the project where we will deploy our API.

Once we have created our API in API Gateway, we will proceed to configure the API by creating a specification document using OpenAPI:

```
swagger: '2.0'
info:
  title: API_NAME
  description: Sample API on API Gateway with a Google Cloud
Functions backend
  version: 1.0.0
schemes:
  - https
produces:
  - application/json
paths:
  /dogs:
```

```
get:
   summary: get all dogs
   operationId: dogs
   x-google-backend:
     address: https://REGION-PROJECT_ID.cloudfunctions.net/
getDogs
   responses:
     '200':
       description: A successful response
       schema:
         type: string
```

Here, we have the following:

- API_NAME is the name of the API created in API Gateway.

- PROJECT_ID is the ID of the project where the API was deployed.

- REGION is the region where the cloud function was deployed.

The value of the address parameter corresponds to the trigger URL of our service deployed in Cloud Functions.

In order to deploy this configuration to our API previously created in API Gateway, we can use the following command:

```
gcloud api-gateway api-configs create CONFIG_NAME \
  --api=API_NAME --openapi-spec=API_DEFINITION_PATH \
  --project=PROJECT_ID --backend-auth-service-account=SERVICE_
ACCOUNT_EMAIL
```

Here, we have the following:

- CONFIG_NAME is the name of the configuration to create.

- API_NAME is the name of the API created in the previous section.

- API_DEFINITION_PATH is the path of the document with the OpenAPI Specification.

- PROJECT_ID is the ID of the project where the API was deployed.

- SERVICE_ACCOUNT_EMAIL is the service account with the cloud function invoker role that will be used to authenticate with the backend service (in this case, Cloud Functions).

Having configured our API, we can then expose our service through an external URL that goes through the API management solution.

## Exposing our service

To expose our service, we use the following command:

```
gcloud api-gateway gateways create GATEWAY_NAME \
  --api=API_NAME --api-config=CONFIG_NAME \
  --location=GCP_REGION --project=PROJECT_ID
```

Here, we have the following:

- GATEWAY_NAME corresponds to the name that we will give to the exhibition of our service.
- API_NAME is the name of the API deployed in API Gateway.
- CONFIG_NAME is the name of our API configuration in API Gateway.
- GCP_REGION is the region where our API was deployed.
- PROJECT_ID is the project where our API was deployed.

To obtain the URL on which we will consume the exposed service, we will use the following command, using the parameters mentioned in the preceding list:

```
gcloud api-gateway gateways describe GATEWAY_name \
  --location=GCP_REGION --project=PROJECT_ID
```

When executing this command, we will obtain the information from defaultHostname, which will correspond to the URL on which we consume our service.

To make a call to our service, we will use the following URL:

https://DEFAULT_HOSTNAME/dogs

Here, DEFAULT_HOSTNAME is the external URL provided by API Gateway to consume our service.

For this particular example, we use the /dogs endpoint, but the endpoint will change depending on what is specified in the OpenAPI configuration file uploaded to API Gateway.

# Protecting our services

In the previous section, we reviewed how to expose a serverless service created in Cloud Functions using API Gateway. If we want to protect our service either through the API_KEY method or by using a service account, we simply have to modify the specification file for our API created in OpenAPI with the following information:

- In the apiKey case, add the following definition:

```
securityDefinitions:
  security_method:
    type: "apiKey"
    name: "key"
    in: "query"
```

- In the service account case, add the following definition:

```
securityDefinitions:
  security_method:
    authorizationUrl: ""
    flow: "implicit"
    type: "oauth2"
    x-google-issuer: "SA_EMAIL_ADDRESS"
    x-google-jwks_uri: "https://www.googleapis.com/robot/
v1/metadata/x509/SA_EMAIL_ADDRESS"
```

Here, SA_EMAIL_ADDRESS is the email of the service account used to authenticate with the services:

```
Finally, to indicate which endpoint of the service are
going to be protected, we have to add the following
specification (by way of example) to the selected
endpoints:
paths:
  "/dogs":
get:
    summary: get all dogs
    operationId: dogs
    security:
    - security_method: []
```

If you wanted to protect all endpoints of the service, you could add the previous specification at the top level of the document.

# API development best practices

In this section, you will learn how to create services based on good practices such as **REST APIs** and **Domain-Driven Design** (**DDD**) in order to make your APIs easier to understand and use and to facilitate discussions within your organization.

## An overview of DDD

DDD is a concept that allows us to structure our services so that they align with our business domain. A detailed understanding of how to implement DDD within our organization requires a lot of experience, both in developing services and in business domains. In this section, we will briefly summarize the different integrated concepts within DDD and how they relate to each other. This will give us an initial baseline understanding of what DDD is and what its benefits are.

DDD is separated into two key concepts, *tactical design*, which pertains to structuring at the code level, and *strategic design*, which is about structuring at the organizational level.

Within tactical design, we have the following concepts, which we will explain in detail:

- Model-driven design
- Services
- Entities
- Value objects
- Aggregates
- Repositories
- Domain events

- Factories
- Layered architecture:

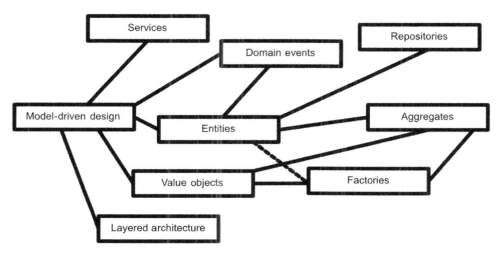

Figure 6.4 – Tactical design

**Model-driven design** refers to the ability to associate the business concepts we already have in our organization in order to model our design. To express the semantics of our domains, the concepts of *services*, *entities*, and *value objects* will be used.

A **service** is what allows us to orchestrate the logic described in a business use case, in conjunction with the use of *entities* and *value objects*.

An **entity** is maintained over time regardless of whether any of its values change; it remains the same element. For example, if I have user A and this user changes their email, the user remains the same, regardless of whether the value has changed.

A **value object**, on the other hand, *is* affected by changes made to its value. In this particular example, it would be the email address, an element that, if it changes, becomes another element. Understanding the concepts of both *entities* and *value objects* within our solution allows us to develop a more robust and decoupled solution, which brings us greater benefits when having to make any changes to our developments.

**Aggregates** are a pattern within DDD, represented as a set of *entities* and *value objects* that it makes sense to treat together. For example, the concept of a purchase order and line items should be treated as a single unit and, when persisted, should be stored together.

To access all the *entities* and *value objects* of the aggregate collections that we have within our domain, the concept of **repositories** is used. Repositories also allow us to abstract from storage in order to avoid direct coupling to data sources.

**Domain events** are any type of event that may exist in our application, such as the creation of a user or the registration of a purchase order. The idea of having these events is to be able to decouple the business logic on their processing.

**Factories** is a design pattern that allows us to encapsulate the creation of aggregate collections to maintain a logical representation and prevent other classes inside the application from interacting directly with internal elements. For example, if we are creating an order in an e-commerce application, we need to take care of creating an address, a list of items, and preferred payment methods. A factory can help us to get this information from external services to create the order.

Finally, a **layered architecture** is what supports all the concepts mentioned and enables us to implement our solution with this division of domains:

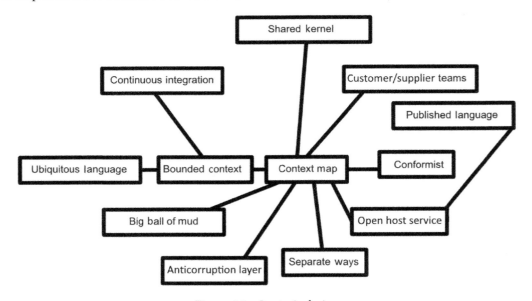

Figure 6.5 – Strategic design

For **strategic design**, we have to consider the following concepts, which will be explained in detail:

- Ubiquitous language
- Bounded context
- Continuous integration
- Context map
- Big ball of mud
- Anticorruption layer
- Separate ways
- Open host service
- Published language
- Shared kernel
- Customer/supplier teams
- Conformist

**Ubiquitous language** refers to being able to maintain a common language between developers and users. This language should be used both for the activities carried out by the business and to describe these activities at the coding level. For example, if we need to define a word for a task status in our application, the word *done* is more common in daily usage than *finished*.

**Bounded context** is the main pattern within DDD, and refers to the ability to group models that have similarities or relationships with each other in contexts in order to provide autonomy and decoupling between the different domains within the organization. This decoupling is reflected when making modifications to service code, reducing the generation of conflicts between different development teams. For example, functionalities related to a user in our application can be part of a bounded context.

**Continuous integration** is the ability of each bounded context to have total autonomy when deploying code to production through the use of CI/CD tools. For example, the use of **Cloud Build** in Google Cloud Platform can help us to create a CI/CD pipeline to deploy code in our project.

The **context map** refers to the relationships that exist between the different bounded contexts identified within the organization, and the relationships between the different teams that are responsible for them. The following definitions are some examples of integrations between multiple bounded contexts.

The **big ball of mud** concept refers to code within the application built without consideration of good architectural or development practices, also known as spaghetti code. It is recommended, as part of the DDD strategy, to separate this code behind an anticorruption layer. For example, a big ball of mud can refer to old legacy code inside our organization.

The **anticorruption layer**, or **ACL**, is implemented between two bounded contexts and allows us to integrate functionalities of general legacy services with our modern applications by translating the request/response specification of an API according to the bounded context in which it is found. For example, we can create an ACL to integrate our modern system with an on-premises API. Later, if we need to integrate with a newer version of this service, we need only to change the ACL and not modify the code in our modern system.

The concept of **separate ways** refers to the freedom to be able to work with different methodologies or technologies within different bounded contexts. For example, one bounded context can use Node.js to develop its microservices and another bounded context can use Java. They also can use different methodologies, such as **Waterfall** or **Agile**.

**Open host service** is the ability of a bounded context to open a communication channel with another bounded context, for example, by exposing an API inside the organization.

**Published language** refers to the documentation provided by the open host service so that one bounded context can consume another bounded context. Examples of a published language include the Swagger documentation for a service, which is created based on the OpenAPI Specification.

**Shared kernel** considers the development of common functionalities defined by a context map between different bounded contexts, in order to centralize these functionalities and thus reduce duplication in development. For example, the use of a shared library of authentication between two bounded contexts could be considered as an example.

**Customer/supplier teams** refers to scenarios in which teams from different bounded contexts need to integrate and one of them is the supplier and the other the customer. For example, to determine priorities within the integration, the customer team (it could be a project that needs to integrate with an API inside the organization) must be available to the supplier team (it could be an exposed API inside the organization) to resolve any questions about the integration. On the other hand, the supplier team must give priority to the integration of the customer team in order to avoid blockages.

**Conformist** refers to the relationship between two bounded contexts where one of them has no interest in making any changes to facilitate integration. For example, this scenario often occurs in an organization where it is necessary to integrate a new functionality with an existing and well-established system.

The concepts described in tactical and strategic design give us a vocabulary that equips us to address important considerations in the development of our services. This helps to improve both developments at the coding level and the interactions between the different teams responsible for these services within the organization.

# REST

**REST**, or **Representational State Transfer**, is an architecture design style of APIs that can be implemented in the creation of our services to facilitate the use and understanding of the services.

For an API to be considered REST, it must comply with six core principles:

- **Client-server**: Separation of user interface responsibilities from information storage responsibilities.

- **Stateless**: Each call to the service must contain all the information necessary to execute the request, without the need to resort to context information on the server.

- **Cacheable**: The possibility of storing a response to be retrieved and used later, without the need to make a new request to the source of the information.

- **Uniform interface**: Identification of resources, manipulation of resources through representations, self-descriptive messages, and hypermedia as the center of the application state.

- **Layered system**: An ordering of the architecture through hierarchical layers, where each component of the architecture can only interact with its predecessors or successors.

- **Code on demand (optional)**: The possibility of extending the functionalities of the service through scripts.

Regarding the identification of resources and referring to the point of a uniform interface, each resource will be associated with a URL in its plural form. For example, if we have a resource of the dog type, the URL to access this resource will be /dogs.

When we talk about executing actions on a particular resource, we associate the HTTP verbs with the **CRUD** actions:

- **Create**: POST
- **Read**: GET
- **Update**: PUT/UPDATE
- **Delete**: DELETE

In this way, every time I want to get the resources of the dog type, I will make a call of the GET type to the /dogs resource. This call will return a list of all the resources of the dog type that are available.

If I want to get a particular resource, I will make a GET call to the dogs resource accompanied by a unique identifier of the resource, for example, GET /dogs/1 for resource 1 and GET /dogs/2 for resource 2.

If I want to update an existing resource, I will make a PUT call to the dogs resource accompanied by the unique identifier of the resource plus the information to be modified. For example, if we want to modify resource 2, we will make a call to PUT /dogs/2 and, within the body of the request, we will send the information to be modified.

If I want to delete an existing resource, I will make a DELETE call to the dogs resource accompanied by the unique identifier of the resource. For example, if we want to delete resource 2, we will make a call to DELETE /dogs/2.

Finally, if we want to create a new resource, we will make a POST call to /dogs and, within the body, all the information necessary to create this resource.

In this way, whenever we are confronted by a REST-type API, we know immediately how to create, obtain, update, and delete a resource using the corresponding HTTP verbs on the resources.

In addition to the points reviewed in this section, for an API to be considered REST, it is important to consider the following set of good practices in order to ensure that our API has easy usability, maintenance, and security:

- **HTTP and REST**: A data-oriented design paradigm rather than function-oriented design.

- **For easier usability**: Design according to RESTful best practices, focused on consumption and consistency, and provide a clear statement of the value proposition the API represents to developers. Avoid premature optimization and hide unnecessary complexity from developers. Remember, developers likely do not have time to learn the inner workings of our system and should not need to; they simply want the data they need to enrich their application.

- **For ease of maintainability**: Follow a standard design pattern in interface and logic design and practice maintainability during the design process of the API, as it can't be added later on.

- **Protect APIs**: Enforce a consistent set of security policies and protocols across all APIs – private and public. Employ authentication such as OAuth/OpenID Connect in conjunction with **Transport Layer Security** (**TLS**) to protect data and control who accesses it, and consider spike arrests and per-app usage quotas to help maintain API performance.

- **Test and deploy APIs**: Sync the API life cycle with a modern, agile, and iterative **software development life cycle** (**SDLC**) and automate API testing and deployment.

Considering the points reviewed in this section related to a REST API, we can ensure the development of an API that is easily understandable by developers who will use it in order to consume the exposed resources in an optimal way. In addition, following a set of good practices will allow us to add new functionalities in an efficient and safe way.

# Summary

In this chapter, we have learned that API management is a group of concepts that helps us to expose, protect, monitor, and document our services inside an organization. We've also reviewed in detail three solutions that Google Cloud provides for exposing our services (Cloud Endpoints, Apigee, and API Gateway), and seen how DDD and REST practices can help us to create a better API ecosystem within our organization. In the next chapter, we will see how to manage unstructured data within solutions implemented in Google Cloud, in order to handle large amounts of data and take advantage of the benefits of the cloud to reduce costs.

# Section 3: Storage Foundations

In this section, you will learn the basics of cloud storage, understanding the best options for storing unstructured data, structured data, and analytics data, in addition to best practices and general use cases.

This section comprises the following chapters:

- *Chapter 7, Handling Unstructured Data*
- *Chapter 8, Databases and Event Messages in Google Cloud*
- *Chapter 9, Data Management and Database Strategies*
- *Chapter 10, Optimizing Applications with Caching Strategies on Google Cloud Platform*

# 7
# Handling Unstructured Data

In this chapter, you will learn how to store and consume unstructured data such as images, videos, and files to solve different challenges in your solutions efficiently and optimally, using the services provided by Google Cloud.

We will cover the following topics in this chapter:

- Different real-world use cases for cloud storage
- How to reduce costs using different tiers
- Backing up and deleting files automatically
- Protecting my data with security best practices
- Integrating cloud storage with my application

## Technical requirements

- **Google Cloud SDK 317** or later: https://cloud.google.com/sdk
- **pyOpenSSL** library: https://pyopenssl.org/en/stable/

# Different real-world use cases for cloud storage

**Cloud storage** is a fully self-managed unstructured data storage solution within Google Cloud, allowing an unlimited amount of information to be stored in different parts of the world with low latency and high durability.

In the following sections, we will identify some of the different use cases for which we can use Google's cloud storage service.

## Worldwide delivery

Any application that displays multimedia content to its users, such as social networks, web pages, or streaming platforms, needs a place to store the content that it shows to its users, such as its images, videos, or documents. This content needs to be consumed regularly, be available in different regions, and have the minimum latency between its source of origin and the consumer:

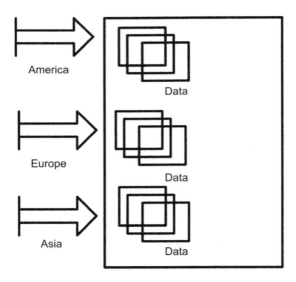

Figure 7.1 – Worldwide delivery

# Analytics

Data analytics solutions require the constant consumption of high volumes of data by **extraction, transformation, and loading** pipelines, better known as **ETL** within our processes. For this, we need a solution that allows us to consume this data in such a way that it is as close as possible to the computing service and within the same region, so as to reduce both the latency in consumption and the amount of network traffic from the source of the data:

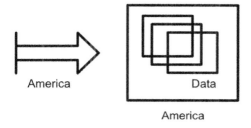

Figure 7.2 – Analytics

# Backup

In all our solutions, we should consider making frequent backups of user-generated information, to allow it to be restored in the event of an error either on the part of the user or in the implementation of solution functionality. Having a storage service allows us to frequently access previously stored information in order to partially or fully (in disaster recovery scenarios) restore data in our application.

# Disaster recovery

Although this scenario is less common than a partial restoration, like the one mentioned in the previous section, the consequences of a disaster and associated information loss can potentially have a much greater impact. In some cases, it could mean the bankruptcy of an organization, as seen throughout history. This is why, as our application grows and generates more and more information, it is necessary to have a plan to recover data in the event of a disaster, such as an attack on our services or some natural disaster. For this, we need to store a copy of all our data that can be restored in its entirety in a way that the cost of keeping this data remains justifiable to the business.

## Audit

In some cases, due to existing laws or regulations in each country, it may be necessary to store the information generated by our users or our applications to enable the authorities to carry out audits on our data. To comply with these regulations, we need solutions that allow us to store this information for long periods (generally greater than a couple of years), sacrificing the ability to readily access this information in order to reduce storage costs.

## Optimizing costs regarding storage use cases

Already understanding some of the use cases where we can use the Google Cloud unstructured data storage solution, we can begin to review how to optimize costs for each of these cases to maximize the benefits of cloud storage and thus take care of our wallet.

If you want to see all the features of cloud storage, you can check the following link: `https://cloud.google.com/storage`.

# How to reduce costs using different tiers

Depending on what we use our cloud storage bucket for, and according to the different use cases reviewed in the previous section, we can select different classes to optimize the costs of our solution. Next, we will review the four options in terms of balancing the availability of the data versus the cost of storage:

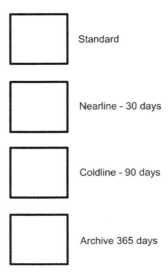

Figure 7.3 – Storage classes

# Standard

The **Standard** class is intended for frequent data access use cases, such as the consumption of multimedia data for social networks, web pages, or streaming platforms or other cases where data is stored for short periods as data and analytics ETL pipelines that require intensive consumption and the realization of transformations.

Depending on the specific case, it is possible to configure our cloud storage bucket to make data available regionally (ideal for data processing and analytics cases that are in the same region) or multi-regionally (ideal for cases where the information is consumed by different users in different parts of the world and multiple regions, such as social networks or streaming platforms).

It is also possible to obtain the best of both worlds by using dual-region configuration, obtaining high availability between regions, and low latency. This is ideal for analytics solutions, which are often critical for the business and therefore require greater availability.

# Nearline

The **Nearline** class is designed for storing data that is accessed infrequently, with a minimum storage commitment of 30 days. The access costs of this data are higher than those of the Standard type, but those costs are offset by the reduced cost of storing such data.

The ideal scenario for using this class is for data backups or analytical scenarios where data is processed every 30 days.

# Coldline

The **Coldline** class is intended for data storage with a minimum commitment of 90 days, having lower storage costs than the Nearline type class, but at the same time higher costs for obtaining this data.

The ideal scenario for using this class includes information backups and data archiving.

# Archive

The **Archive** class is intended for storing data with a minimum commitment of 365 days. It has the lowest storage cost of all the classes, but at the same time, the highest cost for obtaining said data.

The ideal scenario for using this class is the storage of data for long periods, in order to satisfy regulatory requirements or disaster recovery plans.

# Explaining storage pricing

As mentioned before, different classes allow us to obtain the maximum benefit in terms of costs depending on the use case of our bucket in cloud storage.

Next, we will review the factors for which we are charged when using the cloud storage service:

- **Data Storage**: Storage costs per GB.

- **Network**: Outbound traffic costs from our bucket.

- **A Class Operations**: Create object and bucket operations and list existing objects.

- **B Class Operations**: Get objects, buckets, and metadata operations.

To measure the benefit of using the correct class according to our use case, we will carry out an example assuming that we are storing 100 GB of data for 1 month, comparing the different classes:

- **Standard**: $0.020 * 100 GB = USD 2

- **Nearline**: $0.010 * 100 GB = USD 1

- **Coldline**: $0.004 * 100 GB = USD 0.4

- **Archive**: $0.0012 * 100 GB = USD 0.12:

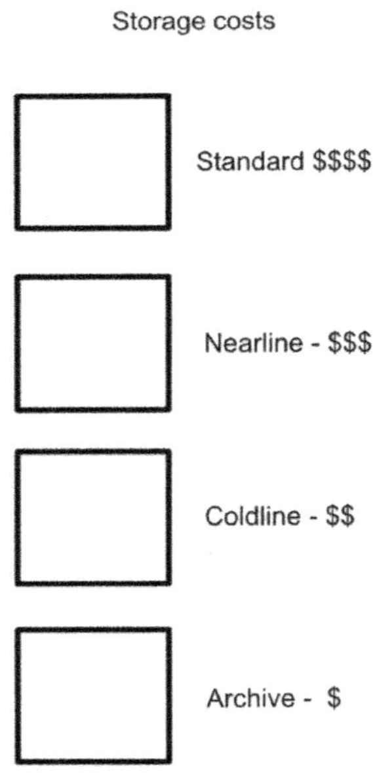

Storage costs

Standard $$$$

Nearline - $$$

Coldline - $$

Archive - $

Figure 7.4 – Storage pricing

We can notice a difference of up to almost 20 times between the Standard class and the Archive class when it comes to storage. But what if we now want to obtain the information previously stored in our bucket, performing a type B operation (for example, getting an object from the bucket) to obtain the existing 100 GB:

- **Standard**: $0.004 * 100 GB = USD 0.4

- **Nearline**: $0.01 * 100 GB = USD 1

- **Coldline**: $0.05 * 100 GB = USD 5

- **Archive**: $0.50 * 100 GB = USD 50

Although storing information in the Archive class meant almost 20 times lower costs, we observe that if we want to obtain the information stored, we can have 120 times higher costs compared to the Standard class. This is why it is extremely important to use the class most appropriate for the use case we face. Otherwise, instead of obtaining benefits, we could end up having much higher costs:

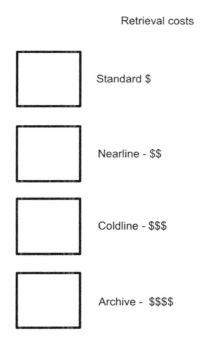

Figure 7.5 – Retrieval pricing

## Cloud storage summary diagrams

We now understand that all this information relating to cloud storage can be complicated. That is why we created this summary diagram with the information reviewed so far regarding cloud storage:

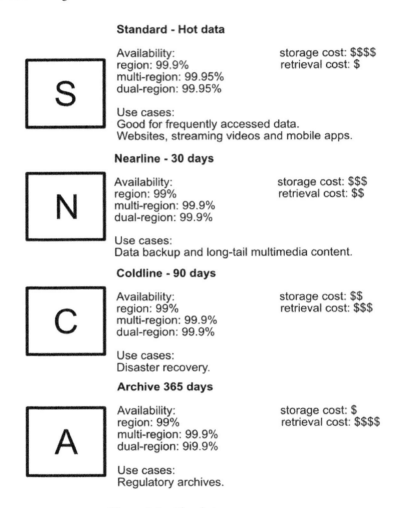

Figure 7.6 – Cloud storage summary

# Backing up and deleting files automatically

The longer our application has to live in operating environments, and the more users or processes that use it, the greater the amount of data generated. Having an automated backup and data cleaning strategy on our solution becomes crucial in lowering costs.

In this section, we will learn how to automate the process of changing the storage class from our bucket, as reviewed in the *How to reduce costs using different tiers* section, and thus obtain the benefits offered in relation to data storage.

We will also review how to protect our data using object versioning and data protection options to avoid the unintentional deletion of buckets and files.

# Managing life cycles

To automate actions on our data in a cloud storage bucket, we can use object life cycle configuration. By doing this, it is possible to create one or more life cycle rules with one or more compliance conditions on a given action.

Possible actions include the following:

- `Delete`: Action to delete an object when all the conditions of a life cycle rule are met
- `SetStorageClass`: Action of changing an object from one class to another when all the conditions of a life cycle rule are met

For an action to be executed, all the conditions associated with the corresponding rule must be met. If there are multiple rules associated with the same action, it is enough that one of the rules is fulfilled to execute that action.

If multiple rules meet their conditions simultaneously, the following prioritization will be taken:

- **Elimination** actions have priority over class change actions.
- **Class change** actions over the class with the lowest storage cost will have priority.

It is important to note that in the case of class changes, it is only possible to move to a class with a lower storage cost. This means that if we are in a class of the Standard type, we can move to a class of the Nearline, Coldline, or Archive type.

# Rule conditions

In this section, we will review some of the options we have for specifying conditions to configure our life cycle rules and thus be able to execute removal or class change actions on our objects:

- `Age`: The condition that is fulfilled when a particular object reaches the indicated age in days

- `CreatedBefore`: The condition that is met when an object is created prior to the specified date

- `CustomTimeBefore`: The condition that is met when an object is created prior to the date specified in the `Custom-Time` field of the metadata

- `DaysSinceCustomTime`: The condition that is met when an object reaches the specified age in days from the date specified in the `Custom-Time` field of the metadata

- `MatchesStorageClass`: The condition that is met when an object corresponds to a specified class

It is important to note that performing an update on any of these conditions in a previously configured life cycle rule can take up to 24 hours to take effect, so the previous rules could take effect up to 24 hours after they were modified.

## Implementing object life cycles

Now that we understand what actions, rules, and conditions are, we can review how to implement life cycle rules in our cloud storage buckets.

For this, the first thing we have to do is create a configuration file in JSON format. In this example, we will create a rule that eliminates all objects more than 30 days old:

```
{
"lifecycle": {
  "rule": [
  {
    "action": {"type": "Delete"},
    "condition": {
      "age": 30
    }
  }
 ]
 }
}
```

After creating our configuration file with the life cycle rules, we will proceed to assign these rules to our bucket in cloud storage. For this, we use the following Google Cloud SDK command:

```
gsutil lifecycle set CONFIG_FILE gs://BUCKET_NAME
```

Here, the following applies:

- CONFIG_FILE: The name of the previously created configuration file
- BUCKET_NAME: The name of the bucket to which the rules will be applied

To review all the configuration options for life cycle rules on a cloud storage bucket, refer to the following link: https://cloud.google.com/storage/docs/lifecycle

# Object versioning

Just as it is possible to version the source code of a project, we can also version our unstructured data within the cloud storage buckets so that we can retrieve a particular version if necessary.

To activate this functionality, simply run the following Google Cloud SDK command:

```
gsutil versioning set on gs://BUCKET_NAME
```

Here, the following applies:

- BUCKET_NAME: The name of the bucket where we will activate the versioning of objects

By activating this functionality, every time an object is replaced or deleted, it will go from a live state to a non-current state with a unique identifier called the generation number. Furthermore, versioned objects can only be obtained if they are explicitly included in the request.

To obtain versioned objects in a request, we can use the following command:

```
gsutil ls -a gs://BUCKET_NAME
```

Here, the following applies:

- BUCKET_NAME: The name of the bucket where we will activate the versioning of objects

To access a particular object, add the generation number to the name of the object, which can be found after the # sign when listing the objects.

For example, when listing the objects, we might receive a list like this:

```
gs://my-bucket/my-object.png#1
gs://my-bucket/my-object.png#2
gs://my-bucket/my-object.png#3
```

To access the object with the generation number 2, we simply add that generation number to the object's name, as seen in this example:

```
gs://my-bucket/my-object.png#2
```

To access the object with a live status, simply call the object by its original name, without adding the generation number:

```
gs://my-bucket/my-object.png
```

This functionality increases storage costs because more than one version of the object will be saved, but it does give you greater control. For example, it gives you the ability to control which versions to store and which not by configuring the following life cycle rules for versioned objects:

- `DaysSinceNoncurrentTime`: The condition that is met when a live object becomes non-current (when it is replaced by another object) for the number of days defined in the condition
- `IsLive`: The condition that is met when an object is in the live (`true`) or non-current (`false`) state
- `NoncurrentTimeBefore`: The condition that is met when a live object becomes non-current (when it is replaced by another object) on a date prior to the one specified in the condition
- `NumberOfNewerVersion`: The condition that is fulfilled when an object has `N` new versions on it, where `N` is specified in the condition

It is also possible to remove a specific version by using the following Google SDK command and adding the generation number to the request:

```
gsutil rm gs://my-bucket/my-object.png#2
```

In this way, it is possible to control the number of versions we have available within our bucket, so as to optimize storage costs.

## Bucket retention policy

One of the ways within Google Cloud in which we can protect the objects in our buckets from inadvertent actions or errors is through a retention policy.

To implement this protection, we execute the following command from the Google Cloud SDK:

```
gsutil retention set SECONDS gs://BUCKET_NAME
```

Here, the following applies:

- SECONDS: The number of seconds the object will be locked for deletion based on its creation in the bucket
- BUCKET_NAME: The name of the bucket for which we are activating the retention policy

This action protects the objects inside the bucket by allowing the deletion only of objects that have met the retention condition in the number of seconds specified in the previous command.

To block the possibility of editing a retention policy previously applied to a bucket, we can use the following command:

```
gsutil retention lock gs://BUCKET_NAME
```

Here, the following applies:

- BUCKET_NAME: The name of the bucket where we will block the possibility of editing the retention policy

It is important to note that, as its name indicates, this retention policy is applied permanently and blocks any action to edit or remove this policy from the bucket. The only way to delete both the objects and the bucket is by waiting for the retention condition to be met.

## Object hold protection

If we want to protect a particular object within a cloud storage bucket, it is possible to use the object hold functionality. This consists of applying a flag within the object's metadata to prevent its removal.

The object hold options define two types:

- **Event-based**: This protects the object while the object is on hold, and also resets the retention time of the object when applying a release
- **Temporary**: This only protects the object while it is on hold.

There is also a default configuration that applies an event-based hold to the entire bucket and thus applies a hold to all the objects created in that bucket.

To apply an event-based hold to all objects in a bucket, we can use the following command:

```
gsutil retention event-default set gs://BUCKET_NAME
```

Here, the following applies:

- BUCKET_NAME: The name of the bucket to whose objects the hold settings will be applied

To disable the configuration, simply apply the following command:

```
gsutil retention event-default release gs://BUCKET_NAME
```

Here, the following applies:

- BUCKET_NAME: The name of the bucket where hold settings on objects will be disabled

To apply a hold to a particular object, we can use the following command:

```
gsutil retention HOLD_TYPE set gs://BUCKET_NAME/OBJECT_NAME
```

Here, the following applies:

- HOLD_TYPE: The type of hold to apply to the object (temp or event)
- BUCKET_NAME: The name of the bucket where the object is located
- OBJECT_NAME: The name of the object to which the hold is to be applied

To free a particular object, we apply the following command:

```
gsutil retention HOLD_TYPE release gs://BUCKET_NAME/OBJECT_NAME
```

Here, the following applies:

- HOLD_TYPE: The type of hold to release on the object (temp or event)
- BUCKET_NAME: The name of the bucket where the object is located
- OBJECT_NAME: The name of the object to be released

In this way, we can apply protection to our objects against deletion in a cloud storage bucket.

# Protecting my data with security best practices

One of the most important things regarding our data is to keep it securely stored so that only authorized users or applications can access it. In this section, we will review how to control access to our data by applying access control policies and encrypting data at rest, among other good data protection practices.

## Access control

Among the options we have to control who or what has access to our data within a cloud storage bucket, there is uniform access and fine-grained access.

Uniform access works in conjunction with Cloud IAM to control access to a particular bucket. It is the recommended access control method to use for data storage in general, especially if the data to be stored is of a sensitive type, such as **personally identifiable information (PII)**, since the configuration has a lower probability of misconfiguration and thus data exposure:

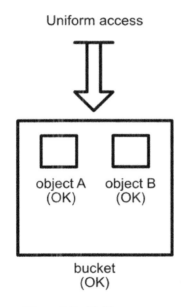

Figure 7.7 – Uniform access

Enabling uniform access control can be executed when a bucket is created for the first time or through the following command from the Google Cloud SDK:

```
gsutil uniformbucketlevelaccess set on gs://BUCKET_NAME
```

Here, the following applies:

- BUCKET_NAME: The name of the bucket to which you want to apply uniform access control

If you want to reverse the operation, you can use the following command:

```
gsutil uniformbucketlevelaccess set off gs://BUCKET_NAME
```

Here, the following applies:

- BUCKET_NAME: The name of the bucket for which you want to revert the uniform access control

It is important to note that once uniform access control is applied, you have 90 days in which you can reverse the operation. After that time, it is not possible to reverse the operation.

Fine-grained access works using Cloud IAM in conjunction with the **Access Control List** or **ACL**, and allows you to control access to either a particular bucket or an object within the bucket. This type of access control should be used if you want to explicitly handle an individual control for each object within the bucket, or if you want to have compatibility to migrate data from cloud storage to **Amazon S3**:

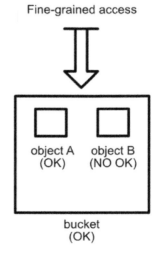

Figure 7.8 – Fine-grained access

To assign a permission to a particular bucket or object, we need two elements that together make up an entry:

- **Permission**: What action can the user or group take
- **Scope**: The user or group that will be able to execute the action

The three permissions that we have available to select are as follows:

- READER: If applied to a bucket, this allows you to list the content of the bucket and read the metadata. If it is applied to an object, it allows the downloading of the object.
- WRITER: If applied to a bucket, this allows you to list, create, replace, and delete objects from a bucket. You cannot apply this permission directly to an object.
- OWNER: If applied to a bucket, this gives both READER and WRITER permissions, in addition to modifying the metadata and the ACLs. If applied to an object, it allows modification of the metadata and the ACLs.

On the scope side, there are two types of special identifier that are important to note:

- allAuthenticatedUsers: Allows access to any user who is authenticated with a Google account
- allUsers: Allows any internet user access, with or without a Google account

To implement ACLs within cloud storage, we can use the Google Cloud SDK and the following commands; for example, if we need to assign read permission to a particular user on a bucket:

```
gsutil acl ch -u SCOPE:READ gs://BUCKET_NAME
```

Here, the following applies:

- SCOPE: Who can perform the specified actions
- BUCKET_NAME: The name of the bucket to apply the ACL to

As good security practice, you should always consider assigning permissions based on the principle of least privilege (see *Chapter 2, Security Fundamentals and Best Practices*), granting only the permissions needed to allow a user to perform their action. In addition, the special scopes of allAuthenticatedUsers and allUsers should only be used on non-sensitive information, since any authenticated person, or worse, any person from the internet, could have access when using these scopes.

Finally, it is important to note that it is possible to assign a maximum of 100 ACL entries to a bucket.

## Data encryption

All data stored in cloud storage buckets is kept encrypted at rest, being decrypted automatically when an authorized user consumes the information.

By default, Google is responsible for both storing and rotating the encryption keys that are used to encrypt and decrypt the information, but depending on the user's needs, it is also possible to manage our own encryption keys, deliver our own encryption keys, and lastly, encrypt the information before sending it to cloud storage.

It is very important to note that although there are options for providing our own encryption keys without Google's management, losing these keys can mean the permanent loss of our data, so it is extremely important to store these keys in a safe place, which cannot be accessed by unauthorized users. Unless there are special needs in the encryption of our data, the management of encryption and storage of keys by Google is the recommended option.

## Signed URLs

In some scenarios, we may need to share access to a file temporarily through a URL without the need for our user to have to log in with a Google account, such as when downloading a file through a link sent to the user's email. For this particular case, Google Cloud offers us the functionality of signed URLs, which allows us to programmatically create a URL that exposes an object stored in a temporary access cloud storage bucket.

To create a signed URL, it is necessary to have a user or service account that has the access permissions to the object in question. In this example, we will review how to generate a signed URL using the Google Cloud SDK and the **pyOpenSSL** library:

```
gsutil signurl -d EXPIRATION_TIME PRIVATE_KEY gs://BUCKET_NAME/
OBJECT_NAME
```

Here, the following applies:

- EXPIRATION_TIME: The period of time during which the signed URL will be available for use
- PRIVATE_KEY: A private key generated from a service account with the permissions needed to access the object

- `BUCKET_NAME`: The name of the bucket where the object is located
- `OBJECT_NAME`: The name of the object to obtain

After executing this command, we must select the URL from the **Signed URL** column that begins with `https://storage.googleapis.com`, which will allow us to access the specified object.

If we want to generate our signed URL programmatically in our application, the following official documentation provides the information needed to understand the steps that need to be carried out:

`https://cloud.google.com/storage/docs/access-control/signing-urls-manually`.

# Integrating cloud storage with my application

Having reviewed the most common use cases of cloud storage bucket storage, how to use classes to reduce storage and consumption costs, and how to have more secure access control to our data, in this final section, we will review how to integrate our data with our application.

## Storing and retrieving objects from cloud storage

Among the basic operations that an application can perform on unstructured data are uploading and downloading it. Depending on the type of file we are working with, there are three ways to upload files:

- **Simple upload**: This option is recommended when the file to be uploaded is of a small size, which means it can be reloaded in the event of failure, and provided that we do not need to upload any type of metadata to the file.

- **Multi-part upload**: This option is recommended when the file to upload is small enough to be reloaded in the event of failure and we need to upload some type of metadata to the file.

- **Resumable upload**: This option is recommended when the file to be uploaded is of a size that requires resuming the upload, or if the size of the file is unknown (as would be the case for streaming data).

In the case of downloading files, the following options exist:

- **Simple download**: When we need to download a file from a source to a destination
- **Streaming download**: When we need to download data from an origin to a process
- **Sliced object download**: When we need to download large files.

To facilitate the implementation of file uploads and downloads within our application, we can rely on the available Google Cloud libraries for different programming languages, such as **C++**, **C#**, **Go**, **Java**, **Node.js**, **PHP**, **Python**, and **Ruby**.

To understand how to upload and download files, we will next look at an example using the Node.js library for cloud storage: `https://github.com/googleapis/nodejs-storage`.

To install the library, we execute the following command:

```
npm install --save @google-cloud/storage
```

This command will install the cloud storage library within our project.

After installing the library, we can implement the following code to upload files from a local environment to cloud storage:

```
const {Storage} = require('@google-cloud/storage');

const storage = new Storage();
async function uploadFile() {

  await storage.bucket(BUCKET_NAME).upload(FILE_NAME, {
    destination: DESTINATION_FILE_NAME,
    metadata: {
      cacheControl: CACHE_CONTROL,
    },
  });
}
uploadFile().catch(console.error);
```

Here, the following applies:

- BUCKET_NAME: The name of the bucket where the file will be stored.
- FILE_NAME: The name of the source file.

- DESTINATION_FILE_NAME: The name of the destination file.

- CACHE_CONTROL: Metadata about cache control policies. If the file is to be updated, use `'no-cache'`. If the file is not to be updated, use `'public, max-age = 31536000'`, where `max-age` corresponds to the time in seconds that the file will be cached.

To download a file previously stored in cloud storage, we can implement the following code:

```
const {Storage} = require('@google-cloud/storage');
const storage = new Storage();

async function downloadFile() {
  const options = {
    destination: DESTINATION_FILE_NAME,
  };

  await storage.bucket(BUCKET_NAME).file(FILE_NAME).
download(options);
}
downloadFile().catch(console.error);
```

Here, the following applies:

- DESTINATION_FILE_NAME: The name of the destination file

- BUCKET_NAME: The name of the bucket where the file is stored

- FILE_NAME: The name of the source file

If we need to upload or download a very large file, or if the size of the file is unknown (as in the case of streaming files), then we need to use `createWriteStream` and `createReadStream`, respectively.

To transmit a file to a cloud storage bucket, we can use the following code:

```
const fs = require('fs');
const {Storage} = require('@google-cloud/storage');
const storage = new Storage();
const myBucket = storage.bucket(BUCKET_NAME);
```

```
const file = myBucket.file(DESTINATION_FILE_NAME);

fs.createReadStream(FILE_NAME)
  .pipe(file.createWriteStream())
  .on('error', function(err) {
    //TODO: handle upload error.
  })
  .on('finish', function() {
    //TODO: upload complete.
  });
```

Here, the following applies:

- BUCKET_NAME: The name of the bucket where the file will be stored
- FILE_NAME: The name of the source file
- DESTINATION_FILE_NAME: The name of the destination file

To stream a file from a cloud storage bucket to a local environment, we can use code like this:

```
const {Storage} = require('@google-cloud/storage');
const storage = new Storage();
const bucket = storage.bucket(BUCKET_NAME);

const fs = require('fs');
const remoteFile = bucket.file(FILE_NAME);
const localFilename = DESTINATION_FILE_NAME;

remoteFile.createReadStream()
  .on('error', function(err) {
  //TODO: handle download error.
  })
  .on('response', function(response) {
    //TODO: download in progress.
  })
  .on('end', function() {
    //TODO: download complete.
  })
  .pipe(fs.createWriteStream(localFilename));
```

Here, the following applies:

- DESTINATION_FILE_NAME: The name of the destination file
- BUCKET_NAME: The name of the bucket where the file is stored
- FILE_NAME: The name of the source file

For all the aforementioned examples, it is necessary to consider having a service account configured with the writing or reading roles in Cloud IAM, which will be used by the library to access the cloud storage bucket.

## How to avoid CORS problems

The **Cross Origin Resource Sharing**, or **CORS**, specification was developed by the **W3C** to handle the restriction that existed when a script hosted in one origin needed to access a resource in another origin and was restricted by the same-origin security policy:

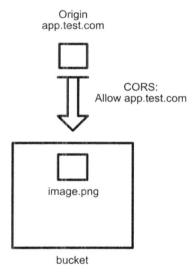

Figure 7.9 – CORS configuration

As the data stored in cloud storage will always be in a different origin to the script that will consume the data, we have to do CORS configuration.

To perform this configuration, we create a JSON file with the following fields:

```
[
    {
        "origin": ["ORIGIN"],
        "method": ["METHOD"],
        "responseHeader": ["HEADER"],
        "maxAgeSeconds": MAX-AGE
    }
]
```

Here, the following applies:

- ORIGIN: The origin domain where the cloud storage data will be consumed
- METHOD: The HTTP method that will be allowed to make queries from the origin to the bucket in cloud storage
- HEADER: The headers of the HTTP request that will be allowed from the origin to the bucket in the cloud storage
- MAX-AGE: The amount of time in seconds for which the browser will make a request before performing a pre-flight (a small request that is sent by the browser before the actual request) again.

After generating the file, it is necessary to run the following command from the Google Cloud SDK:

```
gsutil cors set FILE_NAME gs://BUCKET_NAME
```

Here, the following applies:

- FILE_NAME: The name of the JSON file previously created with the CORS configuration
- BUCKET_NAME: The name of the bucket to which the CORS configuration will be applied

In this way, we can allow our files to be consumed from an origin other than cloud storage without encountering problems caused by the same-origin security policy.

# Summary

In this chapter, we've reviewed how to use cloud storage to store and consume unstructured data such as images, videos, and files to implement solutions efficiently and optimally. You have seen how classes can be used to optimize costs, how to apply the best security practices via access control to documents, and how to integrate cloud storage with our applications. In the next chapter, we will review how to store structured data in Google Cloud's self-managed database solution, Cloud SQL.

# 8
# Databases and Event Messages in Google Cloud

In this chapter, you will learn how to use Cloud SQL to create your first instance, and will review security considerations as you connect from your local environment and create your first database in Google Cloud. You will also learn how to use **Cloud Firestore** and make use of its dashboard, before learning how to create your first documents. Then, we'll cover how to carry out **create, read, update, and delete** (**CRUD**) operations in Firestore. Finally, you will learn how to decouple applications using an event message queue with Cloud Pub/Sub.

This chapter will cover the following topics:

- First steps in the Cloud SQL and NoSQL world with Firestore
- Differences in designing and integrating a SQL database versus a NoSQL database in your application
- Understanding how to connect to a Cloud SQL instance and the Firestore dashboard
- Decoupling applications using Pub/Sub
- Creating, updating, and showing data in your frontend application

# Technical requirements

For this chapter, you will need to have the Google Cloud **software development kit** (**SDK**) 317 or later. You can find more information on this at the following link: `https://cloud.google.com/sdk`.

# First steps in the Cloud SQL and NoSQL world with Firestore

In previous chapters, we have reviewed fundamental concepts, good security practices, computing solutions, and unstructured data storage. However, most applications need to store structured data (such as tables and columns) or semi-structured data (such as **JavaScript Object Notation** (**JSON**) objects) in order to perform the actions of creating, updating, obtaining, and deleting information.

In this section, we will review what Cloud SQL and Firestore are and what their main features are, and examine how they can help us implement data operations in our applications.

## What is Cloud SQL?

**Cloud SQL** is a fully managed solution for the management of relational databases such as **MySQL**, **PostgreSQL**, and **SQL Server**. Cloud SQL can reduce operational costs by delegating those tasks to Google Cloud. In this way, we can focus on the development of data modeling and the coding of our application.

In addition, thanks to the capabilities of the cloud, it is possible to increase the resources of our instances, such as a **virtual central processing unit** (**vCPU**), **random-access memory** (**RAM**), and storage, to meet the demands of our application without fear of being short of resources.

It also offers us the option of monitoring the use of our resources through the default integration with cloud operations, which enables us to review the use of the CPU, memory, and storage, among other elements, through graphs with time filters.

Cloud SQL has an integrated console in Google Cloud that provides an overview of the latest actions carried out on our instance, user management, the databases in our instances, configuration of backup policies, and read replicas, as well as network control for the exposure of our instance both within our private network and toward the internet.

Finally, Cloud SQL is able to reach an availability of up to 99.95% to ensure the operation of our applications.

## Firestore

**Firestore** is a self-managed, scalable, and serverless NoSQL document-model database that allows us to store our applications' information without worrying about resource demands, thanks to built-in auto-scaling.

It also has access control directly connected to Google **Cloud Identity and Access Management** (**Cloud IAM**), which allows security to be managed by assigning roles and delegating authentication and authorization to that service.

Firestore allows us to perform **Atomicity, Consistency, Isolation, Durability** (**ACID**) operations on stored documents, which gives us considerable flexibility in how we structure our data. The existence of multiple libraries for different programming languages accelerates the integration of our application with our data.

Finally, Firestore has strong consistency and regional and multi-regional replication, being able to reach an availability of up to 99.99%, to ensure the operation of our applications.

# Differences in designing and integrating a SQL database versus a NoSQL database in your application

In this section, we will review the differences between SQL and NoSQL databases, examine how the new latter type of database varies from the traditional model, and consider when it is recommended to use each of them.

## SQL versus NoSQL databases

**Structured Query Language** (**SQL**) allows the access and manipulation of information in a relational database. When we talk about a SQL database, we mean that SQL is used on that particular database.

**NoSQL**, on the other hand, means **not only SQL**, indicating that this type of database provides more flexible schemas and structures than those found in traditional databases.

If we make a connection with the two types of databases reviewed in the previous section, Cloud SQL corresponds to a service that allows us to manage databases such as MySQL, PostgreSQL, and SQL Server—databases that use SQL to perform inquiries about stored information.

Firestore, in contrast, is a semi-structured database, meaning that it does not use the traditional structure of tables, rows, and columns. Instead, it uses rather flexible schemas, different from SQL (but sometimes inspired by it), on which other methods are used to obtain information.

Depending on the type of workload we face, it may be convenient to use a database of either a SQL or a NoSQL type, a point that we will consider in the next section.

## Which database is better for my workload?

Depending on the type of application that we are going to develop, one database type could be more appropriate than another.

As a general principle, if the data that our application is going to consume is structured, then the recommendation is to use one of the databases available in Cloud SQL, such as MySQL, PostgreSQL, or SQL Server.

Among the recommended workloads for Cloud SQL are those that involve structured data; it is not recommended for analytical operations.

Otherwise, if the data that our application is going to consume is semi-structured, the recommendation is to use a documentary database such as Firestore.

Among the workloads where Firestore is recommended are those that involve semi-structured data, but not analytical operations.

On this basis, we can form a first view about which database to select, depending on the application that we are going to build. For more details about different cases, strategies, and good practices, we can consult *Chapter 9* of this book, *Data Management and Database Strategies*.

## Traditional schema versus semi-structured database in Firestore

Unlike traditional structured databases (composed of tables, rows, and columns) that we can use in Cloud SQL, Firestore, being a semi-structured database, has the following concepts for structuring data:

- **Documents**: A base storage unit within Firestore that contains a set of keys and values to store information.

- **Collections**: A logical container for existing documents in Firestore, which we reference by means of a unique **identifier (ID)** provided by the user or created automatically by Firestore. Although Firestore is a schemaless database, allowing each document to contain different fields, it is recommended that existing documents within a collection have something in common in order to facilitate searches.

An example of a document within Firestore is given here:

```
{
name:"Alice",
age: 32
}
```

Within a collection, we can have multiple documents with different values in both the name and age fields. We can also include different fields within our documents. An example of a case where this type of variable schema may be required could be the display of product information, as we can see in the following code snippet:

```
{
productType:"computer"
storageType:"SSD"
}
{
productType:"car"
topSpeed:250
}
```

In this case, we have two products with different properties, which—by means of the option of not having a rigid schema—we can express in the same collection.

It is also possible to order information in a hierarchical way, using sub-collections.

To understand how this hierarchy is displayed, look at the following document, which includes a reference to another document located in another collection:

```
//classroom collection
{
name: "classroom-1"
homeworks: homeworks
```

```
}

//homeworks collection
{
name: "homework-1"
}
{
name: "homework-2"
}
{
name: "homework-3"
}
```

In this example, we have a document within the `classroom` collection that contains a reference to a `homework` sub-collection where various documents are located. By referencing documents, it is possible to maintain order and limit the document size.

In this way, we can use the advantage of a semi-structured database to create more complex structures and thus satisfy the differing needs of our applications.

A diagram of a traditional schema versus a semi-structured database is provided here:

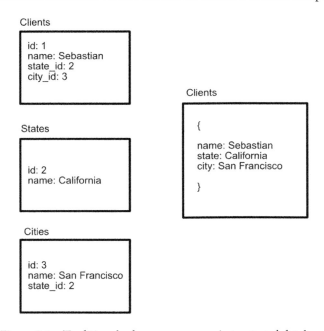

Figure 8.1 – Traditional schema versus semi-structured database

# Understanding how to connect to a Cloud SQL instance and the Firestore dashboard

In this section, we will review how to create instances in Cloud SQL and Firestore, in addition to examining access through the Google Cloud console and exploring the different options offered by these two database services.

## Creating and connecting to a Cloud SQL instance

In order to create a Cloud SQL instance within the Google Cloud console, the first thing to do is to access `https://console.cloud.google.com/sql/` and click on the **CREATE INSTANCE** button.

Once inside the Cloud SQL section for creating instances, we have to select which type of self-managed instance we want. Among the options available at the time of writing this book are the following:

- MySQL
- PostgreSQL
- SQL Server

After selecting the type of instance to create, select the instance ID, the password to use, and the database version to use. In addition, you must select whether the instance will be in a single zone (**Single zone**, recommended for non-production environments) or will have instances in multiple zones (**Multiple zones**, recommended for live environments). It is also possible to modify the type of machine, storage, networking, and backups, among other options.

You can see an overview of this in the following screenshot:

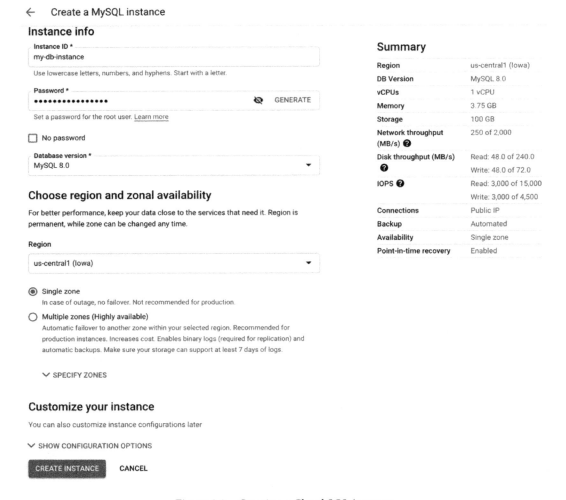

Figure 8.2 – Creating a Cloud SQL instance

Once the characteristics of our instance have been selected, we can proceed to select the **CREATE INSTANCE** button.

Having already created an instance, we can proceed to explore the dedicated Google Cloud console for this service.

In the first section, **Overview**, we can see how resources such as the CPU, memory, and storage of our instance have been used over a period from **1 hour** to **30 days**, as illustrated in the following screenshot:

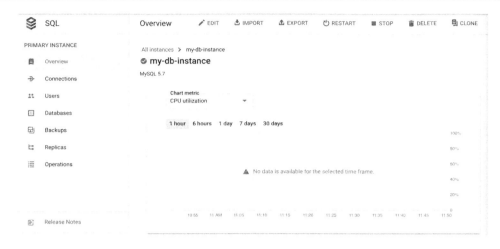

Figure 8.3 – Cloud SQL overview

In the second section, **Connections**, it is possible to configure how we will connect to our instance. If we want to connect from an application within the network where an instance was created, simply enable the **Private IP** option, and we can connect using the **Private IP** option, **port**, **username**, and **password**.

If it is necessary to connect to an instance from outside the network, we have to use the **Public IP** option, as illustrated in the following screenshot:

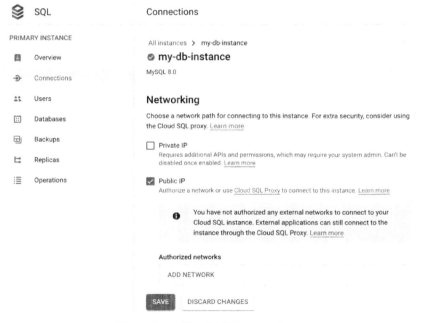

Figure 8.4 – Cloud SQL connections

As exposing a database to the internet is an insecure process, it is also necessary to carry out one of the following steps:

- Enable the **Consumer IP** option from the **Authorized networks** section.

- Create a connection through **Cloud SQL Proxy.** (To learn how to configure a Cloud SQL proxy, you can visit the initial documentation through the following link: `https://cloud.google.com/sql/docs/mysql/connect-admin-proxy`.)

The advantage that a connection through Cloud SQL Proxy has over the use of consumer **Internet Protocol** (**IP**) enablement is that the consumer's IP address may be modified, potentially creating a need to constantly enable new IP addresses used by the consumer. Because Cloud SQL Proxy uses a service account with the `roles/cloudsql.client` role, it is not necessary to be constantly authorizing consumer IPs.

In the third section, **Users,** we can observe and create new users within an instance. Each user created in this section can be restricted to access the instance from any host or from a specific IP range. You can see an overview of this section in the following screenshot:

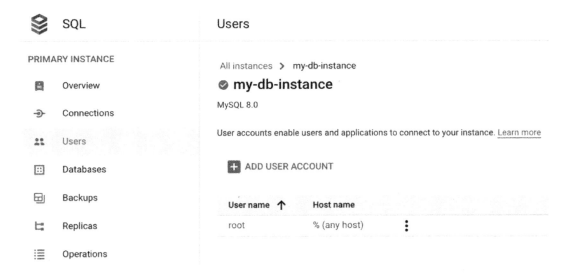

Figure 8.5 – Cloud SQL users

In the fourth section, **Databases**, it is possible to observe and create new databases within our instance, and it is also possible to select the name of the database, the character set, and the collation. If you want to create a new database within a previously created instance, just click on **CREATE DATABASE** and fill in the requested parameters. Once a database is created, you can connect using the credentials of the users created in the previous section. You can see an overview of this section in the following screenshot:

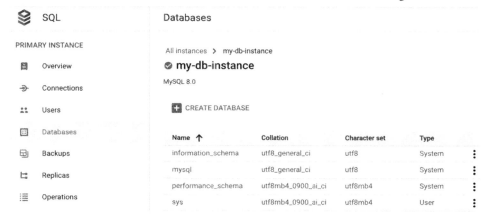

Figure 8.6 – Cloud SQL databases

In the fifth section, **Backups**, it is possible to restore our database from a previously generated backup, create a backup on demand, or configure the current backup policies for a created instance. You can see an overview of this section in the following screenshot:

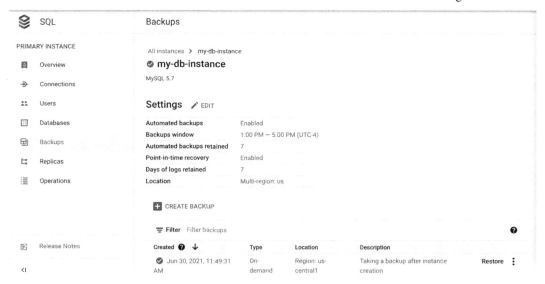

Figure 8.7 – Cloud SQL backups

In the **Replicas** section, it is possible to create a replica instance in read mode, to have a failover in case the zone where our database is located fails. You can see an overview of this section in the following screenshot:

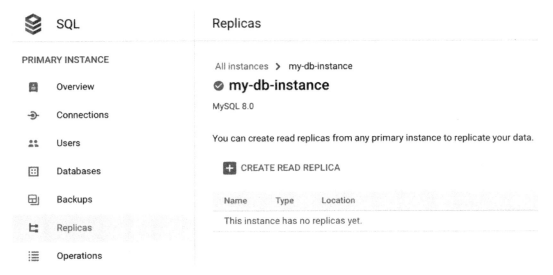

Figure 8.8 – Cloud SQL replicas

In the last section, **Operations**, it is possible to monitor the operations carried out on our instance. In this particular case, we can see the backup operations that have been executed. You can see an overview of this section in the following screenshot:

Figure 8.9 – Cloud SQL operations

# Configuring a Firestore instance and viewing the Firestore dashboard

Firestore has a dashboard that we can access through the Google Cloud console, via the following link: `https://console.cloud.google.com/firestore/`.

The first time we enter the dashboard, we have to create an instance in our project by pressing the **SELECT NATIVE MODE** button, as illustrated in the following screenshot:

| | Native mode | Datastore mode |
|---|---|---|
| | Enable all of Cloud Firestore's features, with offline support and real-time synchronization. | Leverage Cloud Datastore's system behavior on top of Cloud Firestore's powerful storage layer. |
| | SELECT NATIVE MODE | SELECT DATASTORE MODE |
| API | Firestore | Datastore |
| Scalability | Automatically scales to millions of concurrent clients | Automatically scales to millions of writes per second |
| App engine support | Not supported in the App Engine standard Python 2.7 and PHP 5.5 runtimes | All runtimes |
| Max writes per second | 10,000 | No limit |
| Real-time updates | ✓ | ✕ |
| Mobile/web client libraries with offline data persistence | ✓ | ✕ |

Figure 8.10 – Creating a Firestore instance

Then, we must select where our database will be, choosing between regional (lower latency and lower cost) or multi-regional (higher availability and higher cost).

Once our database is created, we can proceed to access the Firestore dashboard. Using this dashboard, we can access our data, create indexes, import and export data, view the usage of an instance, and configure security rules.

In the first section, **Data**, we can access all the collections, documents, fields, and values held in our Firestore database. You can see an overview of this section in the following screenshot:

Figure 8.11 – Firestore data section

In this example, we can see the display of a collection called myCollection that has a document called myDocument, which in turn is made up of a field called myField and a value called myValue. We have options for eliminating fields, documents, and collections, and for creating filters for existing fields in documents using operators, as illustrated in the following screenshot:

## Filter for documents in 'myCollection'

### Add filters

Choose a field to filter by

| myField |

### Add a condition (optional)

Only show documents where the specified field is...

| (==) equal to ▼ |

| String ▼ | myValue |

### Sort results

○ Ascending order
○ Descending order

### Preview query code

```
.collection("myCollection")
    .where("myField", "==", "myValue")
```

APPLY      CLEAR FILTER      CANCEL

Figure 8.12 – Firestore data filters

In the second section, **Indexes**, we are able to see and create composite indexes, which will allow us to perform compound queries. You can see an overview of this section in the following screenshot:

Figure 8.13 – Firestore indexes screen

In the third section, **Import/Export**, we can access import and export operations on our database. You can see an overview of this section in the following screenshot:

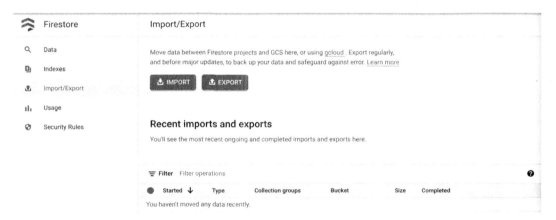

Figure 8.14 – Firestore Import/Export section

In the **Usage** section, we can see the number of read, write, and delete operations that have been applied to our database. You can see an overview of this section in the following screenshot:

Figure 8.15 – Firestore Usage section

In the last section, **Security Rules**, it is possible to access the security rules applied to the Firestore database for web and mobile clients that directly access a database using Firebase.

In this chapter, we focus on using Cloud IAM through a backend to be able to access the database using the following roles:

- `roles/datastore.user`: Read and write permissions on Firestore
- `roles/datastore.viewer`: Read-level permissions on Firestore

Already having our service account together with the roles indicated in the upper part of the page, we can connect using one of the available Firestore libraries, which will be seen in detail in the *Creating, updating, and showing data in your frontend application* section.

# Decoupling applications using Pub/Sub

**Pub/Sub** is a messaging service that allows us to decouple applications that produce and receive events, creating a much more robust system due to the high availability and consistency that the service provides.

Before looking in detail at the different functionalities of Pub/Sub, it is important to understand the fundamental concepts of this technology, since we will mention them frequently in this section. These are presented here:

- **Topic**: Corresponds to a resource created within Pub/Sub where publishers will send their generated messages
- **Subscription**: Corresponds to a resource that represents the flow of messages from a specific topic to a particular subscriber
- **Message**: Corresponds to the information and attributes that are sent to a topic through a publisher and received by the subscribers to that topic

## Pub/Sub types

Among the types of service that Pub/Sub offers us are the following:

- **Pub/Sub**: Multi-zone-type Pub/Sub version, with automatic provisioning, unlimited storage per topic, message retention of up to 7 days, and global endpoint exposures
- **Pub/Sub Lite**: Pub/Sub version of a zonal type that allows reduced costs, provision of resources before being used, maximum storage of 10 **terabytes** (**TB**) per topic, unlimited message retention, and exposure of regional endpoints

## Pub/Sub

If we select the **Pub/Sub** type, our service will scale automatically, which is ideal for scenarios where there is not a constant flow of messages and where we have to be prepared for message peaks. In addition, being a global resource, both topics and subscriptions to these topics can occur in different Google Cloud projects.

## Pub/Sub Lite

If we select the **Pub/Sub Lite** type, our service will have a limited capacity for resources established (number of partitions and storage). This is ideal for scenarios where the flow of messages is predictable and known in advance. If you want to increase the capacity of your service, it is possible to do so manually. In addition, as it is a zonal-type resource, both the topics and the subscriptions must be in the same project and zone.

# Relationship options

Within the relationship options between publishers and subscribers when using Pub/Sub, we can find the following scenarios:

- **Fan in**: Multiple publishers send messages to multiple topics that are consumed by a single subscriber. This is also known as a **many-to-one** relationship.

- **Fan out**: A publisher posts a message on a topic that is consumed by multiple subscribers. This is also known as a **one-to-many** relationship.

- **Many-to-many**: Multiple publishers send messages to multiple topics that are consumed by multiple subscribers.

You can see a diagram of these Pub/Sub patterns here:

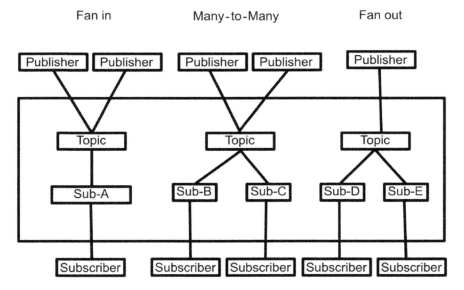

Figure 8.16 – Pub/Sub patterns

# Publishing a message

To post a message within a Pub/Sub topic, the first thing we need to do is create a topic within Pub/Sub. For that, we use the following command from the Google Cloud SDK:

```
gcloud pubsub topics create TOPIC_ID
```

Here, TOPIC_ID is the ID with which a topic will be created.

Once a topic is created, we must assign the necessary permissions to the service account that we will use in our project to publish a message to the topic. For this, we can assign the `roles/pubsub.publisher` role.

Once we have the role that allows us to publish our message, we can proceed to code implementation. In this particular example, we will use Node.js, so we will install the Pub/Sub library using the following command:

```
npm install @google-cloud/pubsub --save
```

If you need to use another programming language, you can go to the official documentation for examples in the various programming languages supported by the Pub/Sub library, at `https://cloud.google.com/pubsub/docs/publisher`.

Then, to publish a message on the topic, we implement the following code:

```
const topicName = 'TOPIC_NAME';
const data = JSON.stringify({field: 'value'});

const {PubSub} = require('@google-cloud/pubsub');

const pubSubClient = new PubSub();

async function publishMessage() {

  const dataBuffer = Buffer.from(data);

  try {

    const messageId = await pubSubClient.topic(topicName).publish(dataBuffer);

  } catch (error) {
    //TODO: Handle error.
  }
}

publishMessage();
```

TOPIC_NAME is the name of the topic in which you want to publish a message (projects/PROJECT_ID/topics/TOPIC_ID).

In this way, we can publish our first message in a Pub/Sub topic.

# Consuming a message using pull and push subscriptions

Within the different types of subscriptions available within Pub/Sub, we find the following:

- **Push**: In this type of subscription, Pub/Sub sends a request with a message to the subscribing application every time a message reaches a topic.
- **Pull**: In this type of subscription, the subscribing application is responsible for generating a request in order to obtain a message from a topic.

For scenarios where multiple topics within Pub/Sub must be processed by a single webhook, where there are webhooks implemented in **Google App Engine** (**GAE**) or Cloud Functions, or where it is not possible to configure dependencies in the webhooks such as credentials or client libraries, it is recommended to use push subscriptions.

To create a push subscription, use the following command from the Google Cloud SDK:

```
gcloud pubsub subscriptions create SUBSCRIPTION_ID
 --topic=TOPIC_ID -push-endpoint=PUSH_ENDPOINT
```

Here, the following applies:

- SUBSCRIPTION_ID is the ID with which a subscription will be created.
- TOPIC_ID is the ID of the topic on which a subscription will be created.
- PUSH_ENDPOINT is the **Uniform Resource Locator** (**URL**) of the webhook where a message received by a topic will be received.

In this way, we can configure a subscription that calls the indicated endpoint every time a message arrives on the topic.

In situations where there is a high message-flow rate (greater than one message per second), where the efficiency of message processing is critical, or where it is not possible to expose endpoints for webhooks with **Secure Sockets Layer** (**SSL**) certificates, it is recommended that pull subscriptions are used.

In order to create a pull-type subscription, use the following command from the Google Cloud SDK:

```
gcloud pubsub subscriptions create SUBSCRIPTION_ID
--topic=TOPIC_ID
```

Here, the following applies:

- `SUBSCRIPTION_ID` is the ID with which a subscription will be created.
- `TOPIC_ID` is the ID of the topic on which a subscription will be created.

Unlike push-type subscriptions, where Pub/Sub is responsible for sending messages to our application through the indicated endpoint, in pull-type subscriptions we must constantly pull messages from a topic.

For this, we need to have a service account with the necessary permissions to obtain these messages, to which we assign the role of `roles/pubsub.subscriber`.

Once we have this role enabled, allowing us to read our messages, we can proceed to code implementation. In this example, we will use Node.js, so we will install the Pub/Sub library using the following command:

```
npm install @google-cloud/pubsub --save
```

If you need to use another programming language, go to the official documentation where there are examples in the programming languages supported by the Pub/Sub library, at `https://cloud.google.com/pubsub/docs/pull`.

Then, to read a message from a topic to which we are subscribed, we implement the following code:

```
const subscriptionName = 'SUBSCRIPTION_NAME';
const timeout = TIMEOUT_IN_SECONDS;
const {PubSub} = require('@google-cloud/pubsub');
const pubSubClient = new PubSub();


function listenForMessages() {

  const subscription = pubSubClient.
subscription(subscriptionName);
  const messageHandler = message => {
    //TODO: get message information from message.data
```

```
        message.ack();
    };

    subscription.on('message', messageHandler);

    setTimeout(() => {
        subscription.removeListener('message', messageHandler);
    }, timeout * 1000);
}
listenForMessages();
```

Here, the following applies:

- `SUBSCRIPTION_NAME` is the name of a subscription associated with a topic to consume the message.
- `TIMEOUT_IN_SECONDS` is the time in seconds for which a subscription listening will pull for new messages.

In this way, we can create a subscription that allows us to programmatically obtain messages from our application.

# Creating, updating, and showing data in your frontend application

In this section, we will review in detail how to interact with the Firestore database to create, update, obtain, and delete documents within our collections, from the installation of dependencies to the implementation of sample code to cover each of the operations.

## Firestore dependencies

In this section, we will use the Firebase `Admin` library and the Node.js programming language for various examples of integration with Firestore.

To install the Firestore library in a Node.js project, we can use the following command:

```
npm install --save @google-cloud/firestore
```

In addition, it is necessary to assign the `roles/datastore.owner` role to the service account that will be used to run the sample code.

If you need to use another programming language, go to the official Firebase documentation at https://firebase.google.com/docs/firestore.

# Creating a document

Information stored in the Firestore NoSQL database is stored in documents that contain fields with the values we want to save. Unlike a relational database, where the necessary schemas must already exist before we can add rows of information, in Firestore we can add both the collection and a document programmatically without a need for them to already exist.

To add a first document to a collection, we can use the following code:

```
const data = {
  fieldOne: 'valueOne',
  fieldTwo: 'valueTwo',
  lastField: 'lastValue'
};

// Add a document in collection "myCollection" with ID
'myDocument'
const res = await db.collection('myCollection').
doc('myDocument').set(data);
```

If the document does not already exist, it will be created. Otherwise, if the document already exists (that is, there's a document in the collection with the same ID), then the original document will be replaced.

If we do not have a specific ID that we want to add to our document, we can use the add() method to add it to our collection, as illustrated in the following code snippet:

```
// Add a document in collection "myCollection"
const res = await db.collection('myCollection').add(data);
```

In order to specify the types of data that will be used in each of the documents, unlike with a structured database where the data types are defined at the time of creating a table, it is enough to only use the data types supported by the programming language we are using.

For example, in the case of Node.js, we can use the following data types within our collections:

```
stringExample: 'stringValue',
booleanExample: true,
numberExample: 12345,
dateExample: admin.firestore.Timestamp.fromDate(new
Date('January 1, 2021')),
arrayExample: [1,2,3,4,5],
nullExample: null,
objectExample: {
    fieldOne: 'valueOne',
    fieldTwo: 'valueTwo'
}
```

# Updating a document

In the event that you want to update an existing document, you can use the `merge` option to replace or add new fields to the document without replacing the existing ones.

For example, suppose we have in our `myCollection` collection a document with an ID of `myDocument` with the following structure:

```
const data = {
    fieldOne: 'valueOne',
    nestedfieldTwo:
{
fieldOne: 'valueOne',
fieldTwo: 'valueTwo'
},
fieldThree:[1,2,3]
};
```

If we want to add a third field to it, we can use the following code:

```
const collectionRef = db.collection('myCollection').
doc('myDocument');
await collectionRef.set({
    fieldFour: 1
}, { merge: true });
```

The final document will then look like this:

```
const data = {
  fieldOne: 'valueOne',
  nestedfieldTwo:
{
fieldOne: 'valueOne',
fieldTwo: 'valueTwo'
},
fieldThree: [1,2,3],
fieldFour: 1
};
```

If we only want to update a field of a document, we can use the update method, as shown in the following example:

```
const collectionRef = db.collection('myCollection').
doc('myDocument');
await collectionRef.update({fieldOne: 'newValueOne'});
```

This results in the following code:

```
const data = {
fieldOne: 'newValueOne',
  nestedFieldTwo:
{
fieldOne: 'valueOne',
fieldTwo: 'valueTwo'
},
fieldThree: [1,2,3],
fieldFour: 1
}
```

If we need to update a nested field within a document, we can use the following code:

```
const collectionRef = db.collection('myCollection').
doc('myDocument');
await collectionRef.update({
  'nestedFieldTwo.fieldTwo': 'newValueTwo'
});
```

This then yields the following code:

```
const data = {
fieldOne: 'newValueOne',
  nestedFieldTwo:
{
fieldOne: 'valueOne',
fieldTwo: 'newValueTwo'
},
fieldThree: [1,2,3],
fieldFour: 1
}
```

If we need to add an array value from our document, we can use the following methods:

```
const collectionRef = db.collection('myCollection').
doc('myDocument');
await collectionRef.update({
  fieldThree: admin.firestore.FieldValue.arrayUnion(4)
});
```

If we want to remove an array value, we can run the following code:

```
await collectionRef.update({
  fieldThree: admin.firestore.FieldValue.arrayRemove(1)
});
```

This yields the following object:

```
const data = {
fieldOne: 'newValueOne',
  nestedFieldTwo:
{
fieldOne: 'valueOne',
fieldTwo: 'newValueTwo'
},
fieldThree: [2,3,4],
fieldFour: 1
}
```

Should you need to increment a numeric value in your document, you can use the following code:

```
const collectionRef = db.collection('myCollection').
doc('myDocument');
const res = await collectionRef.update({
  fieldFour: admin.firestore.FieldValue.increment(1)
});
```

This gives the following object:

```
const data = {
fieldOne: 'newValueOne',
  nestedFieldTwo:
{
fieldOne: 'valueOne',
fieldTwo: 'newValueTwo'
},
fieldThree: [2,3,4],
fieldFour: 2
}
```

## Transactions

Transactions are blocks of instructions that are executed atomically. This means that for a transaction to be successful, all operations included in the transaction must be executed. In the event that one of the operations is unsuccessful, all the operations within the transaction are reversed.

To execute a transaction, we can use code such as this:

```
const documentRef = db.collection('myCollection').
doc('myDocument');
try {
  await db.runTransaction(async (t) => {
    const doc = await t.get(documentRef);
    const newValue = doc.data().counter + 1;
    t.update(documentRef, {counter: newValue});
  });
```

```
} catch (e) {
  // TODO: Handle transaction error.
}
```

In this transaction, a document is obtained through its document ID (myDocument), the counter field of the document is obtained, a unit is added to it, and the field in the document is updated.

Note that within a transaction, all the operations related to reading must precede the document modification operations. The operations within the transaction block will be retried if the document on which read operations are executed is modified. For example, suppose we need to read a value from a document *A* in the transaction and later use this value to update a document *B*. If an external operation updates the value from document *A* at the same time as the execution of the transaction, then the transaction will retry the operations in order to retain consistency in the whole operation.

## Batch writes

If we do not need to perform read operations on the documents, we can use batch writes to execute up to 500 operations.

To execute a batch command, we use code such as this:

```
const batch = db.batch();
const documentRefOne = db.collection('myCollection').
doc('myDocumentOne');
batch.set(documentRefOne, {myField: 'myValue'});
const documentRefTwo = db.collection('myCollection').
doc('myDocumentTwo');
batch.update(documentRefTwo, {myField: myNewValue});
const documentRefThree = db.collection('myCollection').
doc('myDocumentThree');
batch.delete(documentRefThree);
await batch.commit();
```

In this way, we can execute various atomic modification operations.

# Getting a document from a collection

In order to obtain a specific document from a Firestore collection, it is necessary to refer to the collection and document by their IDs, as shown in the following example:

```
const collectionRef = db.collection('myCollection').
doc('myDocument');
const doc = await collectionRef.get();
```

To validate that the query made has actually obtained a document, and thus that no errors have occurred, we can use the `exists` method on the reference to our document, as shown in the following example:

```
if (!doc.exists) {
  //TODO: Handle no document found case.
} else {
  //TODO: Render doc.data() of the document.
}
```

If the query made does not manage to obtain a document, we must handle this scenario in our frontend. We could display a message saying that the information the user was looking for was not found, and then allow them to continue interacting with the application. Otherwise, if the query execution does manage to obtain a document, we can use the `data()` method to obtain the associated object and thereby access each of the existing fields for display in our application frontend.

# Getting a list of documents from a collection

In some cases, we may want not to search for a document by a particular ID, but instead list documents within our application through some condition defined by an existing field within the documents.

For example, suppose we have a collection that stores documents with the following structure:

```
const data = {
name: 'myDocument',
isActive: true
}
```

We could then obtain just the documents where the value of the isActive field is equal to true, by means of the following code:

```
const collectionRef = db.collection('myCollection');
const snapshot = await collectionRef.where('isActive', '==',
true).get();
```

The following operators can also be used within our filter:

- < (less than)
- <= (less than or equal to)
- == (equal to)
- > (greater than)
- >= (greater than or equal to)
- != (not equal to)
- array-contains
- array-contains-any
- in
- not-in

In order to check whether or not a filter applied to our query has brought documents to our list, we can perform the following validation, verifying whether the list obtained is empty:

```
if (snapshot.empty) {
   //TODO: Handle no document list found case.
}


snapshot.forEach(doc => {
//TODO: Render doc.data() for each document in the list.
});
```

If the query made does not manage to obtain any document in the list, the frontend should display a message to the user to the effect that the information being sought was not found and should then allow them to continue interacting with the application. If, on the other hand, query execution does add documents to the list, we can use the data() method to obtain the associated objects and display each of the documents obtained on the frontend.

Finally, if a list to be obtained does not have any particular conditions—we want simply to obtain all documents that may exist in a collection—then it is enough to carry out the query without the `where()` filter, as in the following example:

```
const snapshot = await collectionRef.get();
```

In this case, where the number of documents obtained may be high due to a lack of filters, it is recommended to use query cursors so as to obtain documents gradually, and thus display them in a controlled way in our frontend. Let's look at those now.

# Query cursors

In order to control the number of documents that are obtained by executing a query, we use query cursors.

For example, if we want to limit the number of documents obtained from a collection, we have the option of using a simple cursor in our query, using the following methods:

- `startAt(fieldValuesOrDocumentSnapshot)`: Indicates the starting point for obtaining the documents, including the selected element

- `startAfter(fieldValuesOrDocumentSnapshot)`: Indicates the starting point for obtaining the documents, excluding the selected element

- `endAt(fieldValuesOrDocumentSnapshot)`: Indicates the end point for obtaining the documents, including the selected element

- `endBefore(fieldValuesOrDocumentSnapshot)`: Indicates the end point for obtaining the documents, excluding the selected element

This is very useful when we have an application that allows constant browsing of content, such as reviewing social media content. In order not to obtain all the content at once, which would mean obtaining a gigantic number of documents, we can perform a query that obtains the first $N$ documents and subsequently obtains the next $N$ documents.

# Compound queries

When we need to create more complex queries to obtain our documents, involving the use of more than one filter, we use compound queries. If our query includes only equality operators, just add another `where` statement inside the query, as in the following example.

Suppose we have a document with the following structure:

```
const data = {
name: 'myDocument',
type: 'myType',
firstValue: 10,
secondValue: 50,
isActive: true
}
```

We can filter for more than one field using equality operators with the following code:

```
const collectionRef = db.collection('myCollection');
const snapshot = await collectionRef.where('type', '==',
'myType').where('isActive', '==', true).get()
```

If it is necessary to combine equality operators with inequality operators, it is also necessary to create a composite index in order to combine these operators in a query.

For example, if we wanted to perform the following query, we would have had to previously create a composite index:

```
const snapshot = await collectionRef.where('type', '==',
'myType').where('firstValue', '<', 20).get()
```

However, in Firestore, it is not possible to create queries that involve inequality operators on more than one field of a document in the same query.

For example, the following query would be invalid:

```
const snapshot = await collectionRef.where('secondValue', '>',
10).where('firstValue', '<', 20).get()
```

## Sub-collection queries

If we have documents that are part of a sub-collection, we can obtain those documents by referring to the ID of the sub-collection, as shown in the following example:

```
const querySnapshot = await
db.collectionGroup('mySubCollection').where('isActive', '==',
true).get()
```

For this query to allow us to obtain documents associated with the sub-collection, it is necessary to have previously created a composite index on that sub-collection.

# Deleting a document

If we need to delete a document from a collection within Firestore, we simply have to execute the `delete()` method, as shown in the following example:

```
const res = await db.collection('myCollection').
doc('myDocument').delete();
```

If, on the other hand, we only need to remove a field from a document, we can use the `FieldValue.delete()` method and update the field of our document with this value, as shown in the following example:

```
const FieldValue = admin.firestore.FieldValue;
const collectionRef = db.collection('myCollection').
doc('myDocument');

const res = await collectionRef.update({
  myDocumentField: FieldValue.delete()
});
```

To delete an entire collection, it is necessary to delete all the documents that exist within the collection. It is recommended that documents are deleted using batch writing instructions until all documents in the collection are deleted.

# Some points to remember when using Firestore

If you are going to use Firestore in your application, here are some points you can consider before storing your data:

- Documents have fundamental limits that you can't exceed.
- Collections and sub-collections have different strengths.
- Think ahead to how you want to access your data, and then store it that way.
- Work backward from the query you want to execute to the data structure that will store the data.

# Summary

In this chapter, we have reviewed the fundamental concepts of Cloud SQL and Firestore and the most important differences to consider when thinking about using them in our applications. We have looked at how to create a Cloud SQL instance with both MySQL and Firestore and explored both consoles within Google Cloud. Finally, we examined how to integrate with Firestore and how to create, read, update, and delete information from our applications. In the next chapter, we will review in detail which type of database to use depending on the different scenarios we may face, define strategies to implement different data schemas, and learn about best practices in the area of data management and databases.

# 9
# Data Management and Database Strategies

In this chapter, you will learn how to decide which database to use according to the use case. You will also learn best practices about data management in the cloud, such as how to design your primary key, data backup, data retention, and other related topics.

The following topics are covered in this chapter:

- How to choose which database fits your needs
- Data management strategies for your databases in Google Cloud
- Database and application management best practices

## Technical requirements

There are no specific technical requirements for this chapter.

# How to decide which database fits your needs

Within Google Cloud, we have multiple storage options depending on the workloads we face. For example, we have options for relational databases such as Cloud SQL, semi-structured data storage with **Firestore**, high-frequency data ingestion capacity with Bigtable, and global information replication with Cloud Spanner.

In the following sections, we will review these four databases in a general way and, in more detail, review different use cases in which we can make the most of these different database options.

## Cloud SQL

**Cloud SQL** is a fully managed database service for relational databases such as **MySQL**, **PostgreSQL**, and **SQL Server** that allows the operational costs associated with ensuring availability and generation of backups to be reduced by delegating them to Google Cloud.

## Cloud Spanner

**Cloud Spanner** is a fully managed relational database with unlimited scalability, strong consistency, and up to 99.999% availability. It optimizes performance automatically, allowing us to spend our time scaling our business rather than operating and scaling our database.

## Bigtable

**Bigtable** is a fully managed NoSQL-type database that allows latencies of less than 10 ms to be attained and is capable of managing millions of requests per second. It also offers zero downtime when applying configurations and easy integration with data processing tools.

## Firestore

**Cloud Firestore** is a NoSQL, serverless, flexible, and scalable database that allows data to be automatically replicated in multiple regions and scaled to zero if no one is performing operations. It also includes functions to facilitate data synchronization and data management when applications are in offline mode.

# Choosing the right database

When selecting which database we are going to use within the Google Cloud offer, we can consider some of the following points:

- **Data structure**: Is the data to be stored structured or semi-structured?

- **Data volume**: How much data do I want to store in my database?

- **Latency**: Is the reading and writing speed with which we obtain and store the data in our application important?

- **Throughput**: How often will I read and insert data into my database?

Which database you choose will depend on the answers to some of these questions. To simplify the choice, we are going to make a comparison between Cloud SQL, Cloud Spanner, Bigtable, and Firestore according to the different cases that we may face, in order to finally understand this choice through a selection diagram.

Based on the first question, if our data to be stored is structured, we can choose one of the first two options mentioned in the preceding list, Cloud SQL or Cloud Spanner.

To better understand which would be more convenient, we need to answer the second question. If the amount of information I need to store in my database is less than 10 TB, then Cloud SQL would be preferable.

In addition, Cloud SQL offers options for MySQL, PostgreSQL, and SQL Server, which becomes an excellent option in scenarios where our application is not being built from scratch and needs to be migrated from an on-premises environment.

Some scenarios for the use of Cloud SQL are the development of **ERP**, **CRM**, **e-commerce**, **web**, and **SaaS-type** applications.

Otherwise, if the amount of information needed to store is greater than 10 TB, Cloud Spanner is recommended. In addition, Cloud Spanner offers the distribution of information in multiple locations with high throughput.

Some scenarios for the use of Cloud Spanner are the development of applications based on gaming, global financial ledgers, supply chains, and inventory management.

If we find ourselves needing to store semi-structured data, we could choose to use either Bigtable or Firestore.

In order to select the optimal database, we can think about our latency and throughput needs. If the needs of our application are to have low latency and high throughput, the correct choice in this case would be Bigtable.

Scenarios for using Bigtable include the development of applications based on personalization, advertising, recommendation systems, and fraud detection.

On the other hand, if the need for our application is to facilitate the development of applications on a global scale, with the possibility of scaling to zero, then Firestore is the solution.

Scenarios for using Firestore include the development of web, mobile, and IoT applications such as retail product catalogs and social media users' profiles:

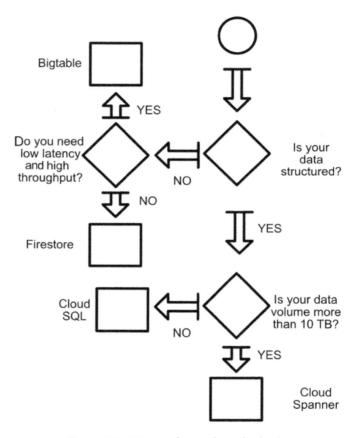

Figure 9.1 – How to choose the right database

# Data management strategies for your databases in Google Cloud

In the previous section, we learned that the choice we make from the different database options offered by Google Cloud will depend on the workloads we face when considering factors such as data structure, data volume, latency, and throughput. In this section, we will focus on factors that allow us to get the best performance from our database, to ensure that applications developed on these databases function optimally.

## What is database sharding?

**Database sharding** is a horizontal partition of data held on a separate server to spread the load.

Some of the database solutions that Google Cloud offers, such as Firestore, Cloud Spanner, and Bigtable, do database sharding in order to give the benefits of horizontal scaling.

One of the problems of database sharding is hot-spotting, a performance problem that we are going to review in the next section.

## What is hot-spotting, and why should you avoid it?

**Hot-spotting** is a problem that occurs when very close data is written within the same server in databases that distribute their data (such as Cloud Spanner, Bigtable, and Firestore). One of the factors responsible for this problem is the creation of custom identifiers or primary keys in our databases with a monotonous pattern of increment, in other words, creating documents with identifiers such as these:

- **Id1**
- **Id2**
- **Id3**
- **Id…N**

In this section, we will review strategies for designing identifiers or primary keys that avoid this problem, which directly affects the performance of our database operations:

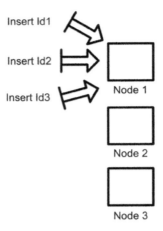

Figure 9.2 – Hot-spotting

## Defining a key structure for high-write applications in Bigtable

Bigtable is a database that stores its data in a key/value format, where joins cannot be performed and transactions only apply to a particular row. Furthermore, each table has only one index, which corresponds to the key of the row; therefore, each key of the row must be unique.

The rows within Bigtable are ordered depending on the row key; therefore, to avoid hot-spotting problems and performance problems, when storing our files, it is important to pay attention to key design.

Keys that begin with a timestamp should be avoided, to avoid writing data to just a single node, which considerably reduces performance by not taking advantage of the benefits of a distributed database. If one of our keys begins with a value of the timestamp type, which increments monotonically, it must be accompanied by a value with a high cardinality (such as a value corresponding to a user ID) in order to avoid this trouble.

Although using the user ID to solve the hot-spotting problem can be a good strategy, we must consider aspects of the consumption of our application that could play against us. One is that in some scenarios, new users could be the ones who consume the application the most, generating a hot-spotting problem. This is why user identifiers should not be sequential. To avoid this problem, it is recommended to reverse the user ID before adding it to the end of the row brace.

# Key design in Cloud Spanner

In Cloud Spanner, the writing of rows in the database is assigned by split units, which depend on the distribution of the primary keys of our tables. As more rows are added to a table, a split grows to a maximum of 8 GB of data before creating another split to support the load.

If the design of our keys presents a hot-spotting problem, all the rows will begin to be written to a single split unit until it reaches 8 GB, create another split to support the new load, and so on.

To avoid falling into the problem of hot-spotting when designing the primary keys in a database implemented in Cloud Spanner, we need to ensure that when creating a primary key consisting of more than one value from a table, any value that increases sequentially comes at the end of the key (unlike in Bigtable, where the value of the row key should not start with this type of value).

For example, if we have a key that is composed of a user identifier plus a timestamp-type value (such as a login date), the timestamp value that has monotonically incrementing behavior should always go to the end of the primary composite key. Then, when these values are entered into the database, they are ordered and entered in different servers and not only in a single server.

For example, say we have a primary key that looks like this, `PRIMARY KEY(date,id)`, with the following values:

- `id: INT64`
- `date: TIMESTAMP`

We will have values where the `date` field is at the beginning of the composition of the key, with an increment of the monotonic type, and the `id` field depends on the user who performs the action, that is, it increases or decreases randomly. Because rows are written in the order of the first field of the key, the result is that a single database server receives the entire load:

- `(1616970751,2000)`
- `(1616970752,1500)`
- `(1616970753,11200)`

On the other hand, if we generate a primary key composed of the same values, but in the reverse order – `PRIMARY KEY (id, date)` – the rows will be written ordered by the `id` field, which will allow the pattern with which they are written to be random (depending on the users who connect to the system):

- `(2000, 1616970751)`
- `(1500, 1616970752)`
- `(11200, 1616970753)`

Another way we can force the database to distribute the load evenly is by creating a hash of our composite key and adding it to the beginning of the key.

For example, create a key with the following structure, `PRIMARY KEY(hash,date,id)`, where `hash` has the following value:

- `hash: hash_function(date,id)`

Finally, it is possible to use a **universal unique identifier** (known as a **UUID**) as the primary key to avoid hot-spotting problems, since values are generated randomly for its creation. However, the use of a UUID as the primary key brings some disadvantages, such as needing more bytes to store the data and loss of the relationship between the stored values and the primary key, due to its random generation.

# Defining keys for Firestore to avoid hot-spotting

Firestore allows the creation of automatic identifiers for documents that are created in the database. However, if there is a need to create our own identifiers, it is possible to indicate that programmatically in the application code.

It is very important to correctly define the syntax of the identifiers that our custom documents will have, since otherwise, as we have seen throughout this section, we could be affected by the hot-spotting problem.

Firestore uses the scatter algorithm to locate documents within the database, and that algorithm is affected when the document identifiers have the previously mentioned pattern. To avoid this problem, it is recommended that Firestore creates your identifiers automatically, or you create custom identifiers with incrementing patterns that are not sequential.

In this way, we can mitigate one of the causes of the hot-spotting problem, thus improving the performance of our Firestore queries.

# Database and application management best practices

In this section, we will review a compilation of good practices for designing and developing in the cloud on our databases.

## Keep your Cloud SQL small

It is recommended when possible to keep Cloud SQL instances as small as possible. Instead of having a large instance of Cloud SQL, with lots of resources, it is better and simpler to manage smaller instances, with resources distributed among those instances:

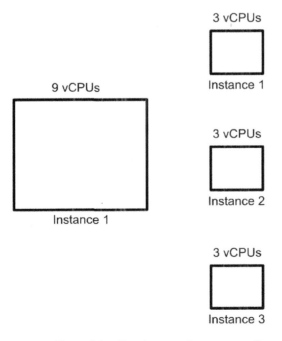

Figure 9.3 – Keeping your instance small

In addition, within these instances, it is not recommended to have more than 10,000 tables, since this can affect both the response times of the instance and the SLA coverage delivered by the cloud provider. The latter is because if the instance does not respond, it is not possible to carry out maintenance operations that directly affect the availability of the service.

If it is necessary to perform a large transaction on the instance, it is recommended that you separate this transaction into transactions that are smaller and faster to perform in order to make it easier and faster to retry a transaction in the event of failure.

## Be prepared to fail

It is always recommended that our applications have ways to manage errors in connection with our database instances so that an error does not end up collapsing the source of information in our solution and so that we can maintain data integrity. It is recommended to implement techniques such as exponential backoff (perform retries in a controlled way through delays in requests) in the case of connection errors and to manage the connection pool in order to not exhaust the maximum number of connections available within the database and make the service unavailable:

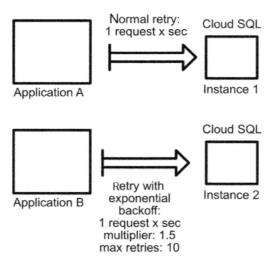

Figure 9.4 – Be prepared to fail

It is also important to test our application by simulating cases of service unavailability to understand how it behaves and recovers in such an event. This can be tested by changing the machine type of a Cloud SQL instance and seeing whether our application connects to the instance and performs operations again without problems. Configuring a retry policy with a window of at least 10 minutes is recommended, together with the use of exponential backoff in order not to saturate the database.

# Improve the speed of your database to import data

You can increase the speed at which information is imported into a Cloud SQL instance by increasing CPU and RAM. Depending on the case, this can be done temporarily in order to reduce costs and take advantage of the vertical scaling that cloud services offer us.

It is also possible to speed up importing by disabling the `autocommit` option, wrapping the operation in a single transaction using the `-single-transaction` option and including the largest number of rows per insert operation.

# Have a recovery plan

Although it seems obvious, many applications do not have backup policies for their data, which means that in the event of human error, an attack, or a disaster, they are vulnerable to losing their data.

Within Cloud SQL, it is possible to use *backups* and *point-in-time recovery* to mitigate this problem.

Backups allow you to recover the information of an instance at the exact moment where the backup was executed. However, there are some limitations, such as the fact that the storage of these backups relates to the instance on which they were created, so if the instance is eliminated, so too is the backup. It is only possible to use the backup in the instance where it was created.

Furthermore, it is not possible to make a backup of a specific table or database, only of a complete instance.

On the other hand, to use point-in-time recovery to recover an instance at a specific point in time, it is necessary to create a new instance, without having the ability to apply it to the existing instance.

Finally, there are *exports*, which, unlike *backups* and *point-in-time recovery*, are slower to generate and require a place to be stored. However, they do not depend on a particular instance and are thus the most robust solution of the three:

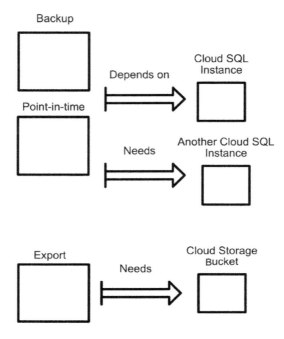

Figure 9.5 – Having a recovery plan

# Optimize query execution in Cloud Spanner

If we want to improve the performance of information retrieval using Cloud Spanner, we can optimize queries that are executed frequently.

For example, if we constantly execute a query that performs a WHERE clause on the database with different parameters, we can replace the literal value with a query parameter, as shown in the following example:

```
SELECT c.cityId FROM Cities AS c WHERE c.CityName = @name;
```

We can do that instead of having to do this:

```
SELECT c.cityId FROM Cities AS c WHERE c.CityName = 'Santiago';
```

This enables the query to take advantage of caching and be reused by Cloud Spanner, which reduces operating costs and makes execution faster.

Another way to optimize the execution of queries on Cloud Spanner is by using secondary indexes, which speed up query execution by avoiding full scans of the tables to be consulted.

For example, suppose we need to execute the following query:

```
SELECT c.cityId FROM Cities AS c WHERE c.population = 1000;
```

If we create a secondary index on the population field, then a full scan on the entire table is avoided; the query is performed only on the much smaller data source that contains the information from the population field in the index table.

## Optimize bulk loading in Cloud Spanner

In order to optimize the data load within Cloud Spanner, we can adopt the following practices.

As a first practice, it is advisable to send write requests that are within the limits that Cloud Spanner handles. If we do not follow this recommendation, we will elicit retry errors that will considerably increase the latency in the processing of these operations. To control these limits efficiently, it is recommended not to exceed 65% CPU load for instances in a single region and not to exceed 45% for instances that are distributed across multiple regions.

Also, it is recommended to optimize the distribution of requests to Cloud Spanner by grouping requests into 1 MB to 5 MB batches for best performance. Each write operation executed against the database contains overhead, so by doing this you will maximize throughput and the amount of information per write operation. You must ensure that the number of rows involved in the operation does not exceed 20,000, however, since this is the limit that Cloud Spanner supports per commit.

## Optimize update operations in Cloud Spanner

If it is necessary to perform data update operations within Cloud Spanner using **data manipulation language (DML)**, it is recommended to add a WHERE clause associated with a primary key of the data to be modified. In that way, you avoid executing a full scan on the table and executing locks on the information that is being obtained. Also, if you want to run multiple data update operations, use **Batch DML** in order to send multiple operations in a single request, thereby reducing latency.

## Bigtable test best practices

To understand whether the design of our keys in Bigtable is having the desired effect, it is possible to perform some tests. For this, we can create a table and load it with at least 30 GB of test information.

Subsequently, it is recommended to run a load test so that Bigtable can balance the information.

Then, run a simulation of reads and writes to the database for at least an hour before using the **Key Visualizer** tool to understand whether the design of our keys is generating hot-spotting problems.

Also, with the help of Cloud Monitoring, it is possible to get a picture of the CPU utilization in Bigtable nodes to help determine whether any of the nodes are experiencing overload.

## Firestore location cases

The decision about where our database will be located is fundamental and depends on the needs of our application.

For example, if our application requires high availability, it is recommended to select a multi-regional location. Then, if there is any unavailability of service in a particular region, our database can continue to function.

In the event that our application requires access to information in the database with low latency, it is recommended to select a regional location, selecting the same region where our computing solution will be found:

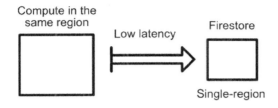

Figure 9.6 – Firestore location

# Avoid hot-spotting due to read and write operations in collections

In this chapter, we have seen that one of the causes of the hot-spotting problem is the creation of sequential identifiers for our documents. It is also important to consider that the management of writing and deletion within our database is important to avoid hot-spotting. This problem can occur when adding documents at high speed to a collection containing few documents, deleting documents at high speed, or writing to the database at high speed without a gradual increase in traffic.

In order to avoid this, it is necessary to increase traffic gradually, to allow Firestore to be prepared for the increase in traffic. It is recommended in this case to start with 500 operations to the database for 5 minutes. After the first 5 minutes, increase the number of operations by 50%, and so on. This technique is called the 500/50/5 rule.

# Reading and writing documents from Firestore

It is recommended not to write to a document at a frequency greater than one operation per second. Exceeding this frequency of write operations on a document can lead to contention errors in Firestore.

If there is a need to update a numeric field at a frequency greater than one operation per second, as could be the case with a counter, it is recommended to use distributed counters. A distributed counter is a document with a sub-collection of *shards*, where the value of the counter does not depend on a single value, but rather corresponds to the sum of all the values of the shards of multiple documents.

Having very few shards within a document can cause contention errors within our solution, but on the other hand, if we have many shards within a document, the meter reading speeds will be affected, since it is necessary to count a higher number of values.

If it is necessary to have a high writing speed, it is recommended to have a high number of shards within the document (having more document shards allows us to increase the limit to write values within the database). If it is necessary to have high reading speeds, we can copy the counter value to another document in order to have a higher speed of reading when obtaining the total value of the counter (reading a static value is faster than making a sum operation every time to read a value).

# Reduce costs and remove limits with indexing exemption

Firestore automatically takes care of generating indexes for each field that exists within a document. Although the creation of indexes is a good practice to improve query performance, it should be used moderately, since the more indexes there are within the database, the greater the time taken for writing and the cost of storage will be.

We can use the so-called index exemptions in order to indicate to Firestore that we do not want it to index specific fields that we do not intend to use to perform searches.

For example, we can consider omitting the use of indexes when we have very large values stored in documents (in order to improve costs related to storage), when sequential values are written to documents in a very accelerated way (to eliminate the limit of writing 500 writes per second), and when we have very long arrays within our documents (in order to remove the limit of 40,000 indexes per document).

# Summary

In this chapter, we have reviewed how to decide which database to use, depending on the kind of workload that we need to implement. We have looked at what hot-spotting is and how to avoid this problem when we design our primary keys. Finally, we have learned the best practices around performance, error handling, and the reduction of costs and latency. In the next chapter, we will review how to optimize our application's performance using caching strategies.

# 10
# Optimizing Applications with Caching Strategies on Google Cloud Platform

In this chapter, we will learn how to create a caching strategy for our applications and how to create, implement, and manage these strategies using **Memorystore's** fully managed service for **Memcached** and **Redis**.

In this chapter we will cover the following topics:

- How, when, and why you should use a caching strategy in your applications
- Handling high traffic volumes with Memorystore for Memcached
- Optimizing your application with Memorystore for Redis

# Technical requirements

For this chapter, you will need Google Cloud SDK 317 or later (`https://cloud.google.com/sdk`).

# How, when, and why you should use a caching strategy in your applications

Generally, when developing an application, we focus on developing its functionalities and may neglect other important aspects such as security and performance. A data caching strategy within our application allows us to take care of the performance aspects within our application. In this section, we will answer the questions of why, when, and how to implement a caching strategy.

## Why is having a cache strategy important?

Although some applications can work autonomously, without needing to integrate with other services, most applications need to obtain information either by accessing services or databases.

This is not a problem when our application generates small traffic against these services or databases, and it only faces latency problems when it's accessing a service that is very far in terms of location from our computing resources:

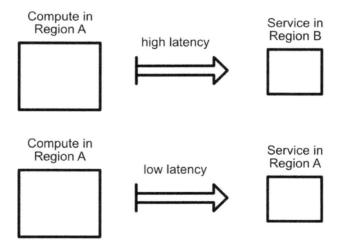

Figure 10.1 – High latency versus low latency due to location

But when we come across a scenario where the flow of interactions is considerably greater, we will notice that other problems related to network egress costs start to appear. These include services that do not have the capacity to support this flow of calls. This, in turn, increases the cost of using services and databases due to the increase in computing capacity:

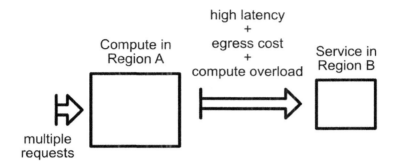

Figure 10.2 – Service-to-service integration issues

To address these problems, we can consider implementing a data caching strategy, which allows us to keep a copy of the data in memory and near our computing resources. This avoids us having to constantly make direct calls to services and databases, thus reducing data access latency, network egress costs, and resource use.

In addition to these benefits, data caching allows us to keep the services operational if the data sources present some unavailability in the system. We can increase the availability of our applications by keeping a copy of this data in our cache.

However, although it seems that implementing a cache strategy is the silver bullet that solves all our problems, it is not possible to implement this solution in all scenarios. So, in the next section, we will review when we can make use of this strategy to get these benefits.

Finally, it is important to highlight that data caching is not always cheap. In some scenarios, data caching could result in added cost related to memory resources.

## When can we implement a cache strategy?

As we mentioned in the previous section, we should consider implementing a data caching strategy if we want to reduce latency in data access, reduce network egress costs, and reduce the resource utilization load that's imposed on data sources.

Data caching consists of making a temporary copy of the data so that we can access this data much faster and cheaper. When we're considering whether to implement a data caching strategy, we must verify that the data we are going to access does not change over time or has a low rate of change. Otherwise, our users could be presented with data that is outdated relative to the original data.

If we find a scenario where our users constantly consume information with a zero or very low frequency of change, we can implement a data caching strategy that copies this information into a database that stores our information in memory.

Another point to consider is the response that the user requesting the data may receive. If multiple users consume a common data source and the response to this request is the same, the caching strategy is still valid.

However, if the response to the request from these multiple users consists of multiple responses, due to ad hoc queries for each request to the same data source, the caching strategy will not have the effect we are expecting. This is because caching will be carried out for each request that's made and the rate of reuse for the copied information will be very low.

This scenario is different compared to the case where multiple users receive the same response to a request, thus being able to take advantage of the copied data without needing to obtain the information at the source for each request.

A final factor to consider is the tolerance that our application may have to the eventual consistency of the data. For example, if we have a scenario where we need to obtain the prices of products from an external service, displaying an outdated price to the user may have legal consequences that generate a great problem for the business, so this scenario is not considered tolerable.

On the other hand, if we have a scenario where we need to obtain restaurant ratings in an application, it is possible to show an average close to reality at certain time intervals, without being exposed to a critical problem such as keeping out-of-date prices. Therefore, this scenario is more tolerable.

Now that we understand why and when to consider using a caching strategy, we will review how to implement this strategy and the two services that Google Cloud offers for implementing it in our applications.

## How can we implement a caching strategy?

Now that we know why and when to implement a caching strategy in our applications, let's review some available options to bring this strategy to reality.

One of the first options we have is to cache our data locally; that is, in the place where our applications are computed:

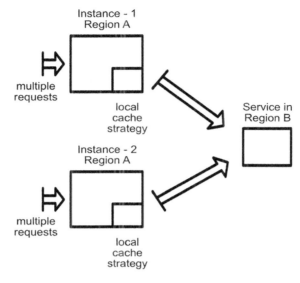

Figure 10.3 – Local caching

This is a quick way to implement caching in our application as it does not require us to implement another component. It also allows us to experience the advantages of the strategy in a more agile way, since this is normally considered a first step before we opt for other solutions.

However, implementing data caching while using this solution also has its disadvantages. By storing data within our server to manage caching, our application becomes a stateful solution, thus bringing problems that we have mentioned in previous chapters into view, such as inconsistency in obtaining data.

Depending on the number of computational instances that we have in our solution, it is possible to encounter scenarios where a user makes a request that was previously stored in one instance (generating what is known as a cache hit) and not in another instance (generating what is known as a cache miss), which means we can't obtain 100% of the benefits of data caching.

Another problem with this solution is that as the number of instances increases, the greater the possibility of obtaining a cache miss (failing to obtain information about the request from the cache). This overloads the data sources even further, meaning that the benefit of reducing the use of resources is not obtained.

Finally, it is possible to experience problems when instances are restarted or new deployments are made, thus erasing all the information that was previously stored in memory so that there is no data in the cache to attend to future requests. This problem is called a cold start.

We can also implement caching in our applications via an external cache; that is, in a component that can be distinguished from the instances where computation is performed:

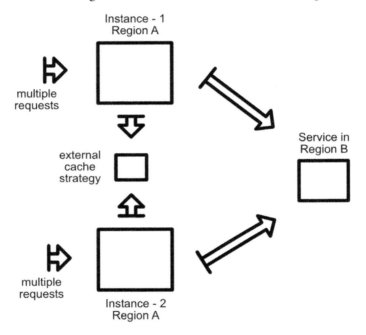

Figure 10.4 – External caching

By implementing an external cache, we can address many of the problems that we reviewed earlier.

By having cached data stored in a centralized place, outside our instances, users are not faced with the problem of accessing information that may be inconsistent. This is caused by the aforementioned differences in information storage in different instances.

The number of existing instances in the solution no longer becomes a problem that can affect the data sources, since validating whether the data is in cache or not will be done through an external component. Thus, the amount of cache miss caused by the increasing number of instances in our solution is reduced.

Finally, if any of the instances are restarted or a new deployment is carried out, we will not encounter cold start problems in our solution because we are no longer depending on the memory of the instances for the data that is in the cache.

Although this solution involves a higher operational cost – due to the need to create a new component, perform an installation, and manage this new solution – in the following sections, we will see that Google Cloud, through its self-administered services, solves these problems for us. This allows us to focus on developing our application as we can delegate all the tasks related to how it operates to Google Cloud.

In the next section, we are going to discuss how to handle high traffic volumes with Memorystore.

# Handling high traffic volumes with Memorystore for Memcached

**Memorystore for Memcached** is a highly scalable and fully managed service built on top of the open source technology known as Memcached, a high-performance system for caching objects in memory to accelerate the use of dynamic web pages and reduce the load on databases.

The implementation of Memcached in Memorystore allows us to access the service through any library that uses the Memcached standards. This allows us to use various programming languages so that we can develop and migrate the tasks of existing applications that are using this technology.

One advantage of this fully managed service is that we can implement an instance composed of a cluster and one or more nodes without the complexity of performing an installation from scratch. This also means we can focus on developing our application while operational tasks are delegated to Google Cloud.

For more information about Memcached, go to the official documentation at `https://memcached.org/about`.

# Creating a Memcached instance

The first thing we need to do before we start exploring and connecting to Memcached is create an instance in our Google Cloud project. For this, we will use the Google Cloud SDK.

To create our instance, we must execute the following command using suitable parameter values:

```
gcloud memcache instances create INSTANCE-NAME --node-
count=NUMBER-OF-NODES --node-cpu=NUMBER-OF-CPUS --node-
memory=MEMORY-PER-NODE --region=REGION --zones=ZONE
```

These schematic parameter values have the following meanings (substitute your own values when building your command string):

- INSTANCE-NAME: The name of the instance to create.
- NUMBER-OF-NODES: The number of nodes in the cluster (instance) to create.
- NUMBER-OF-CPUS: The number of virtual CPUs for each node (even values only).
- MEMORY-PER-NODE: The amount of memory per node. Depending on the number of vCPUs that's selected in [number-of-cpus], you must choose at least 0.9 GB memory per vCPU, with a maximum of 256 GB.
- REGION: The region where the nodes will be created.
- ZONE: The zones where the nodes will be created. (If you want to add more than one zone, you can add multiple zones separated by commas.)

Once our instance has been created, we can review our instance using the following command:

```
gcloud memcache instances describe INSTANCE-NAME
--region=REGION
```

Here, we have the following:

- INSTANCE-NAME: The name of the created instance.
- REGION: The region where the instance was created.

By doing this, we can verify that our instance was created correctly, as well as the configuration that it was created with.

# Connecting to a Memcached instance

Having already created our first instance of Memcached in a GCP project, we can now perform a connection test to verify that the instance is working correctly. For this test, we will use a computing instance that we've created in Compute Engine. This must be created in the same region and zone where our instance was previously created.

To create our compute instance on Compute Engine, we can use the following command from the Google Cloud SDK:

```
gcloud beta compute --project=PROJECT_ID instances create
memorystore-memcached-test --zone=ZONE --machine-type=n1-
standard-1 --subnet=default
```

Here, we have the following:

- PROJECT_ID: The project ID where the Memcached instance was created.

- ZONE: The zone where the Memcached instance was created.

In the following diagram, we can see how the different components we created interact to address the caching solution:

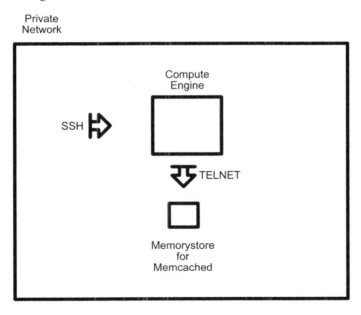

Figure 10.5 – Memorystore for Memcached

Now that we've created our instance, we can access the instance by entering the `Compute Engine | VM instances | SSH` section.

Once we're inside the previously created instance, we must install the telnet client to connect to one of the nodes of our instance. We can do this by using the following command:

```
sudo apt-get install telnet
```

Once the telnet client has been installed, we can connect to one of the nodes of the previously created instance using the following command:

```
telnet NODE_IP_ADDRESS 11211
```

Here, we have the following:

- `NODE_IP_ADDRESS`, which is the IP of one of the nodes of the instance we created of Memcached in Memorystore (to obtain this address, we can use the `gcloud memcache instance describe` command, which we used in the *Creating a Memcached instance* section.)

Once we've connected to the node, we must set a key/value within Memcached using the `set` command using the following structure:

```
set KEY META_DATA EXPIRY_TIME LENGTH_IN_BYTES
```

An example of using this command can be seen here:

```
set mykey 0 0 4
test
```

Here, we have the following:

- `KEY`: The name of the key to set and later retrieve the stored value.
- `META_DATA`: Metadata related to the current operation. In this case, `0`.
- `EXPIRY_TIME`: The expiration time in seconds of the value to store. In this case, `0` = no expiration time.
- `LENGTH_IN_BYTES`: Length in bytes of the value to store. In this case, test = 4.

Once the value has been created, we can obtain it using the following command:

```
get mykey
```

Get the value using the following command:

```
test value
```

If everything was configured correctly, we should be able to set and obtain the value stored in the `mykey` key. This allows us to successfully connect to a Memcached instance for Memorystore within our Google Cloud project.

In the next section, we are going to discuss how to optimize the performance of our applications using Memorystore for Redis.

# Optimizing your application with Memorystore for Redis

Memorystore for Redis is a fully managed service that allows us to use a Redis in-memory data store to build applications that require caching data access strategies with queries that have sub-millisecond latency.

Among the advantages of using Redis in Memorystore is the option to select different service tiers that can be adapted to the needs of our application, from basic tiers for development tests to standard tiers with an availability of up to 99.9% in multiple zones and up to 300 GB of memory for data caching. In addition, being a cloud service, it allows us to scale vertically, should our application require more resources.

In terms of security, the Redis instances in Memorystore are protected by private IPs, which means that someone can't access the instances from the internet, but only through resources that are within our own private network, thus reducing the attack surface considerably.

Being a fully managed service, we can focus on developing our application, and tasks such as infrastructure provisioning, replication, failover, and monitoring can be delegated to Google Cloud.

Finally, Redis in Memorystore, like Memcached, complies with all protocol standards, which allows us to code our new applications as if we were using a Redis instance in an on-premises environment, but with the advantages of the cloud.

For more information about Redis, take a look at the official documentation at https://redis.io/.

## Creating a Redis instance

The first thing we must do before using Redis on Google Cloud is create an instance in our project. To do this, we will use the Google Cloud SDK.

To create our instance, we must execute the following command:

```
gcloud redis instances create INSTANCE-NAME --size=SIZE
--region=REGION --redis-version=VERSION
```

Here, we have the following parameters:

- INSTANCE-NAME: The name of the instance to create
- SIZE: The amount of memory to create for the instance
- REGION: The region where the instance will be created
- VERSION: The version of Redis to use

Once our instance has been created, we can review the information of our instance using the following command:

```
gcloud redis instances describe INSTANCE-NAME --region=REGION
```

Here, we have the following parameters:

- INSTANCE-NAME: The name of the created instance
- REGION: The region where the instance was created

By doing this, we can verify that our instance was created correctly, as well as the configuration that it was created with.

## Connecting to a Redis instance

Having created our first instance of Redis in a GCP project, we can now perform a connection test to verify that our instance is working correctly. For this test, we will use a computing instance that has been created in Cloud Functions with a **Serverless VPC Access** connection type. This will allow us to access the private network where our instance is located.

To create a Serverless VPC Access connection, the first thing we must do is enable the API by executing the following command:

```
gcloud services enable vpcaccess.googleapis.com
```

After enabling the API, we can create the connection using the following command:

```
gcloud beta compute networks vpc-access connectors create
CONNECTOR_NAME \
--region REGION \
--range IP_RANGE \
```

Here, we have the following parameters:

- CONNECTOR_NAME: The name of the connector.

- REGION: The region where the serverless service lives.

- IP_RANGE: The unreserved internal IP network. The IP range uses CIDR notation.

Once the Serverless VPC Access connector has been created, we can deploy the cloud function to where the code will be found. This will help us test the connection to our Redis instance in Memorystore:

### Index.js

```js
const {promisify} = require('util');
const redis = require('redis');

const REDISHOST = REDIS_INSTANCE_IP;
const REDISPORT = REDIS_INSTANCE_PORT;

const redisInit = redis.createClient(REDISPORT, REDISHOST);
const redisIncreaseCount = promisify(redisInit.incr).
bind(redisInit);

exports.increaseCount = async (req, res) => {
    const response = await redisIncreaseCount('counter');
    res.writeHead(200, {'Content-Type': 'text/plain'});
    res.end(`Visit count: ${response}`);
};
```

Here, we have the following parameters:

- `REDIS_INSTANCE_IP`: The IP address of the Redis for Memorystore instance
- `REDIS_INSTANCE_PORT`: The port of the Redis for Memorystore instance

Then you need to create the `package.json` file with the Redis dependencies:

---

**Package.json**

```json
{
  "name": "memorystore-redis-test",
  "version": "0.0.1",
  "dependencies": {
    "redis": "^3.0.0"
  }
}
```

To deploy this cloud function in our GCP project, we must use the following command:

```
gcloud functions deploy increaseCount \
--runtime nodejs10 \
--trigger-http \
--region REGION \
--entry-point increaseCount \
--vpc-connector projects/PROJECT_ID/locations/REGION/
connectors/CONNECTOR_NAME
```

Here, we have the following parameters:

- `REGION`: The same region where we have our Redis for Memorystore instance
- `PROJECT_ID`: The same project where we have our Redis for Memorystore instance
- `CONNECTOR_NAME`: The Serverless VPC Access connector's name

In the following diagram, we can see how the different components we've created interact to address the caching solution:

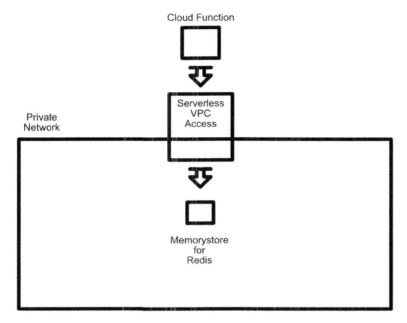

Figure 10.6 – Memorystore for Redis

Finally, to test that the connection from Cloud Functions to the Redis instance works correctly, we can execute a GET call to the following endpoint:

```
https://REGION-PROJECT_ID.cloudfunctions.net/increaseCount
```

Here, we have the following parameters:

- REGION: The same region where we have our Redis for Memorystore instance
- PROJECT_ID: The same project where we have our Redis for Memorystore instance

If everything has been configured correctly, we should see an increment in the counter every time we make a call to the endpoint. This means that we can get and modify a value correctly in Redis for Memorystore within our Google Cloud project.

## Summary

In this chapter, we learned about the importance of having a data caching strategy in our applications to improve the user experience, reduce costs, and reduce resource utilization on our servers. We also explored how to implement these solutions in the Memorystore service offered by Google Cloud for Memcached and Redis. In the next chapter, we will learn how to create logs within our application, which allows us to detect problems quickly and effectively.

# Section 4: SRE for Developers

In this section, you will learn the basics of **site reliability engineering** (**SRE**) so that applications can be made easier to debug and monitor. Also, you will learn how to configure alerts if certain functionalities of your application are presenting problems so as to correct those problems in time.

This section comprises the following chapters:

- *Chapter 11, Logging on Google Cloud Platform*
- *Chapter 12, Cloud Monitoring, Tracing, and Debugging*

# 11
# Logging on Google Cloud Platform

In this chapter, you will learn how to create both functional logs and error logs, and how to use Cloud Logging to review the flow of your application, filter by results, detect errors, and thus diagnose issues in your applications in a fast and effective way.

In this chapter we will cover the following topics:

- Introduction to Cloud Logging, the logging solution of GCP
- Learning logging best practices in the cloud
- How to enable an application to create custom logs
- How to watch logs and make advanced logging queries on Cloud Logging
- Real-case logging examples using Cloud Logging and Cloud Monitoring

## Technical requirements

Google Cloud SDK 317 or later is required: `https://cloud.google.com/sdk`.

# Introduction to Cloud Logging, the logging solution of GCP

**Cloud Logging** is a solution that allows the management and analysis of log events in real time, storing them safely so that they can be searched and analyzed.

It allows us to ingest personalized logs from any data source, offering a complete fully managed service that removes any worries about storage limits for our log events.

Through **Logs Viewer**, it is possible to access a visualization panel where we can observe previously registered log events, filter them by key parameters, and carry out more advanced queries in order to obtain specific information that allows us to diagnose errors in our applications.

To cater for the creation of our own custom logs, we can use the **Cloud Logging Ingestion API** and thus write logs from any origin.

With the help of **Cloud Monitoring**, a **Google Cloud Platform** (**GCP**) monitoring service, we can configure alerts based on the log events we record, and automate auditing and monitoring operations on our applications.

If we need to perform advanced analytics operations, we can export our log events in real time to the **Google Cloud BigQuery** data warehouse solution to use the capacity of SQL queries on our log events.

We can also configure different retention periods for log events in order to reduce costs by using shorter retention periods or to comply with compliance policies by increasing retention periods in line with these policies, by exporting the log events to **Cloud Storage buckets**.

In addition, thanks to audit logging, it is possible to review data access and administration operations in multiple Google Cloud services in order to help the security areas of our organization comply with the established access policies.

Finally, thanks to **log buckets**, we can control which users have access to which logs by using **Cloud Identity and Access Management** (**Cloud IAM**) to assign roles and permissions to our users.

In the next section, we will review good practices for fundamental event logging and for using Cloud Logging.

# Learning logging best practices in the cloud

When we are developing an application in our local environment, it is possible to perform debugging operations in order to gain insight into the contribution of different functions and lines of code to the operation of our application, and thus be able to correct unwanted behaviors or errors in encoding.

However, from the moment we deploy our application in an environment other than our local environment (such as a production environment) and it begins to be used by users, we lose visibility and control, and the task of detecting problems in something becomes much more complex.

The correct implementation of logs in our applications is therefore very important to facilitate the detection of bugs and problems in production environments.

Next, we will review general good practices related to the implementation of logs as a way of reducing the difficulty of troubleshooting tasks, thus helping us to detect errors more effectively.

## Use libraries in your application to record logs

Although it is possible to create a log registry from scratch, using existing libraries can speed up the process of implementing the log event registry while maintaining established standards in our development, such as the registration of logs at different levels and categories. In addition, we have the possibility of integrating logs with external services that allow us to centralize the registration of events.

## Don't create all logs on a single level

Logs have different levels of registration in order to simplify reading when debugging our application.

Levels of log records include the following options:

- **Debug**: This log type should be used in order to understand how our application works, to help correct errors in the logic of our code.
- **Info**: This type should be used to record events triggered by the user or by the system in order to see that our application keeps working correctly.
- **Warn**: This log type should be used to record events that could cause an error, such as closeness to the service quota limit used by the application, to help prevent (or understand the cause of) an error.

- **Error**: This log type should be used to record error events that arise with integration to external systems or internal functionalities.

This separation in the levels of registers will allow us to easily access certain events generated by our application, and gain access to more information when it is necessary to carry out debugging operations and protect the exposure of sensitive information in production environments:

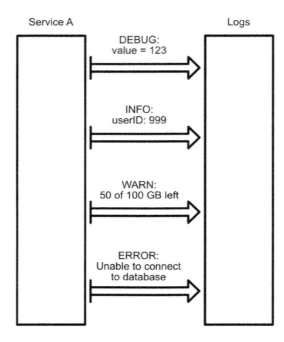

Figure 11.1 – Log severity

## Categorize your logs correctly

In the previous section, we discovered that log events can be recorded at different levels, to facilitate reading and to protect the exposure of information depending on the environment where our application is deployed.

In addition to the correct registration of our log events by level, it is necessary to categorize logs so as to identify in which part of the code the event is occurring and what is producing the event.

For example, if we are logging an event in a particular class within our code, the log should include a reference to this class, so that we can understand the origin of the event.

If an event is generated by a particular system or user, the log should also include non-sensitive information that allows filtering the event in order to carry out a diagnosis that excludes events carried out by third parties.

# Add meaningful descriptions

It is recommended to add meaningful descriptions to log events. These descriptions should provide information about the context in which an event has occurred, in order to help us understand the event.

For example, if we find an error of the *Operation Failed* type, it is much more difficult to understand and has much less context than an error of the *Operation Failed: User not found {"user": 12345}* type. The second type of error gives us much more information about the cause of the error, and thus it is easier to make a proper diagnosis.

Although adding this type of information is good practice, it is important not to add sensitive information to the log registry.

# Make your logs understandable to both humans and machines

Although in the previous section we reviewed why it is important to add meaningful descriptions to the logs, it is also important for process automation to keep our logs easily understood by machines.

For example, a log of the *Operation Failed: User 12345 not found* type is simple to understand for a human but more difficult to parse for a machine since it is necessary to code regular expressions in order to extract information of interest, such as the user's ID. This same log but with a more structured description, such as *Operation Failed: User not Found {"user": 12345}*, will be simpler to process in code and thus more readily supports automated operations.

# Add unique event IDs

In scenarios where our events must go through multiple components before being processed in their entirety, the audit process can become very complex if we do not have well-configured logs that allow us to make correct diagnoses.

In these cases, it is extremely important to have unique event identifiers that are created at the beginning of the process and are propagated by the various components. This allows the logs to be filtered to extract only the logs referring to a particular event, not other logs that are irrelevant and do not add value:

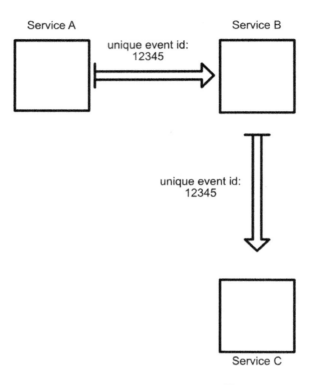

Figure 11.2 – Use unique event IDs

# Review your logging ingestion metrics

Unlike when we are operating on an on-premises environment and we have storage limitations, in Google Cloud, we can often forget storage management and simply save all the events that occur without worrying about the cost that this may have in the future.

While the costs of Cloud Storage are generally low, it is always important to be aware of what we are storing in order to keep track of our expenses in the cloud, no matter how small they may be.

For this, Google Cloud offers us a section called **Logs Storage**, which allows us to access a list of the size of the log events that have been ingested in the previous month, how much we have ingested this month, and what the ingestion projection is according to current behavior:

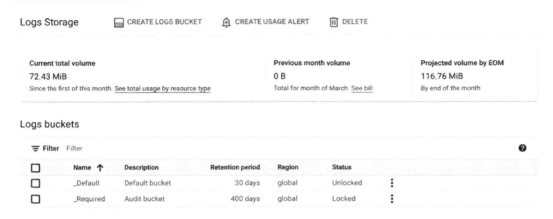

Figure 11.3 – Logs Storage

# Exclude logs for cost optimization

As we reviewed in previous sections, strategies for optimizing costs when we record log events include reducing the retention period of events or storing in Cloud Storage buckets that have classes optimized for long-term storage, such as the `Coldline` or `Archive` classes.

However, there is a third option: excluding some log events that are not useful to generate diagnostics or audits, in order to reduce the number of log events ingested in Cloud Logging and thus reduce the costs associated with this service.

An example of this is the exclusion of events that are successful within our system, such as events with `200 OK` codes. Instead of monitoring these types of events, we should consider monitoring only events with error codes, since these should be less frequent and will provide us with more meaningful data for the analysis of problems within our systems. Doing so will also reduce ingestion costs relating to the use of the Cloud Logging service.

# How to enable an application to create custom logs

Having already reviewed what Cloud Logging is and what some of the best practices for recording log events in the cloud are, we can proceed to look at how to enable our applications to record logs in Cloud Logging.

In this section, we will review options to allow our applications to record logs using Google Cloud services, to enable us to carry out troubleshooting, analysis, and auditing tasks.

# Enabling an app to create custom logs

Depending on the service we use in Google Cloud to deploy our applications, we will have to perform different tasks to enable the logging from our application to Cloud Logging.

For example, in the case of Cloud Functions, Cloud Run, **Google Kubernetes Engine (GKE)**, App Engine, and Compute Engine, the integration with Cloud Logging is done by default; we only have to worry about using the Cloud Logging library to record our logs.

We will use a base application created in Node.js using the Cloud Logging library and deployed in Cloud Functions in order to show an end-to-end example.

First, we proceed to create a cloud function using the GCP console. For that we will select the following options:

- **Function name**: `cloud-logging-test`
- **Region**: `us-central-1`
- **Trigger type**: HTTP
- **Authentication: Allow unauthenticated invocations**

Then we click on the **SAVE** and the **RUNTIME, BUILD AND CONNECTIONS SETTINGS** buttons.

In the **Runtime** section, we choose the following options:

- **Memory allocated: 256 MB**
- **Timeout: 60 seconds**
- **Runtime service account: App Engine default service account**

Then we are going to click the **NEXT** button, which will take us to a section where we can add our code and dependencies.

In the **Runtime** section, we will select **Node.js 10**.

In the **Index.js** section, we are going to add the following code:

**Index.js**

```
const { Logging } = require('@google-cloud/logging');

const logging = new Logging();
const log = logging.log('cloud-logging-test');
```

```
exports.helloWorld = (req, res) => {

const METADATA = {
  resource: {
    type: 'cloud_function',
    labels: {
      function_name: 'cloud-logging-test',
      region: 'us-central1'
    }
  }
};

const data = {
  event: 'userSearch',
  value: '12345',
  message: 'User not found'
};

const entry = log.entry(METADATA, data);
log.write(entry);

res.status(200).send("OK");

};
```

This code registers a custom log in Cloud Logging in order to register particular events in a way that is humanly understandable (descriptions found in the message parameter of the log) and readily understood by a machine (event parameters and values).

In the **package.json** section, we will add the following code:

### package.json

```
{
  "name": "cloud-logging-test",
  "version": "0.0.1",
  "dependencies":{
    "@google-cloud/logging": "9.2.1"
```

```
    }

}
```

This code will be responsible for adding the Cloud Logging dependencies in order to interact with the Cloud Logging API and record our custom logs.

After these modifications, we click on the **DEPLOY** button.

In order to trigger the registration of our custom log, we will enter our cloud function again by clicking on the name of the function: **cloud-logging-test**. Then, we go to the **TRIGGER** section and finally, click the trigger URL.

Once our cloud function is executed, we can go to the **Cloud Logging / Log Explorer** section and execute the following filter in the **Query builder** section:

```
resource.labels.function_name="cloud-logging-test"
```

In this way, the logs generated from our cloud function will be filtered so that we can see the custom event log we just created:

Figure 11.4 – Structured logs

# Using Cloud Storage for cost optimization

Once we are generating log events within Cloud Logging, it is possible to create sinks that point to Cloud Storage buckets in order to optimize storage costs.

The first thing we will do before sink configuration is to create a `Coldline` class bucket that will serve as storage for our log events.

For that we will use the Google Cloud SDK by executing the following command in Cloud Shell:

```
gsutil mb -c COLDLINE gs://BUCKET_NAME
```

Here, `BUCKET_NAME` is the name of the bucket to create.

To create our sink, we will go to the **Action / Create Sink** section within the **Log Explorer** section.

In the **Sink details** section, we proceed to add a name for the sink to be created and an optional description. Then, we need to click on the **NEXT** button.

In the **Sink destination** section, we select **Cloud Storage Bucket** as the sink service and then select the bucket previously created in this section; then click on the **NEXT** button.

In the **Choose logs to include in sink** section, we add the following query, to allow the saving of log events associated with the cloud function previously created in this section:

```
resource.labels.function_name="cloud-logging-test"
```

After adding the query, we click on the **NEXT** button.

Finally, we click on the **CREATE SINK** button.

In this way, from now on, all the logs generated from the resources associated with the `cloud-logging-test` cloud function will reach the bucket that we created for the sink.

If we want to see the status of our sink, we can go to the **Logs Router** section of Cloud Logging and look for the sink by the name assigned at the time of its creation.

Here is an example of how the logs are stored in a .json file in the Cloud Storage bucket of the sink that we just created:

```
{"insertId":".........4lkjf2RRS1neM4Pp4jndCi","jsonPayload":
{"event":"userSearch","message":"User not
found","value":"12345"},"logName":"projects/PROJECT_ID/logs/
cloud-logging-test","receiveTimestamp":"2021-04-19T15:40:08
.066590015Z","resource":{"labels":{"function_name":"cloud-
logging-test","project_id":"PROJECT_ID","region":"us-
central1"},"type":"cloud_function"},"timestamp":"2021-04-
19T15:39:51.059999942Z"}
```

To access the logs generated in the sink, simply go to the Cloud Storage bucket that we created and open the .json file inside the folder with the name of our function (in this case cloud-logging-test).

# Using Pub/Sub to trigger events

If we want to automate processes based on the log events that are registered in our applications, it is possible to create sinks that point to Pub/Sub topics in order to create procedures that read these events and perform automated actions.

The first thing we must do before proceeding with the sink configuration is to create a Pub/Sub topic where the log events generated by our application will arrive.

For that we will use the Google Cloud SDK by executing the following command in Cloud Shell:

```
gcloud pubsub topics create TOPIC_NAME
```

Here, TOPIC_NAME is the name of the topic to create.

To create our sink, we go to the **Action / Create Sink** section within the **Log Explorer** section.

In the **Sink details** section, we add a name for the sink to be created and an optional description, before clicking the **NEXT** button.

In the **Sink destination** section, we select **Cloud Pub / Sub topic** as the sink service and we select the topic previously created in this section, then click the **NEXT** button.

In the **Choose logs to include in sink** section, we add the following query, to allow the saving of log events associated with the cloud function previously created in this section:

```
resource.labels.function_name="cloud-logging-test"
```

After adding the query, we click the **NEXT** button.

Finally, we click the **CREATE SINK** button.

In this way, from now on, all the logs generated from the resources associated with the `cloud-logging-test` cloud function will reach the topic that we created for the sink.

Here is an example of how the logs are stored in a Pub/Sub topic of the sink that we just created:

Figure 11.5 – Pub/Sub sink logs

To access the logs generated in the sink, simply go to the **Pub / Sub** section of the GCP console, select the previously created topic, and click on the **View Messages** option (if this is the first time we are obtaining the messages, the console will only ask us to create a subscription). Finally, just click on the **PULL** button and we will be able to see all the log events that have reached our topic.

## Using BigQuery for logs analysis

If we want to perform advanced analytics with the log events generated by our applications, we can create a sink that leaves the log events in a BigQuery table so that we can later execute SQL statements on our logs.

The first thing we need to do before proceeding with the sink configuration is to create a dataset in BigQuery that will serve as storage for our log events.

For that, we use the Google Cloud SDK, executing the following command in Cloud Shell:

```
bq -location=LOCATION mk --dataset DATASET_NAME
```

Here, we have the following:

- DATASET_NAME: The name of the dataset to create
- LOCATION: The dataset location

To create our sink, we then go to the **Action / Create Sink** section within the **Log Explorer** section.

In the **Sink details** section, we add a name for the sink to be created and an optional description. Then we need to click the **NEXT** button.

In the **Sink destination** section, we select the **BigQuery** dataset as the sink service and select the dataset previously created in this section, then click on the **NEXT** button.

In the **Choose logs to include in sink** section, we add the following query, which allows the saving of log events associated with the cloud function previously created in this section:

```
resource.labels.function_name="cloud-logging-test"
```

After adding the query, we click on the **NEXT** button.

Finally, we click the **CREATE SINK** button.

In this way, from now on, all the logs generated from the resource associated with the `cloud-logging-test` cloud function will reach tables within the previously created dataset.

Here is an example of how the logs are stored in a BigQuery table of the sink that we just created:

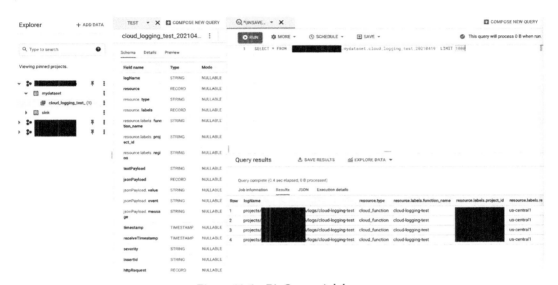

Figure 11.6 – BigQuery sink logs

To access the logs generated in the sink, simply go to the **BigQuery** section of the GCP console, select the previously created dataset, and click on the generated table (in this case `cloud_logging_test_`).

# How to watch logs and make advanced logging queries on Cloud Logging

Having already learned how to create log events in Cloud Logging, it is time to understand how we can take advantage of this stored information to diagnose errors or problems in our applications.

For that, we will begin by looking at the execution of simple to more complex queries that allow us to reach the information we are looking for.

## Our first search query

We ran our first query for the sink creation processes in the previous section. It consisted of the following:

```
resource.labels.function_name="cloud-logging-test"
```

This query indicates that for the function_name parameter found within the labels parameter and in turn the resource parameter, an identical match with the term cloud-logging-test is sought. This corresponds to the name of the cloud function that we used in the previous section.

The execution of our queries is carried out from the **Cloud Logging** section, in the **Query builder** box:

Figure 11.7 – Query builder

Within the options that the **Query builder** section provides (without prejudice to the multiple filter options we have to carry out our custom queries), we can see a **Resource** selector (which allows us to filter the logs by type of resource), **Log name** (which allows us to filter the logs by the name of the log defined in the metadata), and the **Severity** selector (which allows us to filter the logs by the severity level of the logs, such as DEBUG, INFO, and ERROR).

By selecting the different options that Query builder offers, we can observe how our queries are built fully automatically.

For example, if we select Cloud Functions-type resources, called cloud-logging-test, with the log name also being cloud-logging-test and a severity level of INFO, Query builder will create a query such as the following:

```
resource.type="cloud_function" resource.labels.function_
name="cloud-logging-test"
logName="projects/datafusionpoc-310116/logs/cloud-logging-test"
severity=INFO
```

So far, we have only explored query execution with the equality operator, but we can also use the : operator to check for matches that contain the word we are looking for.

For example, if we wanted to filter by the name of the function without the final -test prefix, we could execute the following query:

```
resource.type="cloud_function" resource.labels.function_name:"
cloud-logging"
```

In this way, we would obtain all the logs related to the cloud functions that contained cloud-logging in the name.

By default, when more than one condition is added (as in the previous example), the AND operator is added between the two conditions, so if an OR-type comparison is required between the two conditions, it is necessary to add the OR operator to the form explicity:

```
resource.labels.function_name=" cloud-logging-dev" OR resource.
labels.function_name=" cloud-logging-test"
```

We can also simply add an X keyword inside Query builder to find log events that contain this word in one of their parameters, which allows us to explore it in a more flexible way before generating more advanced queries.

An example of that kind of query is as follows:

```
cloud_function
```

We just added the cloud_function keyword without selecting a specific parameter. Cloud Logging will search any parameter that matches this value.

Finally, before proceeding to more advanced queries, it is possible to use inequality operators such as greater than or equal to or less than or equal to in order to filter specific dates where these log events have been created:

```
timestamp >= "2021-04-10T23:00:00Z" timestamp <=
"2021-04-19T23:30:00Z"
```

## Advanced queries

In the previous section, we reviewed how to generate queries using equality operators such as =, the contains operator, :, and inequalities such as <= or > =. However, in some cases, even these may not be enough to find the events we are looking for.

That is why Cloud Logging allows us to use other operators to generate more advanced queries, including the following:

- NOT: Not including
- (X): Grouping
- :*: Missing value
- =~: Matches a regular expression pattern
- !~: Does not match a regular expression pattern

If we have a previously created filter and we want to exclude specific types of log event, we can use the NOT operator:

```
resource.labels.function_name="cloud-logging-test"
NOT jsonPayload.event="userSearch"
```

This will allow all events that don't have the name userSearch to be displayed in the query result.

For example, if we need to make a query that is based on matching two values (such as filtering by two types of subscription), we can use the grouping operator, (X), as shown in the following example:

```
jsonPayload.type = ("SILVER" OR "GOLD")
```

If we need to add a condition to validate whether or not a field is present in a log event, we can use the : * operator (where the * character is not used as a wildcard), as in the following example:

```
jsonPayload.type:*
```

In this way, it is not necessary to add a default value to validate whether or not the log event has that field available.

If our queries still require greater complexity, we can use regular expressions in order to specify the log events we are looking for in a more exact way.

If we want to filter by a value within our log events that matches a regular expression, we can use the following query:

```
jsonPayload.value =~ "REGEX"
```

To look for values that do *not* match the regex, we can use the following query:

```
jsonPayload.value !~ "REGEX"
```

To learn about all the regular expression operations available to us for use in our queries, see the official documentation at the following link: `https://github.com/google/re2/wiki/Syntax`.

Finally, in order to improve the performance of our queries, try to implement the following recommendations:

- Whenever possible, avoid global searches in your queries (that is, searching for a single value without associating it to a particular field of the logs event).
- Use the equality operator, =, instead of the : operator.
- Perform queries on individual fields if the structure of the log event allows it.

In this way, your queries will have to perform less extensive searches on the log events and their speed will increase considerably.

# Real-case logging examples using Cloud Logging and Cloud Monitoring

In this section, we will review some real cases of Cloud Logging and Cloud Monitoring implementations to bear in mind when working with GCP in our organization.

## Centralization of multiple logs in a GCP project

The examples reviewed in this chapter have shown how to record log events in Cloud Logging from a particular application and project. But in an organization, we are confronted with multiple applications co-existing in multiple projects, and this is when we need to centralize these events to facilitate decision-making and error diagnosis.

One of the options we have for meeting this objective is to use the Cloud Logging bucket sink service, which uses the same storage technology for events registered in Cloud Logging but with the possibility of deriving multiple logs from different projects to a single project. This can facilitate the analysis work of an organization's site reliability engineering teams:

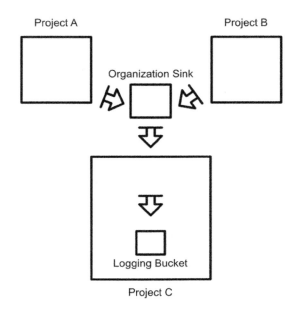

Figure 11.8 – Centralized logs

To achieve this objective, it is necessary to create a dedicated project in which to centralize all the log events generated by the various applications and components existing in the multiple projects of the organization.

Once the base project has been created, a bucket log is created in the same project, which will be the storage source for the log events.

To create a log bucket, we can use the following command from the Google Cloud SDK:

```
gcloud logging buckets create LOGGING_BUCKET_NAME \
    --location=global \
    --project=PROJECT_ID
```

Here, we have the following:

- LOGGING_BUCKET_NAME: The name of the logging bucket to create
- PROJECT_ID: The ID of the created project

After creating the project and its logging bucket, we create a sink that points to our logging bucket. In this case, it is at the organization level, however, so that all existing projects within the organization derive their events from logs to our sink.

To create this sink, we use the following command from the Google Cloud SDK:

```
gcloud logging sinks create SINK_NAME \
logging.googleapis.com/projects/logs-test-project/locations/
global/buckets/LOGGING_BUCKET_NAME \
  --log-filter='logName:cloudaudit.googleapis.com' \
  --description=SINK_DESCRIPTION \
  --organization=ORGANIZATION_ID \
  --include-children
```

Here, we have the following:

- SINK_NAME: The name of the sink to create
- LOGGING_BUCKET_NAME: The name of the created logging bucket
- SINK_DESCRIPTION: Description of the sink to create
- ORGANIZATION_ID: The ID of the organization

To obtain the name of the sink service account, we will use the following command from Cloud Shell:

```
gcloud logging sinks describe SINK_NAME
```

Here, SINK_NAME is the name of the sink created in the previous section.

Once the command is executed, we obtain the value of the service account from the writerIdentify parameter, excluding the serviceAccount: prefix.

After the creation of the sink, it is necessary to go to the project where the logging bucket was created and access the **IAM & Admin / IAM** section within the GCP console to assign permissions to the service account used by the sink to write in the logging bucket.

In the **Cloud IAM** section, we click on the **Add** button, then in the **New member** field, we add the name of the service account. In the **Select a role** menu, select the **Logs Buckets Writer** role.

In this way, our global sink will already have permission to write to the base project's logging bucket.

# Automatic error alerts

We have already learned good practices around the creation of log events, and both simple and complex searches, enabling logs in our applications, and referral to different services in our own project and in external projects.

However, log review can be a daunting task, depending on the size of our organization and the number of applications and services we are using. Automating processes allows us to spend our time automating other, more complex tasks.

For example, instead of reacting to problems reported by our users, we can act proactively by automating the review of these events and automating alerts that allow us to generate a diagnosis before a major problem occurs in our application.

For that, we can create a metric based on an ERROR-level log event and then, if this metric exceeds a certain number of occurrences within a particular time period, trigger an alert through Cloud Monitoring.

Cloud Logging allows us to create a metric based on a filter based on a query. The metric could be based on a query that is associated with a particular component (in this case a cloud function) and a particular log level (in this case ERROR):

```
severity=ERROR
resource.type="cloud_function" resource.labels.function_
name="cloud-logging-test"
```

After creating our query, we can access the **Action / Create logs metric** section.

Then we select the **Counter** option in the **Metric Type** section and the metric we want to use in the **Details** section.

Finally, in the **Filter selection** section, we add the previously created query:

```
severity=ERROR
resource.type="cloud_function" resource.labels.function_
name="cloud-logging-test"
```

We have now created a metric associated with ERROR-level log events for a particular component. Once our metric is created, the GCP console will recommend the next steps, where we will select **Create a metrics based alert**.

If this is the first time we have accessed Cloud Monitoring, a workspace for Cloud Monitoring will be created. Once inside Cloud Monitoring, the type of resource and the metric to be used will be automatically displayed in the **METRIC** section. (In the next chapter, we will learn how to perform this procedure from scratch.)

Then, we proceed to configure the Aggregator and Period parameters with the following values:

- Aggregator: **count**
- Period: **10 minutes**

The time series then includes a count of the errors that occurred in a 10-minute interval.

Later, in the **Configuration** section, we will configure the condition that allows the alert to be executed. We will specify the following configuration:

- Condition triggers if: **Any time series violates**
- Condition: **is above**
- Threshold: **1**
- For: **most recent value**

This means that if there is an increment of 1 in relation to the last value of the time series, the alert will be triggered, which would indicate the existence of errors in the log events.

To continue, we press the **Save** and **NEXT** buttons to configure who should receive the alert, adding emails in the **MANAGE NOTIFICATION CHANNELS** section.

Finally, in the **What are the steps to fix the issue?** section, it is possible to add the name of the alert and optionally steps to fix the incident (if it is a known incident).

In this way, we can specify actions more proactively when we detect particular error events in our applications. It is possible to create multiple alerts, to automate the tasks of the site reliability engineering teams, and thus optimize the use of resources within our organization.

# Summary

In this chapter, we have reviewed best practices relating to logging in the cloud. We also reviewed Cloud Logging, a logging service of GCP, and how to enable our applications to use this service. We looked at the creation of custom logs and advanced queries in order to gain more observability across our applications. Finally, we reviewed some real-world examples. In the next chapter, you will learn how to monitor, trace, and debug applications using GCP services that are part of the cloud operations suite.

# 12
# Cloud Monitoring, Tracing, and Debugging

In this chapter, you will learn how to create dashboards based on the previous chapter's logs and create automated alerts to attend to your application issues. You will also learn how to trace applications, and how to debug and profile an application using Google Cloud tools.

We will cover the following topics in this chapter:

- Your first operational dashboard and metrics
- Optimizing your application with cloud tracing and profiling
- Real case examples using cloud monitoring, debugging, and tracing for applications on GCP

## Technical requirements

Google Cloud SDK 317 or later is required (`https://cloud.google.com/sdk`).

# Your first operational dashboard and metrics

**Cloud Monitoring** is a Google Cloud service that allows us to have greater visibility of the use of resources, availability, and the health of the applications and infrastructure that we are using in the cloud.

With Cloud Monitoring, we can collect multiple metrics in real time, thereby facilitating the work of our organization's **Site Reliability Engineering** (**SRE**) teams and enabling us to create dashboards and charts that allow us to obtain relevant information on the operation of our applications and integrations with multiple Google Cloud services.

In this section, we will start by creating all the basic elements necessary to construct the first dashboard in our project.

## Creating your first workspace

A **Workspace** is a place where the resources in one or more Google Cloud projects or AWS accounts are monitored. From the workspace, we access the metric data of all the projects that we are monitoring, but note that the information is stored in each of the projects, and not within the workspace.

A workspace is associated with a specific project within Google Cloud called the host project. Within this project, all the configurations related to the dashboards, automated alerts, and notifications are stored, so the workspace is directly dependent on the project in Google Cloud where it was created.

To create a workspace, just go to the **Google Cloud console** (accessible at `https://console.cloud.google.com`) and go to the **Operations / Monitoring** section.

The first time we enter this section, a workspace will be created automatically and the project where we are located will be assigned as the host project. In this section, we can access the following features:

- **Overview**: Summary screen where we can view monitored resources, current incidents, uptime checks, graphics, and groups.
- **Dashboard**: Screen where we can see the previously created dashboards.

- **Services**: Screen where we can observe the defined **Service-Level Objective (SLO)** policies.

- **Metrics explorer**: Screen where we can view the existing metrics in the different projects associated with the workspace.

- **Alerting**: Screen where we can observe the incidents that have been triggered, reported, and closed based on the defined policies.

- **Uptime checks**: Screen where we can observe the availability of the monitored resources.

- **Groups**: Screen where we can observe and order the monitored resources by creating groups.

- **Settings**: Screen where we can observe the general intake of metrics, both the current and monthly projections. We can also observe and manage the GCP projects and AWS accounts associated with the workspace.

If we want to have a workspace with multiple Google Cloud projects, it is recommended to create a workspace on an empty host project (this means without any additional resources apart from the workspace).

After creating the workspace in the host project, proceed to enter the **Settings** section and, in **GCP Projects**, click on **Add GCP Projects**. In this section, we proceed to select the GCP projects that will be part of the workspace to be monitored.

You can add up to 375 Google Cloud projects. To request an increase in this limit, you can contact your account team.

Having already created our workspace, we can proceed to the creation of our first dashboard.

# Creating your first dashboard

Having already created our first workspace and associated it with its host project, we can start creating our first dashboard. A dashboard allows us to visualize and analyze metrics that are important for the operation of our applications and infrastructures.

Most Google Cloud services deliver a Cloud Monitoring dashboard by default, which does not require any prior configuration:

Figure 12.1 – Cloud function predefined dashboard

However, if we want to create charts with other types of metrics, or custom metrics, it is possible to create a custom dashboard. To create a custom dashboard, we have to enter the **Dashboards** section within **Cloud Monitoring** and click on **CREATE DASHBOARD**.

Once inside, we can select between various graphics options:

- **Line**: A line-type graph that displays time series information. This type of graph allows the time series information to be shown at its highest resolution.

- **Stacked area**: A stacked area-type graph displaying the sum of the information for all the time series. Furthermore, it is possible to identify individually how each time series contributes to the summation by separating the information into different color bands.

- **Stacked bar**: A stacked bar-type graph, ideal for displaying information that contains infrequent samples. This type of chart has a lower resolution than the two previous chart types.

- **Heatmap**: A heatmap-type graph displaying metric information with a distributed value, showing the distribution of the values in color mode. A use case for this graph is the latency of each request to a given service.

- **Gauge**: A gauge-type graph, ideal for displaying metrics graphically as a percentage; for example, displaying the amount of CPU used in Compute Engine.

- **Scorecard**: A scorecard-type graph, ideal for displaying the last value of a particular measurement compared to the history of such measurements. Ideal for identifying peaks in the use of resources.

- **Text**: Allows text to be added to our dashboard for informational purposes. It also allows the addition of links to internal or external resources.

Simply click on one of these charts to include it in a dashboard.

Each of the charts can request specific information for their generation and, except for the text-type chart, all request the following information:

- **Resource type**: The resource that generates the metrics we want to see displayed in our graph (for example, **VM Instance**)

- **Metric**: The particular metric of the resource we want to see displayed in our graph (for example, **CPU Utilization**)

In this particular example, we will review how to create a line-type graph in our dashboard.

For this, we need to first create a resource on which we can obtain metrics, so we will create a virtual machine in Compute Engine using the following command from the Google Cloud SDK from Cloud Shell:

```
gcloud compute instances create monitoring-test --zone=us-
central1-a --machine-type=e2-medium
```

Once our virtual machine has been created, we will proceed to click on the line-type graph in the **Chart library** section.

This will add a line-type chart to our dashboard editor.

Later, it will be necessary to add a title to the chart and select what type of resource and metric we want to monitor.

In this case, we will select **VM instance** as the resource type and **CPU utilization** as the metric. Then, in the **How do you want to view that data?** section, we will select the **Mean** option, which will allow us to observe the average by time series. In this section, we can select the following options:

- **Mean**: See the averages per time series

- **Min**: See the low points per time series

- **Max**: See the high points per time series

Once the options have been selected, we proceed to click on the **ADD SERIES** button:

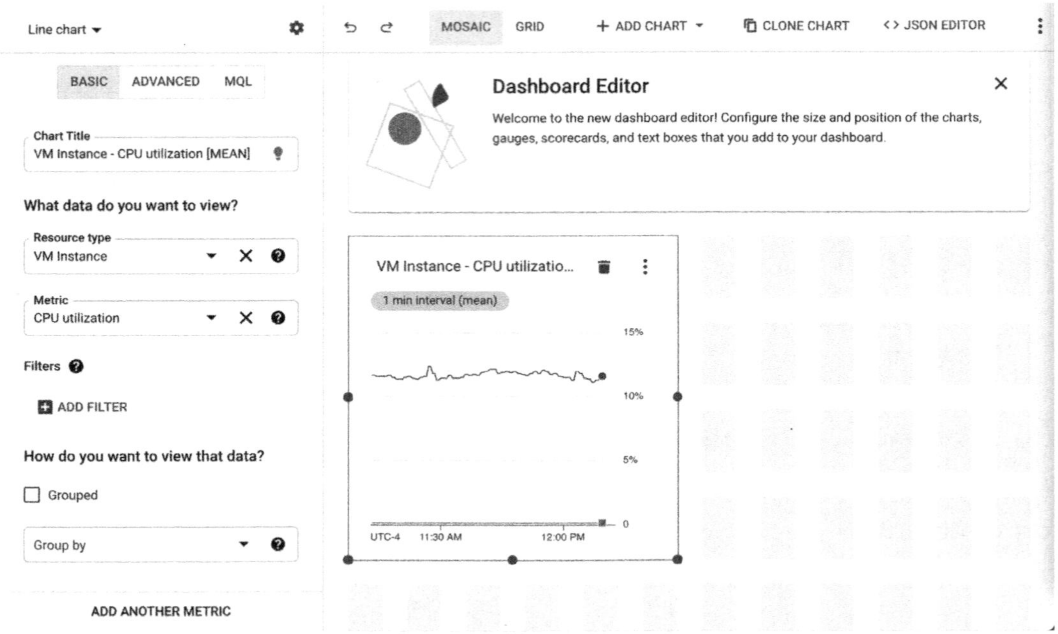

Figure 12.2 – Cloud Monitoring dashboard

As can be seen in this example, we have a large number of resource types on which to obtain metrics and display them in different ways on various charts. In the next section, we will review how to verify that the virtual machine created in this section is available with the configuration of a monitoring service using uptime checks.

# Monitoring your application uptime 24/7

The creation of dashboards is very useful for gaining an overview of our resources, but the more resources we have to monitor, the less visibility we will have. The automation of tasks is therefore very useful for optimizing operational tasks and hence reacting in time to any problem that may occur in our applications.

For that, in this section, we will learn how to create an uptime check for our infrastructure together with the creation of automated alerts that can notify us when a problem is detected based on a previously configured policy.

# Creating an uptime check

An uptime check consists of sending requests regularly to a resource in order to verify that it responds correctly and therefore know that it is available.

To verify the availability of a resource, it is necessary to create an alerting policy, which will allow us to be informed if the resource we are monitoring is not available.

In this example, we will create an uptime check on the Compute Engine virtual machine created in the previous section, called `monitor-test`.

To create an uptime check, we enter the **Uptime checks** section within **Cloud Monitoring** and click on **CREATE UPTIME CHECK**. Then we enter the following settings:

- **Title**: `uptime-check-test`
- **Protocol**: TCP
- **Resource Type**: **Instance**
- **Port**: `22`
- **Applies to**: **Single – Apply to one resource**
- **Instance**: `monitor-test`
- **Check frequency**: **1 minute**
- **Response timeout**: **10 seconds**
- **Log check failures**: **checked**
- **Create an alert**: **on**
- **Name**: `uptime-check-test uptime failure`
- **Duration**: **1 minute**
- **Notification channels**: **Manage Notification Channels**

In the **Notification channels** section, click on **ADD NEW** for **Email** and enter the following information:

- **Email Address**: Your email address
- **Display Name**: `my-email-notification`

Then, click the **Save** button.

Once the notification channel has been created, we proceed to click on the **Refresh** button in the **Alerts & Notifications** section, where we were creating our uptime check, and we will select the previously created notification channel, called my-email-notification.

Before finishing, we click the **TEST** button to verify that the uptime check can connect with the resource that we are going to monitor.

Finally, we click on the **CREATE** button to finish creating the uptime check.

With these steps completed, we will have an uptime check enabled that will determine whether our monitor-test virtual machine is available.

Our uptime check was configured to send requests every minute, so it is enough to wait this long and refresh the page to verify that the uptime check is working correctly:

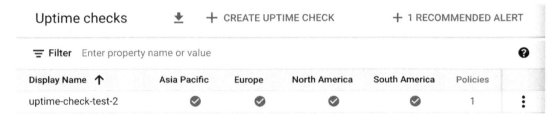

Figure 12.3 – Successful uptime check

It is possible to visualize the success of calls from the different regions to our instance.

To be able to see that the alert configured through the notification channel is working correctly, we will simulate unavailability in our virtual machine. For this, we will go to the **Compute Engine** section in the **Google Cloud** console and select our virtual machine, monitor-test. Then, we will click on the **STOP** button:

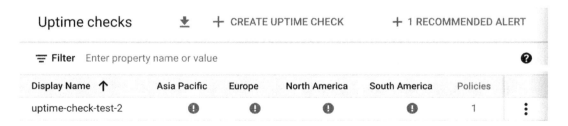

Figure 12.4 – Failed uptime check

In this case, it is possible to visualize that the calls from the different regions to our instance were not successful.

Also, if we configure the notification channel correctly, we will see the following alert in our email:

 Google Cloud                                      VIEW INCIDENT

 **Alert firing**

# Failure of uptime check_id uptime-check-test-2

An uptime check on test2-311919 monitoring-test is failing.

## Summary

**Start time**
April 27, 2021 at 11:06PM UTC (43 sec ago)

**Project**
test2-311919

**Policy**
uptime-check-test-2 uptime failure

**Condition**
Failure of uptime check_id uptime-check-test-2

**Metric**
monitoring.googleapis.com/uptime_check/check_passed

**Threshold**
above 1

**Observed**
6.000

VIEW INCIDENT

Figure 12.5 – Uptime check alert firing

If we go back to the **Compute Engine** section and turn on our instance again, after a minute, we should receive the following email:

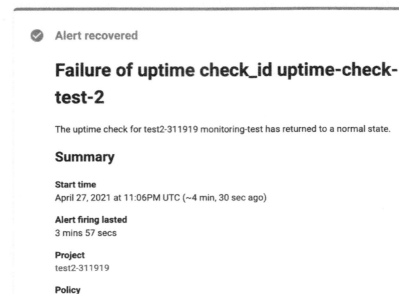

Figure 12.6 – Uptime check alert recovered

In this way, we have verified that with Cloud Monitoring, it is possible to monitor the availability of our resources and trigger alerts when we suffer an incident and when the resource is available again.

In the next section, we will review how to detect problems, this time at the application level, using cloud debugging.

# Finding bugs in your application with cloud debugging

Debugging while the application is under development in a local environment can be a complex task, but performing the same task in an application that is already in production and being consumed by multiple users can be a real pain.

Fortunately, Google Cloud offers us **Cloud Debugger**, a solution that allows us to inspect applications that are running productively without any impact on their operation. Cloud Debugger allows us to inspect the state of an application in real time and capture the values of the variables within our source code, just like when we debug applications that are under development in our local environments.

So as not to affect the performance of an application that is already in production, Cloud Debugger takes a snapshot of the state of the application to carry out its analyses and so identify any bugs within the application.

In addition, Cloud Debugger allows the integration of the snapshot and the state of the application together with the source code in order to facilitate troubleshooting and can integrate with version control systems such as GitHub, Bitbucket, or GitLab.

If it is necessary to review a bug as a team, Cloud Debugger offers collaboration tools that allow particular debug sessions to be shared using a sharing link.

In the next section, we will review how to debug an application already deployed in a Google Cloud project in order to simulate the analysis and search for bugs in a live application.

# Creating our base application

For this example, we will create a virtual machine in Compute Engine and deploy a base application in Node.js to perform a debug operation using Cloud Debugger.

First, we will create the instance of our virtual machine with the Google Cloud SDK in Cloud Shell using the following command:

```
gcloud compute instances create debug-test --zone=us-central1-a
--machine-type=e2-medium --scopes=https://www.googleapis.com/
auth/cloud-platform --tags=http-server
```

After creating the virtual machine, we will configure the firewall rules to allow HTTP traffic to our instance with the following command:

```
gcloud compute firewall-rules create default-allow-http
--direction=INGRESS --priority=1000 --network=default
--action=ALLOW --rules=tcp:80 --source-ranges=0.0.0.0/0
--target-tags=http-server
```

In a live environment, the instance should only allow HTTPS traffic.

Once the firewall rules have been configured, we go to the **Compute Engine** section in the Google Cloud console and select the **SSH connection** option in the **Connect** column corresponding to the previously created instance. This will open a terminal where we can proceed to install our test application.

After accessing our virtual machine, we proceed to install the necessary dependencies to install our base application. For that, we need to install Node and the **Node Package Manager (npm)** using the following link:

https://cloud.google.com/nodejs/docs/setup#installing_nodejs_and_npm

Remember to use the sudo su command before the installation.

To verify that the installation of Node has been successful, we can execute the following command:

```
node --version
```

This command will display the Node version installed.

Once Node is installed, we can create our base application with the following command with the following configuration:

```
npm init
```

- **Package**: debug-test
- **Version**: 1.0.0

You can leave all the other settings as their default values.

Then we will proceed to install the express framework using the following command:

```
npm install express
```

Following the installation of the express dependency, we will install the dependency that will allow us to use Cloud Debugger in our application. For that, we execute the following command:

```
npm install --save @google-cloud/debug-agent
```

Once the necessary dependencies for our application have been installed, we can proceed to create the main file where the application logic will be found by executing the following command:

```
touch index.js
```

After creating the index.js file, we will add the base code of our application.

## Index.js

```
require('@google-cloud/debug-agent').start({
  serviceContext: {
    service: 'debug-test',
    version: '1.0.0',
    enableCanary: false,
    allowExpressions: true
  }
});
const express = require('express')
const app = express()

app.get('/', function (req, res) {

  var name = req.query.name;
  res.send('Hello ' + name);

})

app.listen(80);
```

Once the code has been added to the index.js file, we can run our application by executing the following command:

```
node index.js
```

To access our application in the **Compute Engine** section, we copy the external IP and paste it into a web browser along with the name parameter in the URL, as shown in the following example:

```
http://EXTERNAL_IP?name=Sebastian
```

If we perform all the preceding steps correctly, we should see the displayed text "Hello Sebastian", or whatever name we put in the name parameter, meaning that our application is working correctly.

Having now deployed our base application to the virtual machine, we can proceed to use Cloud Debugger.

## Using Cloud Debugger

To use Cloud Debugger, we go to the **Debugger** section in the **Google Cloud** console. In the **Applications** section, we can see our application with the name debug-test and version 1.0.0. If it is not displayed by default, we must select the version of our application from a drop-down menu in the **Applications** section.

Once our application is selected, we must associate the existing source code and upload it to **Cloud Debugger**. We have the option of loading it directly from our local environment or from a repository such as Cloud Source Repositories, GitHub, Bitbucket, or GitLab.

In this particular example, we will load the source code only from the index.js file in our local environment, but in a live application, this should be done from a source code repository and all the source code corresponding to the application should be loaded.

First, we go to our virtual machine and proceed to download the index.js file by clicking the **Settings | Download file** option icon that appears on the terminal screen. When asked for the **Fully qualifed file path**, we enter index.js. This will allow us to download the file that contains the logic of our application so that we can later upload it to Cloud Debugger.

To upload the code, we go to the **Local files** section and choose **SELECT SOURCE**. On this screen, we proceed to upload the index.js file previously downloaded from our debug-test instance. It is important to note that the file must be inside a folder in order to be uploaded to Cloud Debugger.

Once the file is loaded, we can execute a debug task on our application.

In the next two sections, we will debug using a snapshot and a logpoint.

# Creating a snapshot

A **snapshot** allows us to create a copy of the current state of the application based on a selected execution line. To create a snapshot, just go to one of the lines of source code loaded in **Cloud Debugger** and select the **CREATE SNAPSHOT** option.

Once our snapshot Cloud Debugger has been created, it will remain in listening mode until a request to the application goes through the line that we marked with the snapshot.

For this example, we will execute the same request from the previous section:

```
http://EXTERNAL_IP?name=Sebastian
```

Following execution of the request, the values of the variables we can inspect are displayed in Cloud Debugger, as we can see in the following screenshot:

Figure 12.7 – Snapshot in Cloud Debugger

In this particular example, we see that in the **Variables** section, the name variable contains the value Sebastian, so we verify that Cloud Debugger is indeed taking the state of the application in real time.

In the next section, we will review how to perform a debug task through a logpoint, which allows us to create logs when requests from our applications go through certain places and display code or the values of specific variables.

# Creating a logpoint

`logpoint` allows the addition of a log record in any line of the source code of our application. For this, it is enough to select a line from the source code and add the log that we want to record, as shown in the following screenshot:

Figure 12.8 – logpoint in Cloud Debugger

If our application is deployed on **Compute Engine**, logs will appear in the terminal of the machine itself, like so:

```
LOGPOINT: it works
```

If we want the logs to be registered directly in Cloud Logging, we will have to install the **logging agent** by executing the following commands:

```
curl -sSO https://dl.google.com/cloudagents/add-logging-agent-repo.sh
bash add-logging-agent-repo.sh --also-install
```

In this way, we can view the logs generated in Cloud Logging.

In the next section, we will review how to use the **Cloud Tracing** and **Cloud Profiling** features to detect opportunities for improving our applications and optimizing their performance.

# Optimizing your application with cloud tracing and profiling

The more complex and large the applications are that we are developing, the more difficult it is to understand how they behave or ascertain their resource needs and consumption. Google Cloud offers two services that allow us to better understand how our applications work and thus help us to optimize both performance and resource consumption.

Next, we will review the main characteristics of these two services and how to use them in our applications.

## Cloud Trace

**Cloud Trace** is a distributed tracing service that allows us to collect and track information related to the latency in requests that are made on applications, helping us obtain insights related to the performance of these requests.

This information allows us to detect problems related to bottlenecks within our application and so helps us to explore opportunities for improving the performance of those particular requests.

With Cloud Trace, it is possible to review the requests in particular ways through the multiple filters that the solution provides, thereby helping us to determine the root cause of the latency problems.

In addition, Cloud Trace provides the option to continuously monitor through Analysis Reports, which allows us to detect whether new changes in our application generate performance problems compared to previous versions and so alert us to the need to take pertinent action.

Among the compatibility options offered by Cloud Trace are SDKs for **Java, Node.js, Ruby**, and **Go**. If the application you are building is not using any of the supported programming languages, it is possible to use the Trace API directly.

To obtain more information on this service, consult the official Google Cloud documentation at `https://cloud.google.com/trace`.

# Cloud Profiler

**Cloud Profiler** is a service that allows us to constantly analyze the performance of functions executed in our application by measuring the CPU and memory they use.

This information is displayed in a hierarchical way through graphs that show us which parts of the code may be generating the greatest consumption of resources.

Cloud Profiler can be executed in applications running in live environments with a minimum of impact, thereby enabling real measurements of resource use to be obtained without impacting the performance of our applications.

Among the compatibility options that Cloud Profiler offers us are SDKs for Java, Go, Node.js, and Python.

To obtain more information about this service, consult the official Google Cloud documentation at `https://cloud.google.com/profiler`.

# Using Cloud Trace in our application

For this example, we will use the same application that we used in the previous section. First, we must enable the Cloud Trace service.

To install the necessary dependencies to run Cloud Trace in our application, we go to the previously created virtual machine instance, called `debug-test`, and through the **SSH** option, we open the terminal. Once in the terminal, we execute the following commands in the root directory of the application:

```
npm install --save @opentelemetry/api
npm install --save @opentelemetry/node
npm install --save @opentelemetry/tracing
npm install --save @opentelemetry/plugin-http
npm install --save @opentelemetry/plugin-express
npm install --save @google-cloud/trace-agent
```

This adds the dependencies to our application's `package.json` file.

After installing the dependencies, we proceed to add the following code to the beginning of the index.js file. This code has to be above the code regarding Cloud Debugger dependencies added in the previous section:

```
const opentelemetry = require('@opentelemetry/api');
const {NodeTracerProvider} = require('@opentelemetry/node');
const {SimpleSpanProcessor} = require('@opentelemetry/
tracing');
```

In this way, we load the previously installed dependencies.

Next, we will simulate code execution that generates latency on the requests. We will do this using a for loop, which we add via the following code:

```
opentelemetry.trace.setGlobalTracerProvider(provider);
const tracer = opentelemetry.trace.getTracer('basic');
const span = tracer.startSpan('cloud-trace-test');
span.addEvent('simulate work');
for (let i = 0; i <= Math.floor(Math.random() * 40000000); i
+= 1) { }
span.end();
```

The complete code of our index.js file should look like the following:

### Index.js

```
const opentelemetry = require('@opentelemetry/api');
const {NodeTracerProvider} = require('@opentelemetry/node');
const {SimpleSpanProcessor} = require('@opentelemetry/
tracing');
const { TraceExporter } = require('@google-cloud/opentelemetry-
cloud-trace-exporter');
const provider = new NodeTracerProvider();
const exporter = new TraceExporter();
provider.addSpanProcessor(new SimpleSpanProcessor(exporter));

require('@google-cloud/debug-agent').start({
  serviceContext: {
    service: 'debug-test',
    version: '1.0.0',
```

```
    enableCanary: false,
  }
});
const express = require('express')
const app = express()

app.get('/', function (req, res) {
  opentelemetry.trace.setGlobalTracerProvider(provider);
  const tracer = opentelemetry.trace.getTracer('basic');
  const span = tracer.startSpan('cloud-trace-test');
  span.addEvent('simulate work');
  for (let i = 0; i <= Math.floor(Math.random() * 40000000); i
+= 1) { }
  span.end();
  var name = req.query.name;
  res.send('Hello ' + name);
})

app.listen(80);
```

Once the `index.js` code has been modified to look like the above, we can run our application by executing the following command:

```
sudo node index.js
```

To access our application in the **Compute Engine** section, we copy the external IP and paste it into a web browser, plus the `name` parameter in the URL, as shown in the following example:

```
http://EXTERNAL_IP?name=Sebastian
```

Once the request has been executed, we can go to the **Trace** section in the Google Cloud console.

Within Cloud Trace, we can view the latency associated with the request against our application:

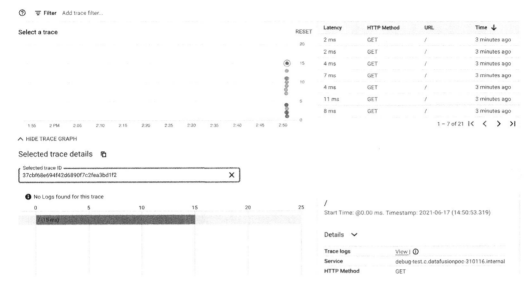

Figure 12.9 – Cloud Trace unique request

In the preceding screenshot, we can see the following sections:

- **Select a trace**: Graph where we can visualize the different requests made to the application.

- **Selected trace details**: We can see in detail a selected request in the **Select a trace** section.

In this case, we generate a trace called `cloud-trace-test` and an event called `simulate work`.

We will proceed to make more requests to have a better visualization of the tool:

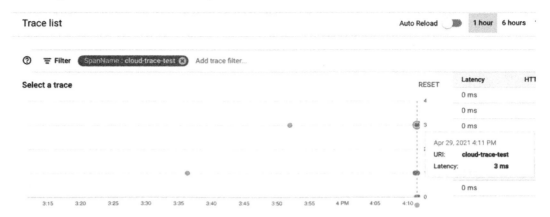

Figure 12.10 – Cloud Trace multiple requests

As you can see, we now have multiple requests with latencies of between 1 and 3 milliseconds. Also, in this case, we filter by **SpanName**, `cloud-trace-test`, to show that it is possible to have multiple traces configured in our application for multiple tasks.

In this way, we can verify in detail each of the requests that our application receives, and so can detect which part of our code may be generating problems. This enables us to evaluate refactoring to improve the performance of the task.

In the next section, we will review how to use Cloud Profiler on our test application to measure the CPU and memory usage of the tasks executed by the application.

## Using Cloud Profiler in our application

To review the functionalities that Cloud Profiler offers us, we will use the application mounted on our `debug-test` virtual machine and that we have been using in the previous sections.

The first thing to do before starting with the Cloud Profiler configuration in our application is to activate the Cloud Profiler API in our project. For this, we will execute the following command from the Google Cloud SDK in Cloud Shell:

```
gcloud services enable cloudprofiler.googleapis.com
```

To install the dependencies needed to run Cloud Profiler in our application, we will go to the virtual machine instance created previously called `debug-test` and, through the **SSH** option, open the terminal. Once in the terminal, we execute the following commands in the root directory of the application:

```
npm install --save @google-cloud/profiler
```

This will add the dependencies to our application's `package.json` file.

Following installation of the dependencies, we add the following code at the beginning of the `index.js` file and under the references to the Cloud Trace dependencies:

```
require('@google-cloud/profiler').start({
  serviceContext: {
    service: 'profiler-test',
    version: '1.0.0',
  },
});
```

Our `index.js` file should look like this:

---

### Index.js

```
const opentelemetry = require('@opentelemetry/api');
const {NodeTracerProvider} = require('@opentelemetry/node');
const {SimpleSpanProcessor} = require('@opentelemetry/
tracing');
const { TraceExporter } = require('@google-cloud/opentelemetry-
cloud-trace-exporter');
const provider = new NodeTracerProvider();
const exporter = new TraceExporter();
provider.addSpanProcessor(new SimpleSpanProcessor(exporter));
require('@google-cloud/profiler').start({
  serviceContext: {
    service: 'profiler-test',
    version: '1.0.0',
  },
});
require('@google-cloud/debug-agent').start({
  serviceContext: {
```

```
    service: 'debug-test',
    version: '1.0.0',
    enableCanary: false,
  }
});
const express = require('express')
const app = express()

app.get('/', function (req, res) {
  opentelemetry.trace.setGlobalTracerProvider(provider);
  const tracer = opentelemetry.trace.getTracer('basic');
  const span = tracer.startSpan('cloud-trace-test');
  span.addEvent('simulate work');
  for (let i = 0; i <= Math.floor(Math.random() * 40000000); i
+= 1) { }
  span.end();
  var name = req.query.name;
  res.send('Hello ' + name);
})

app.listen(80);
```

Now that the code has been modified in index.js, we can proceed to run our application by executing the following command:

```
sudo node index.js
```

To access our application in the **Compute Engine** section, we copy the external IP and paste it into a web browser along with the name parameter in the URL, as shown in the following example:

```
http://EXTERNAL_IP?name=Sebastian
```

The idea is to run multiple requests before heading to the **Profiler** section in the Google Cloud console.

Within Cloud Profiler, we can visualize the resource consumption of the different functions in our application.

Depending on the programming language we are using, we will have different types of profile to select:

- **CPU time**: Information about CPU usage

- **Heap**: Information about the memory allocated in the program's heap when the profile was collected

- **Allocated heap**: Information about the total memory that was allocated in the program's heap, including memory that is freed and no longer in use

- **Contention**: Information about mutex usage

- **Threads**: Information about thread usage

- **Wall time**: Information about the total time to run

In this case, using Node.js for our application, we can access the **Heap** and **Wall time** profile types:

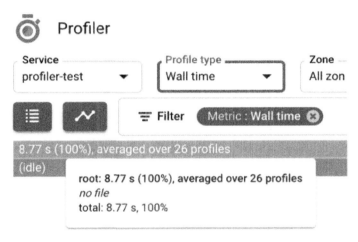

Figure 12.11 – Cloud Profiler Wall time

In this screenshot, we can see that after executing multiple requests, Cloud Profiler gives us average information about the total time it takes to run a block of code. This time takes into account entering and exiting a function, locks, and thread synchronization. This time can never be less than the **CPU time**.

If the **Wall time** value is significantly higher than the **CPU time**, this means that the application is spending a lot of time waiting, which could mean that there is a bottleneck.

If the **Wall time** value is close to the **CPU time**, this means that the application is intensive in CPU usage and that the block of code could be a candidate for optimization:

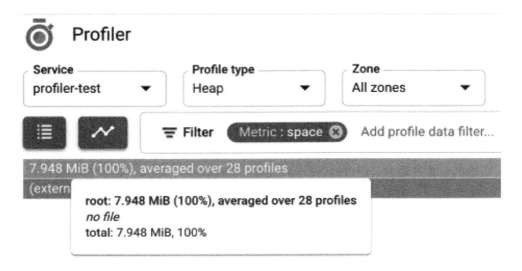

Figure 12.12 – Cloud Profiler Heap

In *Figure 12.12*, we see that Cloud Profiler gives us information about the average total memory allocated in the program's heap at the time of collecting the profile. The profiling **Heap** measurement allows us to determine whether our application is having memory problems and, if it is, to correct this.

This is how, through Cloud Profiler, we can understand how resources are being used to optimize the use of the CPU and memory of our applications.

In the next section, we will review how we can apply everything we have learned in this chapter to actual real-world scenarios.

# Real case examples using cloud monitoring, debugging, and tracing for applications on GCP

## Cloud monitoring SLOs

If you have an externally consumed application and you would like to better measure your customer satisfaction based on the quality of your service, this is possible by creating service-level objectives, or SLOs.

For this, we can create a specific group of alerts that focus on important metrics for our clients. Some recommendations for identifying good SLOs include the following:

- Identify flows within the application that are critical and that directly impact the business (for example, product payment).

- Identify metrics within the application that can determine the user experience and be used as service-level indicators, or SLIs (for example, the latency of operations in our application must be less than 100 ms per action).

- Determine the objectives to be met for our SLOs and how they will be measured (for example, the % of operations with latency under 100 ms must be 99%).

Once the SLIs and SLOs that we are going to use have been identified, we can proceed to use Cloud Logging and Cloud Monitoring to configure these custom metrics and trigger an alert when one of our objectives is not met, so as to identify when there is a problem with our services and allow us to take appropriate action.

For a detailed explanation of how to implement an SLO service in our application, you can review the following link on the official Google Cloud blog: `https://cloud.google.com/blog/products/management-tools/practical-guide-to-setting-slos`.

## Cloud Debugger in the cloud

Deploying our application in cloud environments is always accompanied by the visibility problems that we have when we are not in our local environment.

Generally, when we have a problem in a code block of our application and we do not understand what is happening, we add multiple logs to this code block and deploy the application again in the environment to obtain more information about which lines of code are being executed and what values they contain.

However, thanks to Cloud Debugger we can replace this practice with the `logpoints` functionality, which allows us to add log records without having to modify our source code and deploy our code multiple times to cloud environments.

We can use `logpoints` to print variable values in certain parts of the code and to obtain more information about the behavior of our algorithms.

If you want to know how to get the most out of this tool, you can check the following link on the official Google Cloud blog: `https://cloud.google.com/blog/products/ gcp/diagnose-problems-in-your-production- apps-faster-with- google-cloud-debugger`.

## Cloud Trace cases

The larger and more complex our application, the more difficult it is to perform a performance diagnosis. However, with Cloud Trace, it is possible to greatly facilitate this task.

Because microservice-oriented architectures are very popular today, the best way to monitor the performance of each of the integrations is through the implementation of Cloud Trace in these services and thereby maintain traceability of the critical tasks of our app.

For example, if we have an e-commerce app where the time taken for payment-related activities to be completed can affect whether customers proceed with payments, it is extremely important to have monitoring in place that allows us to take action quickly before an increase in the latency of these activities becomes critical to the business.

This can be done by creating tasks and events using spans in Cloud Trace, as we reviewed in this chapter, only now implementing multiple events in our application, identifying a group of the most critical events.

If you want to know how to use Cloud Trace in multiple projects, to get the most out of this service, you can out check the following link from the official Google Cloud blog: `https://cloud.google.com/blog/products/gcp / viewing-trace- spans-and-request-logs-in-multi-project-deployments`.

## Official documentation resources

If you want to go into more detail regarding the Google Cloud services reviewed in this chapter, you can access the official documentation through the following links:

- **Cloud Monitoring**: https://cloud.google.com/monitoring/docs
- **Cloud Debugger**: https://cloud.google.com/debugger/docs
- **Cloud Trace**: https://cloud.google.com/trace/docs
- **Cloud Profiler**: https://cloud.google.com/profiler/docs

# Summary

In this chapter, we have reviewed how to increase the observability of our applications by creating dashboards with Cloud Monitoring. We also reviewed how to proactively prevent issues in our application, by creating automated alerts, and how to trace, debug, and profile an application using Google Cloud tools. In the next chapter, we will review the sample case study of Hip Local, a community application designed to facilitate communication between people living nearby, which was created by the Google Cloud team to help candidates prepare for the Google Cloud Certified Professional Cloud Developer exam.

# Section 5: Analyzing a Sample Case Study

In this section, you will learn how to prepare the sample case study of Hip Local, a community application designed to facilitate communication between people who are located near to each other, created by the Google Cloud team.

This section comprises the following chapters:

- *Chapter 13, Hip Local Sample Case Study Preparation*
- *Chapter 14, Questions and Answers*

# 13
# HipLocal Sample Case Study Preparation

In this chapter, you'll learn how to prepare the sample case study of HipLocal, a community application designed to facilitate communication between people nearby created by the Google Cloud team. Next, you'll review the executive statement and the existing solution, and review the technical and business requirements. Finally, you'll develop a draft of a solution that meets the needs of the company.

We will cover the following topics in this chapter:

- Pro tips to ace the sample case study
- Reviewing the executive statement, existing solution, and requirements
- Architecting the solution

## Technical requirements

There are no specific technical requirements for this chapter.

# Pro tips to ace the sample case study

Throughout this book, we've reviewed multiple services and technologies provided by Google Cloud to prepare to answer questions related to particular components.

This acquired knowledge will give us better judgment when facing any challenge that involves choosing the optimal technology or service in the cloud.

In order to prepare us to make these decisions in a real-life scenario, Google Cloud offers us example case studies within the certification.

A case study is a fictitious business situation that allows us to apply our knowledge by making decisions, which in this case are decisions about the choice of certain technologies provided by Google Cloud. The case study considers our decision-making not only based on technology, but also on business decisions and objectives.

Throughout this chapter, we will review the **HipLocal** case study, which can be accessed from the following link: `https://services.google.com/fh/files/blogs/master_case_study_hiplocal.pdf`.

In the next section, we will review how the case study is structured in order to understand the information that we can find, which will enable us to facilitate decision-making.

## Sample case structure

Before starting the analysis of the case, it is important to understand what the structure is and what information each of these sections will provide. This will allow us to carry out our analysis in the most efficient way possible. Let's first look at the sections:

- **Company overview**: In this section, we will find a brief summary of the objective of the application, some of its characteristics and functionalities, and how its launch and growth have happened over time.

- **Executive statement**: This statement will show us the C-level vision regarding the high-level evolution that the application must have to achieve the goals proposed by the company.

- **Solution concept**: This section will help us understand in a more grounded way which general objectives must be considered in order to be aligned with the goals of the executive statement.

- **Existing technical environment**: In this section, we can review which technologies are currently used by the application in order to make the best decisions when migrating to the cloud. Generally, we can review technologies such as third-party services, databases used, computing environments, programming languages and frameworks used, and so on.

- **Business requirements**: In this section, we can review the specific objectives related to the business area in order to be aligned with the executive statement.

- **Technical requirements**: In this section, we can review the specific objectives related to the technical area so that we are aligned with the executive statement.

Now that we know what information is available in each section, we'll move on to learning how to organize this information to help facilitate decision-making.

## How to order the case information

One important practice to follow when ordering the case study information is to underline keywords and important phrases and sentences. This lets us focus on the really relevant information and discard valueless information for decision-making.

For this task, we should consider any of the following options:

- **Environments**: Is the current solution in an on-premise environment or is it already in a cloud environment?

- **Services**: Does the current solution consume any third-party services?

- **Open source technologies**: Is there an open source solution that could be replaced by a Google Cloud service?

- **Proprietary technologies**: Are there proprietary technologies that the solution uses that need to be redone?

- **Location**: Does the solution require being in a particular place or serving users in multiple places? Will it be regional or multi-regional?

- **Scaling**: Does the solution need the ability to support request peaks?

If any word within the case study could answer any of the questions that we saw in the preceding list, it should be underlined in order to organize the information we have.

## Map services and technologies with Google Cloud

Some examples of how open sources technologies map with Google Cloud services can be seen here:

- Virtual Machines > Compute Engine
- Apache Kafka > Pub/Sub
- Kubernetes > Google Kubernetes Engine
- MySQL/PostgreSQL > Cloud SQL

- Apache Spark > Dataproc
- Apache Beam > Dataflow
- Apache Airflow > Cloud Composer
- Redis > Memorystore
- Monitoring, Logging, Tracing, Profiling, Debugging > Cloud Operations
- CI/CD > Cloud Build
- Container Repository > Container Registry
- Artifact Repository > Artifact Registry
- Cronjobs > Cloud Scheduler

Although this is a useful exercise for developing an initial view of which services and technologies to tentatively use, it will always be necessary to evaluate whether the technologies we want to use are aligned with the executive statement and business requirements before making a decision.

In the next section, we will review the executive statement of this case study and the existing solution in order to begin evaluating a possible cloud solution design.

# Reviewing the executive statement, existing solution, and requirements

In this section, we will review all the sections in detail and apply the technique of underlining keywords and mapping technologies in order to extract the information necessary for decision-making.

## Executive statement

Let's look at the executive statement. Highlighted words appear in bold:

"We are the number one local community app; it's time to take our local community services **global**. Our venture capital investors want to see **rapid growth** and the same great experience for new local and virtual communities that come online, **whether their members are 10 or 10,000 miles away from each other**."

In this section, we can highlight three important concepts that are worth mentioning.

## Global services

Let's look at the first keyword we highlighted, global. This is a location-based keyword that indicates a need for global services. This indicates that the services have to be multi-regional.

## Rapid growth

Second, let's look at the next keywords, rapid growth. We can associate these keywords with the concept of scaling, which indicates that our solution must have the ability to scale in order to support this growth in the future.

## Distance-agnostic service quality

Finally, we have highlighted an entire phrase that indicates that members at varying distances should have the same experience. This can be linked to the concept of location as the ability to run a multi-regional solution. This can be done by using a caching solution to optimize data consumption.

As we can see, we've left out a lot of information, such as the ranking of the application – that it is the number 1 application of its kind. However, this information is not relevant to the decision-making that needs to be done, so we have filtered it out.

# Existing technical environment

In this section, we will evaluate what options we have for finding solutions based on the existing information. We will refine our choice based on technical and business requirements in the following sections.

We will not define the final solution that we are going to select, but aim to have a wide range of options to understand that there is always more than one option when choosing alternatives in Google Cloud.

"HipLocal's environment is a mixture of **on-premises** hardware and infrastructure running in **Google Cloud**. The HipLocal team understands its application well but has **limited experience in globally scaled applications**.

Their existing technical environment is as follows:

- Existing APIs run on **Compute Engine** virtual machine instances **hosted in Google Cloud**.
- State is stored in a single instance **MySQL database** in **Google Cloud**.

- Release cycles include **development freezes** to allow for QA testing.

- The application has **no consistent logging**.

- **Applications are manually deployed** by infrastructure engineers during periods of slow traffic on weekday evenings.

- There are **basic indicators of uptime**; alerts are frequently fired when the APIs are unresponsive."

Let's analyze everything we've highlighted.

## Hybrid infrastructure

The first thing we can highlight is the application's hybrid infrastructure. This means that a part of HipLocal is in an on-premise environment and another part is in Google Cloud. When we associate this with the concept of environment, the need to make a connection between both environments becomes clear.

To perform this operation, we have four options:

- A simple internet connection

- A VPN

- Partner Interconnect

- Dedicated Interconnect

> **Tip**
> If you want more information about connection methods, you can visit the following link: `https://cloud.google.com/anthos/clusters/docs/on-prem/1.7/concepts/connect-on-prem-gcp`.

## Limited experience – the need for automation

The second point selected indicates that the HipLocal team has limited experience in creating global and scalable applications. Although this could be interpreted in several ways, we can assume that it will be necessary to take full advantage of the capabilities of services that have auto-scaling capabilities.

Here are some of the services that have automatic escalation:

- Cloud Functions
- Google App Engine
- Firestore
- Cloud Storage
- Pub/Sub

There are also other options that can help us achieve auto-scaling. They include creating a group of managed instances that allow the scaling of instances in Google Compute Engine.

## Running APIs on Compute Engine

We can see that the case study mentions that the application APIs are already mounted on Compute Engine. So, we must consider this information in order to make the decision of which auto-scaling strategy to approach. For example, a managed instance group is a good option to allow autoscaling to our compute engine instances.

## Database and storage

The next highlight states that the application's state is stored in a MySQL instance in Google Cloud. We can consider mapping with Cloud SQL, a Google Cloud solution that allows us to build self-managed instances of MySQL, PostgreSQL, and SQL Server. We can also consider Cloud Spanner, a self-managed database that scales globally and automatically. The qualities of Cloud Spanner satisfy both scalability and the global availability of the information, but the migration from MySQL to Cloud Spanner might require data transformation activities before moving the data from one place to another.

## Testing and freezing development

Next, we highlighted the fact that to carry out tests on the platform, it is necessary to freeze the development environment. From this, we can infer that there is no QA environment for carrying out tests. This can be solved by proposing a special environment for testing in the cloud, where the same components that exist in the development environment are replicated.

## Logging consistency

Next, we highlighted the point about the application not logging consistently. If we map services and technologies, we can come across the need for centralized logs with Cloud Logging, part of the Cloud Operations suite. Cloud Logging allows us to centralize the data of the various components that we have in our solution.

## Deploying new features with CI/CD

Now, let's look at the manual deployment of the applications within the solution. If we review services and technologies to meet this need, we can find Cloud Build, which would allow us to perform the CI/CD flow in order to automate the deployment of applications. Having a CI/CD pipeline allows us to implement a DevOps culture within the company, automating application deployments, complying with the optimization of the deployment of new functionalities and their quality according to technical requirements. Depending on the complexity of the application, transforming the application to microservices with a reduced scope of logic per microservice can also help to decouple dependencies and provide more flexibility to deploy changes without impacting the whole solution.

## Uptime indicators

Finally, we saw that there are basic uptime indicators that only respond when the application's APIs are no longer working. For this, we can consider Cloud Monitoring and Cloud Logging within the Cloud operations suite to create alerts based on personalized metrics that allow us to take preventive and not reactive actions.

Some examples of these custom metrics could be log event logs that monitor the use of CPU and RAM memory in order to trigger alerts against anomalous behavior and thus be able to take the corresponding actions.

Having already compiled the information on the current state of the application and evaluated some available options, we will proceed to review the technical requirements in order to be able to reduce the range of options and thus refine our solution.

# Reviewing the technical requirements

In this section, we will look at the relevant information in the technical requirements in order to be able to refine the options evaluated in the previous section. This will give us more background to be able to select our final solution:

- Provide **secure communications between the on-premises data center and cloud-hosted applications and infrastructure**.
- The application must provide **usage metrics and monitoring**.
- APIs require **authentication and authorization**.
- Implement faster and more accurate **validation of new features**.
- **Logging and performance metrics** must provide **actionable information** to be able to provide **debugging information and alerts**.
- Must **scale to meet user demand**.

Let's evaluate everything we highlighted.

## Secure communication between on-premises and the cloud

The first thing that we highlighted is the requirement to have secure communication between the on-premises environment and the cloud. In the *Existing technical environment* section, we could see that we had at least four options to make this connection. However, not all options are equally secure, so based on this requirement we should discard connecting through a simple internet connection as an option. Instead, we should evaluate using a VPN, Partner Interconnect, or Dedicated Interconnect.

Depending on the technical feasibility and based on the requirement to make a secure connection, to connect to Google Cloud, we should opt for Dedicated Interconnect or Partner Interconnect (your connection to Google using these options will be fast, secure, and reliable), and as a last resort use the VPN option (the traffic between Google and your on-premises data center will traverse the public internet but is encrypted).

## Metrics and monitoring

The second requirement deals with the delivery of metrics and monitoring. For this, we can continue considering Cloud Monitoring and Cloud Logging with the use of custom metrics that allow us to generate user usage metrics.

## Authentication and authorization

The third requirement reveals the need to implement authentication and authorization in our APIs. To provide this, we can consider the use of Cloud Endpoints and the implementation of an **extensible service provider** (**ESP**) to prevent unauthenticated calls from reaching our application.

## Speed of feature validation

The fourth requirement covers the need for faster implementation of functionalities within the application. For this, it is essential that the deployments are carried out manually and, as we mentioned in the previous section, we need to automate the CI/CD flows through Cloud Build. We can also include unit test validation within the CI and code quality flow using SonarQube to ensure the quality of these new features.

## Logging and performance metrics

The fifth requirement speaks of the need to record log and performance events, a requirement that we can address with Cloud Monitoring, with performance metrics for Compute Engine and the generation of alerts in case these metrics exceed certain previously defined thresholds.

## Scaling for user demand

Finally, to address the scaling requirement, it is possible to create a group of managed instances that is responsible for creating new instances based on Cloud Monitoring performance metrics. This allows the creation of new instances when the CPU of an instance exceeds a threshold.

As we can see, even after the review of the technical requirements, we still have several options, which we evaluated in the previous section, though others were discarded due to the specific requirements requested.

In the next section, we will subject our options to business requirements in order to further refine the final design of our solution.

# Reviewing the business requirements

In this section, we will look at the business requirements to be able to filter more of the options for our final solution:

- "**Expand the availability** of the application to **new locations**.
- Support **10x** as many **concurrent users**.
- Ensure a **consistent experience** for users when they travel to **different locations**.
- **Obtain user activity metrics** to better understand how to monetize their product.
- **Ensure compliance** with **regulations in the new regions** (for example, GDPR).
- **Reduce infrastructure management time and cost**.
- **Adopt the Google-recommended practices for cloud computing**:

  a. Develop standardized workflows and processes around application lifecycle management.

  b. Define **service-level indicators** (**SLIs**) and **service-level objectives** (**SLOs**)."

Let's evaluate these points in detail.

## Expanding the availability to new locations

The first requirement talks about being able to expand the availability of the application to new locations. This aligns with the goal of the application's global expansion. Based on this, as mentioned before, the solution needs multi-regional support.

The backend of the application, considering a group of instances managed on Compute Engine, can be deployed in multiple regions. So, this needs a load balancer such as Cloud Load Balancer in charge of referring the user to the instances closest to their location.

To manage the data of the application, and to meet the multi-region need, we can consider the option previously seen from Cloud Spanner. This will allow us to have data replicated locally and thus meet the requirement.

## Concurrent user support

The second requirement talks about the need for the application to be able to support 10x as many users. This can be satisfied by Cloud Spanner auto-scaling and the auto-scaling of existing Compute Engine instances in a group of managed instances.

## Obtaining activity metrics

The third requirement covers the need for the application to obtain user usage metrics in order to evaluate how to better monetize the products. This need can be addressed with the use of custom metrics through Cloud Logging.

## Region-specific regulation compliance

The fourth requirement indicates the necessity of compliance with the regulations of each place where the application is available. Google Cloud as an infrastructure complies with various compliance policies, which allows us to meet this need. However, the tasks related to compliance regulations are not only the responsibility of the cloud provider but also of the client who hires their services. So, the application must also comply with these regulations.

## Managing infrastructure time and cost

The fifth requirement addresses the need to optimize the management of the infrastructure's time and cost. Mounting our application in a cloud environment already offers us a significant reduction in time and costs related to the infrastructure, since the tasks related to the operation are covered by the cloud provider. In addition, having our application under a group of managed instances that scale depending on user demand allows us to save on resource use costs.

## Google recommended practices

For the last requirement, it is possible to use Cloud Monitoring in order to define the corresponding SLIs and SLOs and trigger alerts in the event of non-compliance with these indicators.

Now that we've obtained the information we need from the business requirements, having filtered our options further, we can proceed to design the solution.

# Architecting the solution

With all the information collected from each section of the HipLocal case study, we can proceed with proposing a solution.

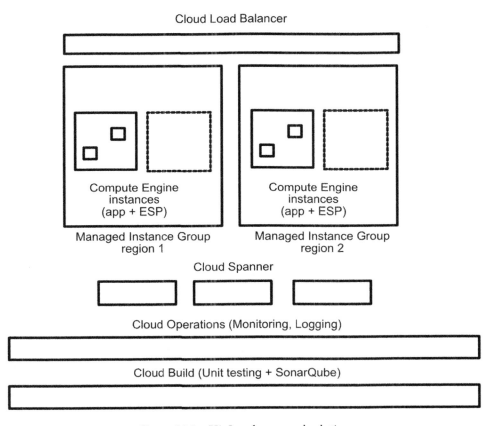

Figure 13.1 – HipLocal proposed solution

Within the solution, we can observe the following elements:

- **Cloud Load Balancer**: Cloud Load Balancer will allow us to redirect user requests to the closest instances to their location in order to comply with the executive statement and business requirements that indicate that the user has to have the same experience no matter where they are (https://cloud.google.com/load-balancing).

- **Compute Engine** and managed instance groups: Compute Engine is where the application APIs are currently deployed. This allows us, together with the managed instance groups, to create new instances based on the user flow that we are receiving and thus comply with the technical requirement that indicates that the solution must scale depending on the user demand and the business requirement that indicates that the solution must support 10x more users (Compute Engine: https://cloud.google.com/compute; managed instance groups: https://cloud.google.com/compute/docs/instance-groups).

- **Cloud Endpoints**: Cloud Endpoints, by deploying an extensible service provider in Compute Engine instances, allows us to comply with the technical requirement for authentication and authorization, preventing unauthorized requests from reaching our application (https://cloud.google.com/endpoints).

- **Cloud Spanner**: Cloud Spanner allows us to store our data in a way that is not a bottleneck for the computing layer and can thus meet both technical and business requirements (https://cloud.google.com/spanner).

- **Cloud Operations**: Cloud Operations, with its Cloud Monitoring and Cloud Logging solutions, allows us to meet the need to keep track of user application usage metrics, track performance metrics, generate preventive alerts, and keep track of SLIs and SLOs (https://cloud.google.com/products/operations).

- **Cloud Build**: Cloud Build allows us to implement a DevOps culture within the company, automating application deployments through the implementation of a CI/CD flow, thus complying with the optimization of the deployment of new functionalities and their quality according to technical requirements (https://cloud.google.com/build).

In this way, we can have a feasible solution in order to be better prepared to tackle the challenge of the HipLocal case study.

> **Important note**
>
> The solution proposed in this section is one of many possible solution options. To be better prepared for the questions that we will encounter in the exam, you should approach this case study again and try to find your own version of the solution.

# Summary

In this chapter, you learned some strategies to help you approach the HipLocal case study, such as underlining important words and phrases and mapping services and technologies with existing solutions in Google Cloud. In addition, we reviewed each of the sections of the case study, evaluating possible solutions in order to reduce the available options by obtaining information on requirements, both from the executive statement and technical and business requirements. Finally, with the information collected, we designed one of multiple solutions based on the information collected.

In the next chapter, we will review sample questions from each of the chapters in order to be better prepared to face the Professional Cloud Developer exam.

# 14
# Questions and Answers

In this chapter, we will review sample questions in order to validate knowledge obtained in this book and to get a notion of the types of questions we might face in the exam.

**Important**: The questions in this book are questions specifically created to validate your knowledge.

To access a set of official questions for certification, you can consult the official documentation through the following link: `https://cloud.google.com/certification/sample-questions/cloud-developer`.

## Technical requirements

There are no specific technical requirements for this chapter.

# Questions

In this section, we will review questions and answers for each of the chapters of the book. Those questions are helpful to validate the specific knowledge obtained in each chapter related to Google Cloud Platform services.

## Google Cloud Platform (GCP) developer fundamentals

1. As a developer, you have been tasked with transforming an application to high availability. Which factor should you consider to meet the requested objective?

   a) Make sure that the application has at least two instances in the same organization.

   b) Make sure that the application has at least two instances in the same project.

   c) Make sure that the application has at least two instances in the same zone.

   d) Make sure that the application has at least two instances in two different zones.

2. Which of the following Google Cloud services is considered a **Platform as a Service (PaaS)** offering?

   a) **Google App Engine (GAE)**

   b) **Google Compute Engine (GCE)**

   c) **Google Kubernetes Engine (GKE)**

   d) Cloud Functions

3. How can we reduce latency when accessing our application data?

   a) By increasing the number of instances of our application

   b) By applying a caching strategy in our application

   c) By increasing the **central processing unit (CPU)** and **random-access memory (RAM)** of our application

   d) By increasing the storage space of our application

4. Which of the following Google Cloud services allows unlimited information storage?

   a) Cloud SQL

   b) GCE

   c) Google Cloud Storage

   d) Secret Manager

5.  Which Google Cloud service allows you to decouple microservices in order to avoid the loss of information transmission in the event of an error?

    a) Firestore

    b) Pub/Sub

    c) Memorystore

    d) Secret Manager

# Security fundamentals and best practices

1.  If we want to minimize the possibility that a part of our application executes unauthorized tasks, which principle should we apply in the configuration of the service accounts of our application?

    a) Principle of least use of resources

    b) **Principle of least privilege (POLP)**

    c) Principle of isolation

    d) Principle of escalation

2.  In which way can we give permissions to users and applications within Google Cloud for other components?

    a) Through **Identity and Access Management (IAM)**

    b) Through the administration manager

    c) By using a username and password

    d) Through certificates

3.  How is the hierarchy of resources composed within Google Cloud?

    a) Organization, folders, projects, and resources

    b) Resources, projects, folders, and organization

    c) Folders, projects, organization, and resources

    d) Resources, projects, folders, and folders

4.  How can I safely store my application credentials?

    a) Directly in the source code

    b) In a relational database

    c) In a non-relational database

    d) In Secret Manager

5.  What is the recommended way to authenticate with a service from an application in Google Cloud?

    a) Service account

    b) Username and password

    c) **Application programming interface (API)** key

    d) Certificates

# Application modernization using Google Cloud

1.  Which commands can we use with the Google Cloud **service development kit (SDK)**?

    a) npm, gcloud, and mvn

    b) gcloud, npm, and bq

    c) gcloud, bq, and gsutil

    d) gsutil, mvn, and gcloud

2.  What kind of test verifies that a particular component is performing a task correctly?

    a) Unit test

    b) Integration test

    c) Load test

    d) **End-to-end (E2E)** test

3.  Which Google Cloud solution can we use to store the source code of our applications?

    a) Google Container Registry

    b) Developer Tools

    c) Cloud Build

    d) Cloud Source Repositories

4.  Which Google Cloud solution can we use to create a **Continuous Integration/ Continuous Delivery (CI/CD)** stream for our applications?

    a) Developer Tools

    b) Cloud Build

    c) Google Cloud SDK

    d) Cloud Composer

5.  Which Google Cloud solution can we use to store the container images of our applications?

    a) Container Registry

    b) Secret Manager

    c) GKE

    d) GCE

# Using Cloud Functions and GAE

1.  With which of these services can Cloud Functions be integrated to receive events?

    a) Cloud Storage, Pub/Sub, and Firestore

    b) GCE, Filestore, and Cloud Storage

    c) GKE, Cloud Run, and Cloud Storage

    d) GAE, GCE, and Cloud Run

2.  What kind of event is received in Cloud Functions when a new object is created in a Cloud Storage bucket?

    a) `google.storage.object.finalize`

    b) `google.storage.object.delete`

    c) `google.storage.object.archive`

    d) `google.storage.object.metadataUpdate`

3.  What precaution should be taken when making asynchronous calls within a Cloud Functions application?

    a) Make calls within the same project.

    b) Wait for the call to finish and return a termination notice to the Cloud Functions application through promises.

    c) Do not make more than two asynchronous calls in a single Cloud Functions application.

    d) Do not make fewer than two asynchronous calls in a single Cloud Functions application.

4.  Which kind of environments are there for GAE?

    a) Standard and flexible

    b) Standard and scalable

    c) Flexible and regional

    d) Flexible and scalable

5.  If we need to test a functionality in production without impacting all our users, which of the following functionalities can we use?

    a) **HyperText Transfer Protocol** (**HTTP**) functions with Cloud Functions

    b) Background functions with Cloud Functions

    c) Call in/call out with GAE

    d) Traffic splitting with GAE

# Virtual machines (VMs) and container applications on GCP

1.  What is the existing VM **Infrastructure-as-a-Service** (**IaaS**) solution on Google Cloud?

    a) GCE

    b) Cloud Functions

    c) Cloud Run

    d) GAE

2.  What is the Kubernetes **Container-as-a-Service** (**CaaS**) solution on Google Cloud?

    a) GCE

    b) GKE

    c) Container Engine

    d) Cloud Run

3.  What is the serverless solution for containers on Google Cloud?

    a) Cloud Functions

    b) Cloud Storage

    c) Cloud Run

    d) Cloud Build

4.  How can we make a group of GCE instances scale automatically?

    a) Through groups of self-administered instances

    b) Through Cloud Build

    c) Through the `manifest.yaml` file

    d) Through Cloud Run

5.  How can we run a bash script on multiple GCE instances?

    a) Through a startup script

    b) Through the GCP console

    c) Through a `manifest.yaml` file

    d) Through Filestore

## Managing APIs on GCP

1. How can we document an API so that it is understood by the various API management services?

   a) Through **HyperText Markup Language (HTML)**

   b) Through the **OpenAPI Specification (OAS)**

   c) Through LaTeX

   d) Through Google Docs

2. Which component is it necessary to implement in our solutions to use Cloud Endpoints?

   a) A storage service

   b) An **Extensible Service Proxy (ESP)**

   c) A router

   d) A computer service

3. How can we protect calls to a service with Apigee?

   a) By verifying an API key in the PreFlow policy

   b) By configuring a reverse proxy

   c) By installing a virtual host

   d) By restricting headers

4. Which of these solutions allows users to create, secure, and monitor APIs in a serverless way?

   a) Cloud Endpoints

   b) API Gateway

   c) Apigee

   d) API Management

5. Which HTTP verbs can we find in a **REpresentational State Transfer (REST)** API?

6. a) GET, POST, PUT, and DELETE

7. b) GET, READ, CREATE, and UPDATE

8. c) CLEAN, UPDATE, RESET, and DELETE

9. d) CLOSE, OPEN, READ, and DELETE

# Handling unstructured data

1. If you have a web page that is consumed from different places in the **United States (US)**, which type of location would you select for your bucket in Cloud Storage?

   a) Region

   b) Multi-region

   c) Dual-region

   d) Zonal

2. If you have analytic processing on a compute layer using `us-east-1`, which type of location would you select for your bucket in Cloud Storage?

   a) Single-region

   b) Multi-region

   c) Dual-region

   d) Zonal

3. If you have auditable information that must be stored for 10 years, which type of class would you select for your bucket in Cloud Storage?

   a) Standard

   b) Nearline

   c) Coldline

   d) Archive

4. If you need to store all the information that is stored in a Cloud Storage bucket, including changes made to the original files, which Cloud Storage functionality would you use?

   a) Object versioning

   b) Bucket retention policy

   c) Object hold protection

   d) Access control

5.  If you need to control access to files within your Cloud Storage bucket at an object level, which access method would you use?

    a) Remote access

    b) Uniform access

    c) Fine-grained access

    d) Unique access

# Databases and event messages in Google Cloud

1.  You are developing an e-commerce platform where each of the products has different information, based on a semi-structured scheme. Which type of database would you use to store the information?

    a) BigQuery

    b) Bigtable

    c) Firestore

    d) Cloud Storage

2.  You need to migrate a MySQL database with the least possible effort to Google Cloud. Which type of service would you use to accomplish this task?

    a) Cloud SQL

    b) BigQuery

    c) Firestore

    d) Bigtable

3.  Your current solution receives messages on a **publisher/subscriber (pub/sub)** topic at a frequency in which the subscriber does not have real-time processing capacity. Which type of subscription would you use to avoid processing problems due to high frequency?

    a) Static

    b) Push

    c) Pull

    d) Automatic

4.  Your current solution receives messages in a pub/sub topic, but the webhook that you have programmed to receive these messages does not allow the installation of external dependencies. Which type of subscription would you use to receive these messages with the aforementioned limitations?

    a) Static

    b) Push

    c) Pull

    d) Automatic

5.  We need to program within our application a query to Firestore that mixes fairness and inequality operators. Which action do we need to perform within Firestore to allow this query?

    a) Composite index

    b) Materialized views

    c) Document partition

    d) Split collections

# Data management and database strategy

1.  We need to design a solution that allows us to receive information from **Internet of Things (IoT)** sensors at a frequency of millions of requests per second. Which kind of database would you use to be able to support this frequency?

    a) BigQuery

    b) Bigtable

    c) Firestore

    d) Cloud Spanner

2.  You need to implement a solution that can support the consumption of data from the US, Europe, and Asia, maintaining the same experience for different users and allowing transactional operations. Which type of database would you use to accomplish this task?

    a) Cloud SQL

    b) BigQuery

    c) Cloud Spanner

    d) Bigtable

3.  You are asked to implement a database that allows you to scale to zero if no one is using the application, to reduce costs. Which type of database would you use to fulfill this request?

    a) BigQuery

    b) Bigtable

    c) Firestore

    d) Cloud Spanner

4.  You have been commissioned to design the keys of a solution that will be implemented in Bigtable. What should you do to avoid hotspotting on your database?

    a) Create partitions for each key.

    b) Create indexes for each key.

    c) Avoid using braces with a sequential increment.

    d) Do not use compound keys.

5.  You have been asked to create a counter in your application that can receive write operations with a frequency greater than 1 second using Firestore. Which strategy would you use to avoid having contention problems within Firestore?

    a) Composite index

    b) Distributed counters

    c) Document partition

    d) Split collections

# Optimizing applications with caching strategies on GCP

1.  Which kind of caching database can be implemented using Memorystore?

    a) MongoDB

    b) Bigtable

    c) Redis

    d) Firestore

2.  You are asked to implement a caching strategy within existing code in Cloud
    Functions. Which action should you consider so that Cloud Functions can
    communicate with Memorystore?

    a) Serverless **virtual private cloud** (**VPC**) access

    b) Firewall rules

    c) Load balancer

    d) Ingress

3.  What are the benefits of implementing a caching strategy in your application?

    a) Simplification of business logic

    b) Reduction of latency and use of resources

    c) Reduction of the number of components to be used

    d) Simplification of the solution architecture

4.  In which of the following scenarios is the use of a caching strategy recommended?

    a) When the source data changes to a low frequency

    b) When the source data changes to a high frequency

    c) When transactional operations are carried out

    d) When having up-to-date data is critical to the operation

5.  Which other benefits related to the availability of our services can the
    implementation of a caching strategy in our applications provide us?

    a) Maintain an additional data source in case of the unavailability of a service.

    b) Simplification of the use of resources.

    c) Increase in computing speed.

    d) Reduction in the use of RAM.

# Logging on GCP

1.  You are asked to create a strategy that allows you to move the log events generated by your applications in Google Cloud so that the analytics team can execute queries in BigQuery. Which type of strategy is the most appropriate to move data from Cloud Logging to BigQuery?

    a) Configure BigQuery to obtain the data from Cloud Logging.

    b) Create a data sink toward BigQuery.

    c) Create a batch process that moves data from Cloud Logging to BigQuery overnight.

    d) Create an event-oriented architecture that allows data to be moved from Cloud Logging to BigQuery.

2.  You have just implemented a log for your application but are having difficulty filtering the different events. Which strategy would you use to solve the problem?

    a) Create a dashboard to view the logs.

    b) Save the logs in a relational database.

    c) Register logs in different projects.

    d) Register logs at the different levels available.

3.  You have a microservices architecture mounted on Google Cloud but you are having difficulties when troubleshooting and following the traceability of your logs. Which modification would you make in the structure of your logs to simplify the troubleshooting activity?

    a) Add a description to the logs.

    b) Add a unique ID to each event.

    c) Register the logs at different levels.

    d) Save the logs in a database.

4.  You are realizing that you are saving many logs that are not necessary for the operation and this is increasing costs considerably. Which modification would you make to reduce the number of logs and operating costs?

    a) Move logs to BigQuery.

    b) Save log partitions in different Cloud Storage buckets.

    c) Exclude logs that have a 200  OK status code.

    d) Migrate the logs to a NoSQL database.

5.  How is it possible to centralize the logs of multiple applications in an organization in a single project?

    a) By creating an organization-level sink that stores the logs in a log bucket

    b) By having a batch process that moves the Cloud Logging data to a centralized project every night

    c) By duplicating application instances in a centralized project to record logs in multiple projects

    d) By creating a filter to save logs in multiple projects

# Cloud monitoring, tracing, and debugging

1.  You are asked to create graphical dashboards for the operations team based on the logs recorded by your applications in Cloud Logging. Which Cloud Operations service would you use to perform this task?

    a) Cloud Trace

    b) Cloud Monitoring

    c) Cloud Debugger

    d) Cloud Profiler

2.  One of your applications is having performance problems and your hypothesis is that some code block is causing the problem. Which Cloud Operations service would you use to identify the problem?

    a) Cloud Trace

    b) Cloud Monitoring

    c) Cloud Debugger

    d) Cloud Profiler

3.  Your application integrates with multiple external services and one of these is creating a bottleneck, but you don't know which one specifically. Which Cloud Operations service would you use to identify the bottleneck?

    a) Cloud Trace

    b) Cloud Monitoring

    c) Cloud Debugger

    d) Cloud Profiler

4.  You are having a problem in production that you have not been able to replicate in your development environment. If you could check the value of a variable of a particular line of code in production, you could solve this problem. Which Cloud Operations service would you use to perform this task?

    a) Cloud Trace

    b) Cloud Monitoring

    c) Cloud Debugger

    d) Cloud Profiler

5.  Your application has critical flows for the user, whereby any problem in the latency of this flow can cause a reduction in business revenue. Which strategy would you use to ensure quality of service?

    a) Create a cronjob that asks for the latency of the service every 10 seconds.

    b) Configure **service-level objectives** (**SLOs**) associated with flow latency with Cloud Monitoring.

    c) Divert all the requirements of that flow to BigQuery and have a team of analysts review the latency of each request.

    d) Trust that the service will always work under the standards that are needed since we are in the cloud.

# Answers

In this section, we will review the answers to the questions in the previous section, with explanations as to why that answer is the correct one.

## GCP developer fundamentals

1.  d) Make sure that the application has at least two instances in two different zones.

    Explanation:

    Having a solution in a minimum of two zones allows our solution to continue working if the other zone is unavailable.

2.  a) GAE

    Explanation:

    GAE was one of the first products offered by Google Cloud and corresponds to a PaaS-type solution.

3.  b) By applying a caching strategy to our application

    Explanation:

    Applying a caching strategy to our application allows us to access a copy of the data source in a closer location, thus reducing latency in accessing this information.

4.  c) Cloud Storage

    Explanation:

    Cloud Storage allows you to store information in the form of objects in an unlimited way, without having to select the disk size beforehand.

5.  b) Pub/Sub

    Explanation:

    Pub/Sub is a Google Cloud service that allows us, through the publisher/subscriber pattern, to decouple the handling of messages between components so that if the subscriber to a message presents unavailability in the service, the message is not lost when the subscriber recovers and can process the message.

## Security fundamentals and best practices

1.  b) POLP

    Explanation:

    The POLP consists of granting the minimum amount of permissions to a user or application in order for it to be able to execute the task that was entrusted to it, thus reducing the attack surface in case any vulnerability in the system is faced.

2.  a) IAM

    Explanation:

    IAM allows us to configure roles to users (through their accounts) and to applications (through their service accounts) to be able to execute actions within Google Cloud.

3.  a) Organization, folders, projects, and resources

    Explanation:

    An organization is the highest level of the hierarchy of resources, then the folders are optional, then the projects, and finally the resources.

4.  d) Secret Manager

    Explanation:

    Secret Manager allows you to store the credentials of your application in a secure and centralized way, being able to take action in case of leakage of these, constantly rotating the credentials.

5.  a) Service account

    Explanation:

    A service account allows an application to authenticate with Google Cloud services through the use of a private key, without the need to use a username and password.

# Application modernization using Google Cloud

1.  c) gcloud, bq, and gsutil

    Explanation:

    gcloud is the command used to perform general operations on the infrastructure in GCP, bq is used to perform operations on BigQuery, and gsutil is used to perform operations on Cloud Storage.

2.  a) Unit tests

    Explanation:

    Unit tests allow us to ensure that a specific component of our solution returns a particular output depending on the inputs it receives, thus avoiding facing unforeseen problems when modifying the code of our application.

3.  d) Cloud Source Repositories

    Explanation:

    Cloud Source Repositories is a Google Cloud solution that allows us to store the source code of our applications and thus integrate it in a simple way with services such as Cloud Build to configure integration flows and continuous delivery.

4.  b) Cloud Build

    Explanation:

    Cloud Build is a Google Cloud serverless solution that allows us to configure CI and CD flows to automatically deploy new functionalities to our applications.

5.  a) Container Registry

    Explanation:

    Container Registry is a Google Cloud solution that allows us to store images created based on the source code of our applications, to be used in the CI/CD flows of our pipelines.

# Using Cloud Functions and GAE

1. a) Cloud Storage, Pub/Sub, and Firestore

   Explanation:

   Cloud Functions allows us to receive events of the creation, update, and deletion of objects in Cloud Storage, receive messages in Pub/Sub topics, and modify documents in Firestore.

2. a) `google.storage.object.finalize`

   Explanation:

   A `finalize` event is received by Cloud Functions when creating a new object in a Cloud Storage bucket.

3. b) Wait for the call to finish and return a termination notice to the Cloud Functions service through promises.

   Explanation:

   If we do not inform Cloud Functions that an asynchronous call has ended, we might experience timeouts and unexpected behaviors.

4. a) Standard and flexible

   Explanation:

   Standard and flexible are the types of environments we can select in a GAE PaaS solution.

5. d) Traffic splitting with GAE

   Explanation:

   With GAE traffic splitting, we can configure the percentage of traffic we will receive in each of the versions of the application we have deployed in GAE in order to perform A/B testing.

# VMs and container applications on GCP

1.  a) GCE

    Explanation:

    GCE is an IaaS solution in Google Cloud that allows us to create VM instances based on an image.

2.  b) GKE

    Explanation:

    GKE is a CaaS solution in Google Cloud that allows us to have a self-managed cluster within our projects.

3.  c) Cloud Run

    Explanation:

    Cloud Run is a serverless solution for containers within GCP that allows us to deploy container images in a fully self-managed way.

4.  a) Through groups of self-administered instances

    Explanation:

    A group of self-managed instances allows us to have an instance template that, based on the behavior of some defined consumption metric, can grow by creating new instances or decrease by eliminating previously created instances.

5.  a) Through a startup script

    Explanation:

    A startup script allows us to configure our GCE instances to execute a bash script when they are created and thus be able to perform configuration operations automatically.

## Managing APIs on GCP

1.  b) Through the OAS

    Explanation:

    The OAS is a standard that allows us to document our APIs so that they can be understood by the various API management services that exist on the market, including those offered by Google Cloud.

2.  b) An ESP

    Explanation:

    An ESP allows calls to be intercepted before they reach our application, and thus they can be validated according to the rules defined in the documentation of our API through the OAS.

3.  a) By verifying an API key in the PreFlow policy

    Explanation:

    The PreFlow flow configuration in Apigee allows us to apply policies before the request reaches our API.

4.  b) API Gateway

    Explanation:

    API Gateway is a Google Cloud solution that allows us to execute the aforementioned tasks in a serverless way.

5.  a) GET, POST, PUT, and DELETE

    Explanation:

    According to the definition of the REST API, GET is used to obtain resources, POST is used for the creation of a new resource, PUT is used for the modification of an existing resource, and DELETE is used for the elimination of a resource.

# Handling unstructured data

1. b) Multi-region

   Explanation:

   Configuring a multi-regional bucket allows us to have greater availability and a reduction in the latency of obtaining data when we have requests from different regions.

2. a) Single-region

   Explanation:

   If we have data-processing scenarios in a particular region, the recommended option is to select a regional bucket in order to improve performance in obtaining data and to reduce latency and usage costs.

3. d) Archive

   Explanation:

   The `archive` class type allows us to obtain the greatest benefit in storing data in exchange for a greater value in obtaining it.

4. a) Object versioning

   Explanation:

   An object versioning configuration allows us to store multiple versions of the same object.

5. c) Fine-grained access

   Explanation:

   A fine-grained access configuration allows us to control access at an object level, unlike uniform access, which allows us to control access at a bucket level.

# Databases and event messages in Google Cloud

1.  c) Firestore

    Explanation:

    Firestore, due to its NoSQL nature and flexible schema, allows us to store different data in our documents in order to fulfill this request.

2.  a) Cloud SQL

    Explanation:

    Cloud SQL is a Google Cloud solution that allows us to create MySQL, PostgreSQL, and SQL Server instances.

3.  c) Pull

    Explanation:

    A pull subscription allows us to obtain messages from a topic at the frequency we deem convenient, in order to be able to control high-frequency message scenarios without the subscriber collapsing.

4.  b) Push

    Explanation:

    A push-type subscription allows us to make calls to webhooks from Pub/Sub without the need to configure dependencies on the subscriber.

5.  a) Composite index

    Explanation:

    When we have a query in Firestore that requires mixing fairness and inequality operators, it is necessary to create a composite index for these values; otherwise, Firestore will indicate an error.

# Data management and database strategy

1.  b) Bigtable

    Explanation:

    Bigtable is a Google Cloud database solution that allows millions of write requests to be received with a latency of fewer than 10 **milliseconds (ms)**, ideal for IoT scenarios.

2.  c) Cloud Spanner

    Explanation:

    Cloud Spanner is Google Cloud's transactional and relational database solution that enables mission-critical operations with unlimited scaling, strong consistency, and 99.999% availability.

3.  c) Firestore

    Explanation:

    Firestore allows scaling to zero if no query is made on the database, thus allowing you to pay only for use of the database.

4.  c) Avoid using braces with a sequential increment.

    Explanation:

    A hotspotting problem occurs when keys are designed that increment in a monolithic way, causing records to be stored in a non-distributed way and thus affecting the performance of the database.

5.  b) Distributed counters

    Explanation:

    Firestore has a document-writing limit of one operation per second. Distributed counters allow you to avoid this limit because of increased latency in obtaining the data.

# Optimizing applications with caching strategies on GCP

1.  c) Redis

    Explanation:

    Redis and Memcached are caching databases that can be implemented using Memorystore.

2.  a) Serverless VPC access

    Explanation:

    Serverless VPC access allows you to create a connection between a serverless service such as Cloud Functions and a VPC in order to access a service such as Memorystore that is not exposed to the internet.

3.  b) Reduction of latency and use of resources

    Explanation:

    Implementing a caching strategy allows you to consume a copy of the source data in a closer location, thus reducing latency and avoiding having to make requests to the source server, thereby reducing resource usage.

4.  a) When the source data changes to a low frequency

    Explanation:

    The ideal scenario for implementing a caching strategy is when the source data has a low frequency of change, allowing us to have a copy of the data for a longer time and thus take advantage of the benefits in a more optimal way.

5.  a) Maintain an additional data source in case of the unavailability of a service.

    Explanation:

    In addition to reducing latency in accessing data, a caching strategy allows our services to continue operating in the event that the source presents service unavailability.

# Logging on GCP

1. b) Create a data sink toward BigQuery.

   Explanation:

   The creation of a data sink toward BigQuery is the simplest solution to solve this problem since it does not require the developing of any solution.

2. d) Register logs at the different levels available.

   Explanation:

   Separating the logs depending on their importance at different levels allows us to make filters in Cloud Logging in order to facilitate the understanding of these events.

3. b) Add a unique ID to each event.

   Explanation:

   Adding a unique ID to each event allows us to cross the different logs generated by our microservices and to understand the causality of each of these events.

4. c) Exclude logs that have a 200 OK status code.

   Explanation:

   Events with a 200 OK status code do not provide us with any type of important information for our operation, therefore we can exclude them and only worry about 500-type error codes, thus reducing the number of logs we receive and diminishing our operating costs.

5. a) Creating an organization-level sink that stores the logs in a log bucket

   Explanation:

   The creation of a sink from Cloud Logging to a log bucket in a centralized project is the most optimal option to achieve the centralization of logs of multiple applications in a single project within an organization.

# Cloud monitoring, tracing, and debugging

1.  b) Cloud Monitoring

    Explanation:

    Cloud Monitoring is a Google Cloud solution that allows you to create dashboards with multiple graphs based on the metrics obtained from Cloud Logging in order to customize the operation of our applications.

2.  d) Cloud Profiler

    Explanation:

    Cloud Profiler allows us to identify the performance of code blocks within our application in order to be able to identify memory leaks in our coding and thus be able to solve them.

3.  a) Cloud Trace

    Explanation:

    Cloud Trace allows us to review the latency between the various integrations that our application has, in order to detect bottlenecks in a particular service.

4.  c) Cloud Debugger

    Explanation:

    Cloud Debugger allows us to create a snapshot of the state of an application in production and thus be able to debug without affecting the performance of our application.

5.  b) Configure SLOs associated with flow latency in Cloud Monitoring.

    Explanation:

    The configuration of SLOs in Cloud Monitoring allows us to be aware of the quality of service that a critical flow may be having for a business and thus be able to take the corresponding action if there is a problem.

# Summary

Although the content of this book covers the entire recommended guide for the exam according to the official documentation, it is recommended to complement the preparation for the exam along with practical experience in GCP in order to obtain the greatest benefits.

The exam has no feedback (it just shows PASS or FAIL), so if you feel your knowledge of a particular service explained in the book is weak after answering these questions, I recommend you to go and read again the relevant chapter of this book in order to reinforce
your preparation, underline key concepts and design, get hands-on experience, and try to imagine the best scenarios of where the services could fit in the development of cloud solutions.

I wish you the best of luck in your preparation for the Google Cloud Certified Professional Cloud Developer exam and with all your future designs and implementations of cloud-native solutions.

# Other Books You May Enjoy

If you enjoyed this book, you may be interested in these other books by Packt:

**Google Cloud for DevOps Engineers**

Sandeep Madamanchi

ISBN: 978-1-83921-801-9

- Categorize user journeys and explore different ways to measure SLIs
- Explore the four golden signals for monitoring a user-facing system
- Understand psychological safety along with other SRE cultural practices
- Create containers with build triggers and manual invocations
- Delve into Kubernetes workloads and potential deployment strategies
- Secure GKE clusters via private clusters, Binary Authorization, and shielded GKE nodes
- Get to grips with monitoring, Metrics Explorer, uptime checks, and alerting
- Discover how logs are ingested via the Cloud Logging API

**Architecting Google Cloud Solutions**

Victor Dantas

ISBN: 978-1-80056-330-8

- Get to grips with compute, storage, networking, data analytics, and pricing

- Discover delivery models such as IaaS, PaaS, and SaaS

- Explore the underlying technologies and economics of cloud computing

- Design for scalability, business continuity, observability, and resiliency

- Secure Google Cloud solutions and ensure compliance

- Understand operational best practices and learn how to architect a monitoring solution

- Gain insights into modern application design with Google Cloud

- Leverage big data, machine learning, and AI with Google Cloud

# Packt is searching for authors like you

If you're interested in becoming an author for Packt, please visit `authors.packtpub.com` and apply today. We have worked with thousands of developers and tech professionals, just like you, to help them share their insight with the global tech community. You can make a general application, apply for a specific hot topic that we are recruiting an author for, or submit your own idea.

# Share Your Thoughts

Now you've finished *Google Cloud Certified Professional Cloud Developer Exam Guide*, we'd love to hear your thoughts! Scan the QR code below to go straight to the Amazon review page for this book and share your feedback or leave a review on the site that you purchased it from.

`https://packt.link/r/1-800-56099-0`

Your review is important to us and the tech community and will help us make sure we're delivering excellent quality content.

# Index

Printed in Great Britain
by Amazon